Full and Present Salvation in Christ

Full and Present Salvation in Christ

Life and Work of Theodor Jellinghaus

KLAUS ARNOLD

◆PICKWICK *Publications* · Eugene, Oregon

FULL AND PRESENT SALVATION IN CHRIST
Life and Work of Theodor Jellinghaus

Copyright © 2018 Klaus Arnold. All rights reserved. Except for brief quotations in critical publications or reviews, no part of this book may be reproduced in any manner without prior written permission from the publisher. Write: Permissions, Wipf and Stock Publishers, 199 W. 8th Ave., Suite 3, Eugene, OR 97401.

Pickwick Publications
An Imprint of Wipf and Stock Publishers
199 W. 8th Ave., Suite 3
Eugene, OR 97401

www.wipfandstock.com

PAPERBACK ISBN: 978-1-5326-1501-6
HARDCOVER ISBN: 978-1-5326-1503-0
EBOOK ISBN: 978-1-5326-1502-3

Cataloguing-in-Publication data:

Names: Arnold, Klaus, author.

Title: Full and present salvation in Christ : life and work of Theodor Jellinghaus / Klaus Arnold.

Description: Eugene, OR: Pickwick Publications, 2018 | Includes bibliographical references.

Identifiers: ISBN 978-1-5326-1501-6 (paperback) | ISBN 978-1-5326-1503-0 (hardcover) | ISBN 978-1-5326-1502-3 (ebook)

Subjects: LCSH: Jellinghaus, Theodor | Salvation—Christianity | Theology, Doctrinal—Germany.

Classification: BT750. A33 2018 (paperback) | BT750 (ebook)

Manufactured in the U.S.A.   04/03/18

I am dedicating this work to the love of my life, best friend, greatest supporter, and encourager, my wife, Martina Arnold.

Contents

Acknowledgments | ix
Abbreviations | x

1   Introduction | 1
2   Historical-Theological Setting | 12
3   Life of Theodor Jellinghaus | 41
4   Doctrine of Salvation I: Doctrine of Reconciliation | 81
5   Doctrine of Salvation II: Doctrine of Redemption | 108
6   Church and Christian Life | 138
7   Assessment of Theodor Jellinghaus's Recantation | 160

Appendix: Biographical Timeline of Theodor Jellinghaus | 181

Bibliography | 187

Acknowledgments

THE AUTHOR OF THIS book acknowledges that many people have contributed to his professional life and development and consequently to the writing of this work. I want to mention the main persons who have influenced and helped me to accomplish this task:

Rev. Thomas Findlay, former professor at European Nazarene College, introduced me to the subject and instilled a desire to do research on Theodor Jellinghaus.

Mr. Sigmar Jellinghaus, great-grandson of Theodor Jellinghaus, who was supportive of the project and gave me access to the family archives.

Dr. Jörg Ohlemacher, professor emeritus at Ernst Moritz Arndt Universität Greifswald, was a true mentor during the process of research and writing. His expertise on the *Heiligungsbewegung* and *Gemeinschaftsbewegung* in Germany in the nineteenth century has been a great resource and inspiration.

Last but not least I want to thank my supervisors at Nazarene Theological College, Dr. Thomas A. Noble and Dr. Geordan Hammond, for their help and guidance especially in connecting the subject to the English context and the Holiness Movement in England and the United States of America in the nineteenth century.

Abbreviations

BIBLICAL TEXTS

Old Testament

Gen	Genesis	Song	Song of Solomon
Exod	Exodus	Isa	Isaiah
Lev	Leviticus	Jer	Jeremiah
Num	Numbers	Lam	Lamentations
Deut	Deuteronomy	Ezek	Ezekiel
Josh	Joshua	Dan	Daniel
Judg	Judges	Hos	Hosea
Ruth	Ruth	Joel	Joel
1–2 Sam	1–2 Samuel	Amos	Amos
1–2 Kgs	1–2 Kings	Obad	Obadiah
1–2 Chr	1–2 Chronicles	Jonah	Jonah
Ezra	Ezra	Mic	Micah
Neh	Nehemiah	Nah	Nahum
Esth	Esther	Hab	Habakkuk
Job	Job	Zeph	Zephaniah
Ps/Pss	Psalms	Hag	Haggai
Prov	Proverbs	Zech	Zechariah
Eccl	Ecclesiastes	Mal	Malachi

New Testament

Matt	Matthew	1–2 Thess	1–2 Thessalonians
Mark	Mark	1–2 Tim	1–2 Timothy
Luke	Luke	Titus	Titus
John	John	Phlm	Philemon
Acts	Acts	Heb	Hebrews
Rom	Romans	Jas	James
1–2 Cor	1–2 Corinthians	1–2 Pet	1–2 Peter
Gal	Galatians	1–2–3 John	1–2–3 John
Eph	Ephesians	Jude	Jude
Phil	Philippians	Rev	Revelation
Col	Colossians		

Journals, Periodicals, Major Reference Works, and Series

AGP — *Arbeiten zur Geschichte des Pietismus.* Edited by Kurt Aland, Erhard Peschke, and Martin Schmidt (vols. 1–19); Kurt Aland, Konrad Gottschick, and Erhard Peschke (vols. 20–24); Kurt Aland, Erhard Peschke, and Gerhard Schäfer (vols. 25–33); Martin Brecht, Gerhard Schäfer, and Hans-Jürgen Schrader (vols. 34–36); Martin Brecht, Christian Bunners, and Hans-Jürgen Schrader (vols. 37–52). Im Auftrag der Historischen Kommission zur Erforschung des Pietismus. Göttingen: Vandenhoeck & Ruprecht, 1967–2007.

AMZ — *Allgemeine Missionszeitschrift.* Monatshefte für geschichtliche und theoretische Missionskunde. Founded by Gustav Warneck. Berlin: Warneck, 1874–1923.

Auf der Warte — *Auf der Warte: Ein Blatt zur Förderung und Pflege der Reichgottesarbeit in allen Landen.* Neumünster: Ihloff, 1904–1940.

BFChTh — *Beiträge zur Förderung christlicher Theologie.* Founded by Hermann Cremer. Gütersloh: Bertelsmann, 1897–1966.

BBKL	*Biographisch-bibliographisches Kirchenlexikon.* 14 vols. and 16 supp. vols. Founded by Friedrich Wilhelm Bautz. Edited by Traugott Bautz. Hamm: Bautz, 1975–2009.
CA	*Confessio Augustana. Das Augsburgische Bekenntnis (1530).* Göttingen: Vandenhoeck & Ruprecht, 1992.
ChW	*Die Christliche Welt.* Protestantische Halbmonatsschrift. Leipzig: Grunow, 1889–1941.
Das völlige Heil	Theodor Jellinghaus. *Das völlige, gegenwärtige Heil durch Christum.* 5 eds. Berlin: different publishers, 1880–1903.
Des Christen	*Des Christen Glaubensweg: Blätter zur Weckung und Förderung des Glaubensweg.*
EGL	*Evangelisches Gemeindelexikon.* Edited by Helmut Burkhardt, Erich Geldbach, and Kurt Heimbucher, 2nd ed. Wuppertal: Brockhaus, 1986.
EKGB	*Einzelarbeiten aus der Kirchengeschichte Bayerns.* Vols. 1–83; continued with vol. 84 as *Arbeiten zur Kirchengeschichte Bayerns.* Nürnberg: Verein für bayerische Kirchengeschichte, 1925–2004.
EKL	*Evangelisches Kirchenlexikon.* 4 vols. and 1 register vol. Edited by Erwin Fahlbusch. Internationale theologische Enzyklopädie. 3rd ed. Göttingen: Vandenhoeck & Ruprecht, 1986–1997.
EKZ	*Evangelische Kirchenzeitung.* Founded by Ernst Wilhelm Hengstenberg. Organ der Evangelisch-Lutherischen innerhalb der Preußischen Landeskirche. Berlin: Oehmigke, 1827–1930.
ELThG	*Evangelisches Lexikon für Theologie und Gemeinde.* 3 vols. Edited by Helmut Burkhardt and Uwe Swarat. Wuppertal: Brockhaus, 1992–1994.
Evangelisches Allianzblatt	*Evangelisches Allianzblatt für diejenigen, welche mit allen Kindern Gottes Gemeinschaft haben.* Blankenburg: Evangelisches Allianzhaus, 1890–1973.

GdP	*Geschichte des Pietismus.* 4 vols. Edited by Martin Brecht et al. for the Historische Kommission zur Erforschung des Pietismus. Göttingen: Vandenhoeck & Ruprecht, 1993–2004.
Heilig dem Herrn	*Heilig dem Herrn: Wochenblatt für Jedermann.* Founded by Ernst Modersohn. Blankenburg: Harfe Verlag, 1910–1941
JETh	*Jahrbuch für evangelikale Theologie.* Edited by Rolf Hille et al. for the Arbeitskreis für evangelikale Theologie. Wuppertal: Brockhaus, 1987–2014.
JGP	*Jahrbücher zur Geschichte des Pietismus.* 3 vols. Edited by Andreas Lindt and Klaus Deppermann for the Historische Kommission zur Erforschung des Pietismus. Bielefeld: Luther, 1974–1977.
KIG	*Die Kirche in ihrer Geschichte: Ein Handbuch.* Founded by Kurt Dietrich Schmidt and Ernst Wolf. Edited by Bernd Moeller. Göttingen: Vandenhoeck & Ruprecht, 1961–2014.
KJ	*Kirchliches Jahrbuch für die Evangelische Kirche in Deutschland.* Founded by Johannes Schneider. Gütersloh: Bertelsmann, 1948–2011.
Licht und Leben	*Licht und Leben. Evangelisches Wochenblatt.* Elberfeld: Licht und Leben, 1889–1926.
MadB	*Mitteilungen aus der Bibelschule und der Evangelisationsarbeit ihrer Mitglieder.* Edited by Theodor Jellinghaus (1899–1906) and Paul Jellinghaus (1906–1913). Berlin: Thormann & Goetsch, 1899–1913.
Mitteilungen	*Mitteilungen aus der Bibelschule und der Evangelisationsarbeit ihrer Mitglieder* (see MadB).
NKZ	*Neue Kirchliche Zeitschrift.* Leipzig: Deichert, 1890–1933.
Philadelphia	*Philadelphia. Organ für evangelische Gemeinschaftspflege.* Stuttgart: Philadelphiaverein, 1891–1921.
PSJ	*Privatarchiv Sigmar Jellinghaus.* Documents in the personal archives of Sigmar Jellinghaus, Heidelberg.

PuN	*Pietismus und Neuzeit.* 39 vols. Edited by the Historische Kommission zur Erforschung des Pietismus. Ein Jahrbuch zur Geschichte des neueren Protestantismus. Göttingen: Vandenhoeck & Ruprecht, 1974–2013.
RCJL	*Das Reich Christi.* Edited by Johannes Lepsius. Zeitschrift für Verständnis und Verkündigung des Evangeliums. Berlin: Wiegand & Grieben, 1898–1911.
Reich Christi	*Das Reich Christi* (see RCJL).
RGG²	*Die Religion in Geschichte und Gegenwart.* 5 vols. and 1 register vol. Edited by Hermann Gunkel and Leopold Zscharnack. Handwörterbuch für Theologie und Religionswissenschaft. 2nd ed. Tübingen: Mohr, 1927–1932.
RGG³	*Die Religion in Geschichte und Gegenwart.* 6 vols. and 1 register vol. Edited by Kurt Galling. Handwörterbuch für Theologie und Religionswissenschaft. 3rd ed. Tübingen: Mohr, 1956–1965.
RGG⁴	*Religion in Geschichte und Gegenwart.* 8 vols. and 1 register vol. Edited by Hans Dieter Betz et al. Handwörterbuch für Theologie und Religionswissenschaft. 4th ed. Tübingen: Mohr, 1998–2007.
Sabbathklänge	*Sabbathklänge.* Illustrierte Wochenschrift für das christliche Haus. Mühlheim, 1881–1915.
TRE	*Theologische Realenzyklopädie.* 36 vols. Edited by Gerhard Müller, Horst Balz, and Gerhard Krause. Berlin: de Gruyter, 1977–2004.
Works (Jackson)	*The Works of John Wesley.* 14 vols. An edition of the complete and unabridged *Works* reproduced by the photo offset process from the authorised edition published by the Wesleyan Conference Office in London in 1872 (originally edited by Thomas A Jackson). Repr., Kansas City: Beacon Hill, 1979.
Works (BE)	*The Works of John Wesley.* Edited by Frank Baker. Bicentennial Edition. Oxford and Nashville, 1975–.

WTJ	*Wesleyan Theological Journal*. Bulletin of the Wesleyan Theological Society. Online resource at Nampa, Idaho: Wesley Center for Applied Theology, 1966–2010.
ZThK	*Zeitschrift für Theologie und Kirche*. Tübingen: Mohr, 1891–2004.

1

Introduction

THE NINETEENTH CENTURY, AND especially the last quarter of it, bears witness to interesting connections and relationships (most of which were reciprocal) in the history of Protestantism between the United Kingdom and the European continent and even the United States of America. One outstanding example is the history and impact of the holiness movement.

This work deals with that movement in general and one of its protagonists in particular, Rev. Theodor Jellinghaus. He was a Lutheran Pietist minister, missionary to India, founder of a Bible school, author of a theological treatise and other publications, speaker at various holiness conferences, theological leader of the *Heiligungsbewegung*[1] and one of the characters at the beginning of the *Gemeinschaftsbewegung* in Germany, a nineteenth century development of the Pietist tradition in Germany.

MOTIVE AND GOAL OF THE WORK

I learned about the work and life of Theodor Jellinghaus during my theological studies. Since I belong to a denomination which has emanated from the American holiness movement, I became fascinated that a German theologian in the nineteenth century tried to build a bridge between Anglo-American and German theological traditions in relation to the doctrine of sanctification.

---

1. Regarding the use of specific German terminology and the methodology of translating German texts, see special paragraph later in this chapter.

After starting with serious research I had the chance to meet some of Theodor Jellinghaus's family, which gave me another boost of motivation for the work. After the death of Dr. Paul Jellinghaus, son of Theodor Jellinghaus and successor of his work, the descendants had decided that the family member with the most interest in the family history should keep the family archives. Because of the total destruction of Berlin during the Second World War most of the archives were lost and destroyed. I had the privilege of meeting Mr. Sigmar Jellinghaus, great-grandson of Theodor Jellinghaus, who has given me access to what was left from the archives.[2]

It is the goal of this work to examine and assess the life and work of Theodor Jellinghaus. Jellinghaus was the only representative of the *Heiligungsbewegung* in Germany who wrote a theological treatise of his understanding of sanctification in relation to other major doctrines of the church. His scholarly contribution was formulated especially in his seven-hundred-and-thirty page *magnum opus*, *Das völlige, gegenwärtige Heil durch Christum* (The Full, Present Salvation through Christ), which went through five editions between 1880 and 1903.[3]

The key event for the life and work of Jellinghaus was his participation in the convention on Christian holiness in Oxford in 1874. Therefore, the approach taken in this work will be to examine the historical context before examining his theology. He wanted to bring the new insights he gained there to revive the Protestant and Pietist traditions in the land of the Reformation. He believed that the doctrine of sanctification by faith in Jesus Christ which he had heard in England was an indispensable consequence of and necessary accompaniment to a clear doctrine of justification by faith in Jesus Christ. His doctrine of salvation focused on a personal faith relationship of the believer with Jesus Christ. In justification the relationship was established by the grace of God through the Holy Spirit; and in sanctification it was sustained through the Holy Spirit in moment-by-moment yielding of the believer to God.

Once he had formulated his doctrine of justification and sanctification, Jellinghaus developed the doctrines of redemption and reconciliation. In fact, the latter became the ontological foundation of his teachings because it provided the basis for both the objectivity and subjectivity of salvation in the person and work of Jesus Christ. It will be demonstrated that his

---

2. In a letter of October 22, 2001 the documents from the personal archives were made available for research.

3. Jellinghaus, *Das völlige Heil*. The fifth edition appeared in 1903. The previous editions were published in 1880, 1886, 1891, and 1898. Nothing of Jellinghaus's publications has been translated into English.

teachings were a distinctive treatment of different influences in his life and learning.

Although the ecclesiology of Jellinghaus was based on the understanding of the established Protestant Church in Germany and rooted in the historical and theological development of the Pietist tradition in Germany (*ecclesiola in ecclesia*)[4], he developed an ecclesiological concept which received an independent character through his doctrines of reconciliation and redemption. This approach and the fact that he formulated his theological understanding in a theological treatise made him unique among the fathers of the *Gemeinschaftsbewegung*. The involvement of Jellinghaus in the *Gemeinschaftsbewegung* must be interpreted from the viewpoint of his ecclesiological concept in the light of his understanding of the kingdom of God and in relation to the Protestant state churches of Germany. His special concern in the *Gemeinschaftsbewegung* was the education of laypersons.

The last phase of his life was characterized by crisis and illness which were related to each other and directly and indirectly led to his so-called recantation. We can only do justice to the overall persona of Jellinghaus if we differentiate between the former (healthy) and later (ill) Jellinghaus. He has to be viewed in the contradictions and tensions within the development of the *Heiligungsbewegung* and the *Gemeinschaftsbewegung* as well as his theological teachings.

This work is the first comprehensive treatment of Jellinghaus which not only focuses on his doctrine of sanctification, but assesses his overall life and work, that is, his theological system and personal involvement in and contribution to the development of the *Heiligungsbewegung* and *Gemeinschaftsbewegung* in Germany.

METHODOLOGY

A mix of biographical study and thematic approach seems to be the best method to look at the life and work of Theodor Jellinghaus. The main themes of his theological thought and his contribution to the *Heiligungsbewegung* and *Gemeinschaftsbewegung* in Germany can only be understood in the framework of important events and developments in his life. From his family background, studies, and experiences as missionary in India and pastor at two different parishes in Germany to the encounter with leading persons of nineteenth century Pietism in Germany and representatives of

---

4. This Latin term means "little church within the church" and refers to an important aspect of Philipp Jacob Spener's view of an ongoing reform of the church. Spener, *Pia Desideria*.

the American holiness movement during a holiness conference in England and the following development of the *Heiligungsbewegung* and *Gemeinschaftsbewegung* in Germany cannot be separated from the formulation of his theological teachings.

There are at least three strengths in this approach. First, it places Jellinghaus in the historical-theological setting of the nineteenth century in Germany. Second, it helps explain the relationship to and the influences of the American holiness movement and the later Keswick movement to his theological teachings. Third, this approach is of assistance in explaining Jellinghaus's theological contribution as a distinctive treatment of different influences in his life and learning.

The leading questions guiding the research were: Who and what influenced Theodor Jellinghaus's life and work? Why did Jellinghaus formulate his thoughts on justification and sanctification the way he did? What was his overall aim? Did Jellinghaus reach his goal? How was Theodor Jellinghaus assessed during his life time until today? What is his theological contribution?

The method and the questions have influenced the procedure for developing this work. First, I have gathered and read all the works published by Theodor Jellinghaus. I have summarized them and correlated the content according to topics and themes to show how his thoughts developed. Second, it was important to research as much as possible about his life: his family, his studies, his ministry and personal relationships and developments in the different phases of his life. The primary sources and the family archives were of great help to develop a personal data sheet in chronological order. This biographical study was then connected to the development of his theological teachings. Third, the different assessments of his thoughts by different theologians were put into dialogue with the different themes of his teachings. This procedure should help to provide a historical-critical approach to the life and work of Theodor Jellinghaus.

TRANSLATION METHODS FOR GERMAN TEXTS AND SPECIFIC GERMAN TERMINOLOGY

Any translations of German works (by Jellinghaus and others as indicated in the footnotes) have been produced by the author. Regarding the methods of translation I have basically followed three types according to Newmark's categories.[5] Rarely did I use the word-for-word translation, which means that the word-order of the source language "is preserved and the words

---

5. Newmark, *Textbook of Translation*.

translated singly by their most common meanings, out of context."⁶ This method was used for book titles.⁷ The second method used is literal translation. In this method, according to Newmark, the grammatical constructions of the source language are converted to their nearest equivalents in the target language "but the lexical words are again translated singly, out of context."⁸ The literal translation method has been applied mostly for short quotations. The method used most commonly in this work has been faithful translation.

> A faithful translation attempts to reproduce the precise contextual meaning of the original within the constraints of the TL⁹ grammatical structures. It 'transfers' cultural words and preserves the degree of grammatical and lexical 'abnormality' (deviation from SL¹⁰ norms) in translation. It attempts to be completely faithful to the intentions and text-realization of the SL writer.¹¹

This method was most appropriate for larger texts and the overall presentation of theological teachings. It was most important to the author of this work to make an effort to be as faithful as possible to the intentions of the writers of the German texts.

When an explanation for the translation is necessary, this is done in the specific chapters (e.g., *Versöhnung, Erlösung, Kirche,* and *Gemeinde*). However, at this point a couple of terms will be explained at the beginning because the terms are either specific to Jellinghaus or appear throughout his writings and this work.

The first term is one that is specific to the teachings of Theodor Jellinghaus. No other theologian used this terminology. Jellinghaus described his doctrine of salvation as *heilistische Erlösungslehre* (I would translate it literally as salvific doctrine of redemption) or *Heilismus* (which is the noun of the adjective *heilistisch*). The word is based on the German term *Heil* meaning redemption, salvation, blessedness, well-being, or even welfare. It seems that Jellinghaus created here a pleonasm in the first use (*heilistische Erlösungslehre*). With the term *heilistisch* or *Heilismus* Jellinghaus wanted to

---

6. Ibid., 45.

7. For example: *Das völlige, gegenwärtige Heil durch Christum* was translated as "The full, present salvation through Christ" or *Mitteilungen aus der Bibelschule* as "Information from the Bible school."

8. Newmark, *Textbook of Translation*, 46.

9. TL stands for target language.

10. SL stands for source language.

11. Newmark, *Textbook of Translation*, 46.

describe his own understanding of salvation, especially the relationship of the doctrines of justification and sanctification, to distinguish it from other teachings in the Protestant tradition in Germany.[12]

The German term chosen for holiness movement (*Heiligungsbewegung*) literally means sanctification movement. I could not find any specific reason why the English designation was not translated literally as *Heiligkeitsbewegung*. However, since the message of the movement focused on the doctrine of sanctification and not on the biblical teaching of holiness in general, the term appears to be most appropriate for the social, historical and theological setting of the movement in Germany. We will use the German term if it refers to the German movement. For the movement in other parts of the world (especially in the United States) the term holiness movement will be used because that is the historic designation.

The last specific German term to be explained in this section is *Gemeinschaftsbewegung*. The most common translation has been "Fellowship Movement."[13] However, it does not fully grasp its original meaning, because the term implies also the sense of confraternity and community. Throughout this work I will use the original German term *Gemeinschaftsbewegung* to describe this movement.

Regarding translation from German to English in this work it is also important to note that the author, although born and raised in Germany, has had most of his theological education (on Bachelor's and Master's level) in English speaking schools and lived in the United States of America for three years as he attended seminary. This is mentioned to emphasize the author's being immersed in the English speaking vocabulary in theological studies, to highlight his familiarity with both languages, and to accentuate his expertise for translating theological texts from German to English.

PRIMARY LITERATURE

The most important source for this work is the main work of Jellinghaus, *Das völlige Heil*. Although each edition reveals the same theological orientation and direction, there are various developments visible in the different

---

12. In a footnote he explains the term himself by stating that others had called his teachings "Methodist" theology and others "new Pietist" theology. However, because he felt that these terms were not accurate he coined the term *heilistisch* or *Heilismus*, since it seemed "understandable, short and hurting nobody" and because it would express a "joyful acceptance of the Savior and the free, full, present salvation, possession of salvation and assurance of salvation and even the salvation of the returning Savior." Jellinghaus, *Das völlige Heil*, 82.

13. See for example the influencing article by Warfield, *Perfectionism*, 1:305–41.

editions. An important methodology has been the creation of a synopsis of the table of contents and a comparison of the content of the chapters of all five editions. Especially in the second and fourth editions there are important enlargements and amendments in regard to his doctrines of reconciliation and redemption, his understanding of faith and his doctrine of baptism.

Jellinghaus's publication is not a dogmatic work in the common sense.[14] It was rather the main textbook of his Bible school and was meant to help train laypersons for involvement in the *Gemeinschaftsbewegung*. In the preface Jellinghaus wrote that he intended it to be biblically, historically and theologically sound, but written in a language that reflected the Pietist tradition and that was readable for laypersons within the *Gemeinschaftsbewegung*.[15]

A second fruitful source was his regular newsletters of his Bible school, the *Mitteilungen aus der Bibelschule* (Information from the Bible school).[16] These regular publications provide a lot of information about his life, ministry, travels, Bible courses, Bible school, and his theological convictions. They also contain interesting comments on the developments of the *Gemeinschaftsbewegung*. Two methodologies used with this source were the development of a chronology of the Bible school and summaries of the different theological teachings. The chronology has been a great tool for the biography of Jellinghaus, and the summaries have aided the interpretation of his other writings.

Jellinghaus wrote two Bible commentaries for laypersons[17] which were designed to start a commentary series on the entire New Testament.[18] However, no other commentaries in this series were published; neither by him nor by any other theologian. The commentaries on John's first epistle and the epistle to the Romans are examples of Jellinghaus's exegesis and focused on his teaching of Jesus as the present Savior in who is victory over sin.

---

14. Theodor Hardeland was probably the first one who had called this work "dogmatics" in 1898. Hardeland, *Heiligungsbewegung*, 28. See also Brandenburg, "Theodor Jellinghaus," 576. Mirbach, "Theodor Jellinghaus," 23. Ohlemacher, "Theodor Jellinghaus," 985.

15. Jellinghaus, *Das völlige Heil*, vi–vii.

16. *Mitteilungen aus der Bibelschule und der Evangelisationsarbeit ihrer Mitglieder* (*MadB*). These were edited by Theodor Jellinghaus from 1899 until May 1906. From edition 23 on (August 1906) until the end of its publication (1913), his son and successor, Dr. Paul Jellinghaus, edited the newsletters. These newsletters were published usually six times a year, but that varied in the history of the school.

17. Jellinghaus, *Erster Johannesbrief* and *Römerbrief*.

18. See his preface to the second edition of Jellinghaus, *Römerbrief*, v–vii.

Other publications by Jellinghaus focused on key teachings of *Das völlige Heil*.[19] In addition he issued a short aid for interpreting the Bible for laypersons.[20] He also published various articles in the *Evangelisches Allianzblatt*[21] (Gazette of the Evangelical Alliance) and other periodicals of the *Gemeinschaftsbewegung*[22] and a practical guide for Christian living.[23] All of these publications do not contain new or different teachings from his *Das völlige Heil*; they were either examples on how he applied his theological teachings or additional interpretations of his basic theological convictions. As these publications were reviewed for this work, they were compared with *Das völlige Heil* and integrated into the appropriate chapters.

SECONDARY LITERATURE AND CURRENT STATE OF RESEARCH

Since the 1970s the research on the *Heiligungsbewegung* and *Gemeinschaftsbewegung* has experienced some attention.[24] Particularly since the last decade of the twentieth century there has been intensive and extensive work on the whole movement as well as specific aspects[25] and outstanding personalities.[26]

19. Jellinghaus, *Heiligungskraft*; *Sieg und Leben*; *Völlige Übergabe*; and *Erst Glaube, dann Erfahrung*.

20. Jellinghaus, *Rechte Schriftauslegung*.

21. Articles from Jellinghaus in the *Evangelisches Allianzblatt* were published between 1892 and 1904.

22. In the main publication of the *Heiligungsbewegung* in the German speaking areas, *Des Christen Glaubensweg*, Jellinghaus contributed articles since its beginnings.

23. Jellinghaus, *Unkeuschheitssünden*. This is an eight-page pamphlet against pre- and extramarital sexual relationships, criticizing especially public persons (politicians and writers) who misused young girls as prostitutes.

24. Drechsel, *Gemeindeverständnis*. Lange, *Gemeinschaften*. Ohlemacher, "Gemeinschaftsbewegung"; Ohlemacher, "Reich Gottes"; Ohlemacher, "Anfänge," 59–83; and Ohlemacher, "Gemeinschaftschristentum."

25. Fiedler, *Glaubensmissionen*; Hollenweger, *Charismatisch-pfingstliches Christentum*; Holthaus, *Fundamentalismus*; and Holthaus, *Heil—Heilung—Heiligung*; Jordy, *Brüderbewegung*; Jung, *Vom Kampf der Väter*; and Jung, *Als die Väter noch Freunde waren*; Lüdke, *Diakonische Evangelisation*; Mehl, *Reich-Gottes-Arbeit*; Ohlemacher, "Evangelikalismus und Heiligungsbewegung im 19. Jahrhundert"; Schmid, *von Oxford*; Streiff, *Methodismus in Europa*; Voigt, *Heiligungsbewegung*; Weyer, *Heiligungsbewegung*; Fleisch, *Heiligungsbewegung*.

26. Baumann, *Johannes Lepsius*; Bister and Holthaus, eds., *Friedrich Wilhelm Baedeker*; Burkhardt, *Christoph Gottlob Müller*; Diener, *Walter Michaelis*; Fuchser, *Carl Heinrich Rappard*; Gerlach, *Carl Brockhaus*; Haubeck, ed., *Lebenszeichen*, Jung, *Julius Anton von Poseck* and *Israel Johannes Rubanowitsch*; Orde, *Carl Mez*; Plathow-Holl, *Eva*

Regarding the life and work of Theodor Jellinghaus the most extensive work has been done by Paul Fleisch.[27] He indicated that he had a special relationship to Jellinghaus. On the one hand, Fleisch saw in Jellinghaus the most thorough theologian of the *Heiligungsbewegung*. In his historical and theological review of the *Gemeinschaftsbewegung* Fleisch laid a special focus on Theodor Jellinghaus and his work. On the other hand, Jellinghaus had asked Paul Fleisch himself to critically assess his theological work. Jellinghaus approached Fleisch during the time he was ill and asked him to help him in the recantation of his theological teachings.[28] Actually, Jellinghaus's work became the overarching benchmark for Fleisch's critical review of the *Heiligungsbewegung*.[29] Ohlemacher, in the preface to Fleisch's second publication on the *Heiligungsbewegung*, is correct in his assessment that Fleisch endeavored to exonerate Jellinghaus from the "perfectionistic excesses" of the movement.[30] Indeed, Fleisch felt that the *Gemeinschaftsbewegung* failed to give Jellinghaus the appreciation and acknowledgment which he deserved.[31] He addressed especially the historical context of the movement and the doctrine of justification and sanctification in Jellinghaus. However, there is not much in his work on Jellinghaus's doctrines of *Versöhnung* (reconciliation) and *Erlösung* (redemption).[32] This is a weakness of Fleisch's work, since the doctrines of reconciliation and redemption not only constituted the ontological foundation for his doctrines of justification and sanctification, but they also shaped his ecclesiological understanding and practical involvement in the *Heiligungsbewegung* and *Gemeinschaftsbewegung*.

---

von Tiele-Winckler; Raedel, *Jean Frédéric Bettex*; Kauffmann, *Franz Eugen Schlachter*; Schirrmacher, *Theodor Christlieb*; Schwarz, *John Nelson Darby*; Seltmann, *Dora Rappard*; Stober, *Christoph Friedrich Blumhardt*; Troeger, *Johannes Lepsius*; Voigt, *Theodor Christlieb*.

27. Fleisch, *Krisis*; Fleisch, *Entwicklung der deutschen Gemeinschaftsbewegung*; Fleisch, *Moderne Gemeinschaftsbewegung*, vols. 1 and 2; and Fleisch, *Heiligungsbewegung*, vols. 1 and 2.

28. Fleisch, *Heiligungsbewegung*, 2:16.

29. Ibid., xxvi.

30. Ibid., xxvii.

31. Fleisch, *Heiligungsbewegung*, 1:5.

32. When speaking of Jellinghaus's doctrines of reconciliation and redemption it is important to note that these are straight translations of the German terminology he preferred: *Versöhnung* and *Erlösung*. The usage of the terms "reconciliation" and "redemption" might be different in most English theological writings; however, because of Jellinghaus's use of the terms in German, the author prefers to use the straight translations to stay as close as possible to Jellinghaus's original terminology.

Except for two brief appraisals of the *Heiligungsbewegung* at the turn of the nineteenth to the twentieth century,[33] most of the assessments of Jellinghaus and his teachings were published in the crisis years of the *Gemeinschaftsbewegung*.[34] All of them focused on his doctrine of sanctification, especially in the light of his so-called recantation. All of them represented one of two viewpoints: They either agreed with the former (healthy) Jellinghaus (or at least wanted to show respect for his contribution) or they approved of the new standpoints of the later (ill) Jellinghaus and rejected especially his teachings on sanctification.

In the second and third decade of the twentieth century the teachings of the *Heiligungsbewegung* in general were reviewed in scholarly works.[35] Two more recent works give special attention to Theodor Jellinghaus. The first was written by Stephan Holthaus, *Heil—Heilung—Heiligung* (Salvation—Healing—Sanctification), in which he summarizes the history and development of the holiness movement and Pentecostal movement in Germany and their relationships (published in 2005). The teaching and ministry of Jellinghaus is treated on sixteen pages in this six-hundred-and-eighty-eight page work, but it does not go beyond the findings and assessment of Paul Fleisch. The second work is a lecture given at the second theological symposium of the *Evangelische Hochschule Tabor* in Marburg in 2011, which was published in 2012. The theme of the symposium was *Die neue Welt und der neue Pietismus—Angloamerikanische Einflüsse auf den deutschen Neupietismus* (The new world and the new Pietism—Anglo-American influences on German New Pietism). The particular lecture was given by Thorsten Dietz and was published as, *Der Einfluss der angloamerikanischen Heiligungstheologie auf Theodor Jellinghaus* (The influence of the Anglo-American holiness theology on Theodor Jellinghaus).[36] Dietz's work is a good summary of the doctrine of sanctification of Jellinghaus. However, Dietz does not present any new or different insights into the life and work of Jellinghaus that go much beyond Paul Fleisch.

---

33. Hardeland, *Heiligungsbewegung*. Clasen, "Heiligung im Glauben."

34. Gelshorn, "Die moderne Gemeinschaftsbewegung"; Gennrich, *Wiedergeburt und Heiligung*; Rietschel, *Lutherische Rechtfertigungslehre oder moderne Heiligungslehre?*; Buddeberg, "Die Heiligung durch den Glauben"; Bunke, "Jellinghaus gegen Jellinghaus"; Heinatsch, *Die Krisis des Heiligungsbegriffes*; Gensichen, "Jellinghaus—und seine Erklärung über seine Lehrirrungen"; Böhme, "Wie ist der Widerruf von Pastor Jellinghaus zu beurteilen?"; Cremer, *Dogma der Gemeinschaftsbewegung*; Ihmels, "Zur Lehre von der Heiligung bei Theodor Jellinghaus"; Warfield, *Perfectionism*, vol. 1.

35. Köberle, *Rechtfertigung und Heiligung*; Reuber, *Mystik*.

36. Dietz, "Der Einfluss der angloamerikanischen Heiligungstheologie auf Theodor Jellinghaus."

Regarding the methodology of examining the secondary literature, all texts were reviewed and assessed according to the theological background of the authors, the theological themes they highlighted in Jellinghaus, the accuracy of representing the teachings of Jellinghaus and their contribution to the study of Jellinghaus.

What is missing in the research of the life and work of Theodor Jellinghaus is an overall assessment of his teachings which examine the relationship of his doctrines of justification and sanctification to his doctrines of reconciliation and redemption and their ecclesiological implications. This work has identified the implications.

To accomplish this objective, it is important to review the historical theological setting in Germany and the holiness movement before it came to Germany. This will establish the framework for the life of Theodor Jellinghaus: his upbringing, education and ministry involvement. In the following two chapters Jellinghaus's doctrine of salvation will be summarized and assessed through his teaching of reconciliation and redemption. In chapter six the ecclesiological implications will be examined. In the last chapter the so-called recantation by Jellinghaus will be reviewed and assessed before conclusions to the life and work of Theodor Jellinghaus will be drawn.

2

Historical-Theological Setting

HISTORICAL-THEOLOGICAL SETTING IN GERMANY

THE BROAD HISTORICAL-THEOLOGICAL SETTING for understanding the life and work of Theodor Jellinghaus is Protestantism in Germany in the nineteenth century in general and the German Pietist tradition at that time in particular.

General Historical-Theological Setting in Germany

When surveying the situation of German Protestantism in the nineteenth century, it is fair to say that two figures were formative in its development: The philosopher Georg Wilhelm Friedrich Hegel (1770–1831) and the theologian Friedrich Daniel Ernst Schleiermacher (1768–1834). The former was the main representative of German Idealism which had strong influences also on the different schools of Protestant theology. The latter became influential through his new approach to religion as feeling (*Gefühl*) and outlook (*Anschauung*), which was a break with the enlightenment and its philosophical approach to theology in terms of metaphysical and ethical absolutes and universal truths. According to Schleiermacher, in the center of any religion must be the experience of absolute dependence (*schlechthinnige Abhängigkeit*) and willful decisions by humanity in the midst of the challenges of the times. Religion as such is interpreted as history of inner experience and dogmas as time-bound expressions of that experience.[1]

Generally speaking three streams developed in German Protestantism in the nineteenth century. There was the conservative stream which assimilated Schleiermacher's critique of the enlightenment without fully adopting it. Within this stream different currents were at work, which were also related in some form or other. Some of these currents developed partly due to the unification of the Lutheran and Reformed churches in Prussia under King Friedrich Wilhelm III in 1817. This politically motivated unification was not welcomed by all, which influenced the development of Reformed Orthodoxy and Neo-Lutheranism. The latter became quite influential and wanted to revive the tradition and importance of the Lutheran doctrines and liturgy in their struggle against the challenges of rationalism.[2] Another current was related to the restoration of the Lutheran tradition, the Erlangen School.[3] It was influenced by the Pietist revival in the first half of the nineteenth century and became known for its emphasis on experience (focusing on regeneration), which allowed individuals to comprehend the truth of dogmatic statements and the object of faith.

The second important stream was theological liberalism which was strongly influenced by Schleiermacher as well. It had a humanistic approach to the study of theology and wanted to become independent from church tradition and dogmas. The secularization of religious themes and the dissolution of church in society and culture were welcomed by its representatives. Theological liberalism was never uniform and developed in various ways. It had great influences, especially on the exposition of the Bible and church history. In Germany it found one of its expressions, in particular, in the so-called cultural Protestantism (*Kulturprotestantismus*) which tried to join Christianity and culture (in this case German culture) by interpreting scientific progress as an expression of cultural progress ordained by God. Some of the most prominent representatives were Ferdinand Christian

---

1. For an overview and more detailed information on Protestantism in Germany in the nineteenth century, see Krumwiede, *Geschichte des Christentums*, 3; Grane, *Die Kirche im 19. Jahrhundert*; Moeller, *Geschichte des Christentums*; Mühlenberg, *Epochen der Kirchengeschichte*; Wallmann, *Kirchengeschichte Deutschlands seit der Reformation*.

2. See also Barth, *Geschichte der protestantischen Theologie*; Kantzenbach, *Zwischen Erweckung und Restauration*; Miltenberger, *Geschichte der deutschen evangelischen Theologie*.

3. See also Beyschlag, *Erlanger Theologie*; Hein, *Lutherisches Bekenntnis und Erlanger Theologie*; Kantzenbach, *Erlanger Theologie*; Winter, *Erlanger Theologie*.

Baur, David Friedrich Strauss, Albrecht Ritschl, Wilhelm Herrmann and Adolf von Harnack.[4]

Between these two streams a third stream tried to mediate, the so-called mediating theology (*Vermittlungstheologie*). This school of thought held on to the traditional understanding of revelation, but believed that ecclesiastical beliefs must be open to change without falling into the other extreme where religion is absorbed into anthropology.[5]

The German Pietist Tradition

The particular historical theological setting of the topic of this work is the German Pietist tradition. Pietism started out as a renewal movement within Protestantism in Germany as a reaction against over-emphasis on doctrinal orthodoxy and religious formality and aimed at emphasizing revival of personal devotion and practical Christianity. It began within the Lutheran and Reformed traditions in the different state churches throughout Germany in the seventeenth century and experienced various developments. One of the most common explanations of the term Pietism points to a work published by Philip Jacob Spener (1635–1705) in 1675 called, *Pia Desideria oder Herzliches Verlangen nach gottgefälliger Besserung der wahren evangelischen Kirche* (Pia Desideria or Earnest Desire for a God-Pleasing Reform of the True Evangelical Church), which became the first comprehensive written expression of Pietism. Spener stressed home Bible studies *(collegia pietatis)*, the active role of laity within church leadership, knowledge and practice of Christianity, restructuring theological education of pastors, and preaching that stressed the renewal of humans (through new birth or regeneration), as well as the fruits of the Christian life. The term Pietism was used around this time in Frankfurt/Main and Leipzig and later all over Germany. First it was used as a pejorative term given to the followers of the movement by its critics, much like the expression Lutherans was used until the mid-sixteenth-century[6] and the term Methodism was used in the early years of its history in Britain in the eighteenth century. Later the followers of the movement bore the name with some pride because in the last quarter of

---

4. See also Courth, *Wesen des Christentums*; Lepp, *Protestantisch-liberaler Aufbruch in die Moderne*; Schröder, *Naturwissenschaften und Protestantismus*; Friedrich and Jähnichen, eds., *Sozialer Protestantismus*; Hübinger, *Kulturprotestantismus und Politik*; Müller, ed., *Kulturprotestantismus*.

5. See also Hirsch, *Geschichte der neueren evangelischen Theologie*. Kattenbusch, *Die deutsche evangelische Theologie seit Schleiermacher*.

6. Schilling, *Martin Luther*, 284.

the seventeenth century it became a strong renewal movement within the Protestant state churches in Germany.

Other important Pietist leaders included August Hermann Francke (1663–1727) who influenced Nikolaus Count von Zinzendorf (1700–1760), who himself was a God-child of Spener and later became the leader of the Moravian Church (*Herrnhuter Brüdergemeine*). Johann Albrecht Bengel (1687–1752), was the author of *Gnomon Novi Testamenti* (Exegetical Annotations on the New Testament) published in 1742 which was used by John Wesley in his *Explanatory Notes Upon the New Testament* (1755). The above mentioned leaders were German Lutherans, but Pietism also had an influence on Reformed Christians and was influenced by them.

Some scholars (like Johannes Wallmann) want to use the term primarily for the first epoch (around 1670–1750) while others (like Martin Brecht) define the term broadly to include movements which were influenced by it.[7] In the second usage of the term, often a differentiation is made between new Pietism and old Pietism. New Pietism includes movements and developments within Pietism which received strong impulses from the Anglo-American holiness movement in the nineteenth century, while old Pietism comprises those groups which were not strongly affected by outside influences.[8] The term Pietism will be used in the broader sense (following Martin Brecht) throughout this work.

Never a fully unified movement, Pietism was separated by geography, liturgy, organization, and doctrine. However, some features were common: (1) a personal relationship with God based upon new birth in Christ; (2) renewal in Christ's image; (3) sanctification, with the goal of attaining a measure of Christian perfection; (4) Bible study, prayer, and spiritual formation in small groups; (5) evangelism and sending missionaries; (6) the authority of Scripture; and (7) expecting the second coming of Christ and rejecting worldliness among Christians.[9]

Another important feature in the history of Pietism is its international character. Throughout its development there have been encounters and reciprocal influences with traditions in other countries, especially the Netherlands and England.[10] John Wesley, for example, had direct contact,

---

7. See especially the discussion in Brecht, "Einleitung"; Wallmann, *Der Pietismus*, 7–8.

8. Lüdke, "Neupietismus—Versuch einer Begriffsklärung," 3–16.

9. Arnold, "Pietism," 408–10. Brecht, "Einleitung"; Wallmann, *Der Pietismus*, 9–27.

10. For a broader discussion, see Deppermann, "Der Englische Puritanismus"; Berg, "Die Frömmigkeitsbestrebungen in den Niederlanden"; Jakubowski-Tiessen, "Der Pietismus in Dänemark und Schleswig-Holstein"; Montgomery, "Der Pietismus in Norwegen im 18. Jahrhundert"; and Montgomery, "Der Pietismus in Schweden im

either personally or by literature, with some of the early leaders of Pietism, especially the Moravians. Although he broke with Zinzendorf and the Moravians, the influence on him and the theological traditions following him should not be underestimated.

The turn of the eighteenth to the nineteenth century was also critical for Pietism in Germany. In the aftermath of the French Revolution (1789), the dissolution of the Holy Roman Empire of German Nations by Napoleon (1806), and the political reshaping of Europe after the congress of Vienna (1815) there were different religious awakenings with Pietist emphases in various parts of Germany. The awakenings were usually restricted to particular areas in Germany,[11] and they did not lead to a unified movement. One of the reasons for that was that Germany was not a nationally unified country until 1871.

It was in the first half of the nineteenth century that new churches and movements from other countries came to Germany: Methodists, Baptists, Adventists, and itinerant preachers (many with German background), who had been influenced by the American and British revivals and awakenings. Reports on great missionary successes in non-Christian areas of the world (especially India, China, and Africa) reached the Pietist circles and sparked interest in missions. Literature was published (much of it translated into German) and mission organizations were founded to promote the Christian faith all over the world.

The last quarter of the century in Germany was characterized, among other phenomena, by the following occurrences: unification to the *Erstes Reich* (1871), industrialization with both unprecedented accumulation of wealth and prosperity and at the same time great poverty and destitution among masses of workers. Connected to industrialization was the growth of the cities with the different side effects of urbanization, philosophical secularization (e.g., Darwin, Marx, Feuerbach), and liberal theology becoming the predominant theological tradition in the Protestant theological faculties. These developments marked a great and fast change in German society and left many people insecure, disoriented and with a sense of instability.

---

18. Jahrhundert"; Laasonen, "Der Pietismus in Finnland im 17. und 18. Jahrhundert"; Dellsperger, "Der Pietismus in der Schweiz"; Streiff, "Der Methodismus bis 1784/1791"; Roeber, "Der Pietismus in Nordamerika im 18. Jahrhundert"; Gäbler, "Evangelikalismus und Réveil"; Laasonen, "Erweckungsbewegungen im Norden im 19. und 20. Jahrhundert"; Filipi, "Die Erweckungsbewegung in Ostmitteleuropa"; Noll, "Evangelikalismus und Fundamentalismus in Nordamerika."

11. For a broader discussion, see Weigelt, "Die Allgäuer katholische Erweckungsbewegung"; and Weigelt, "Die Diasporaarbeit der Herrnhuter Brüdergemeine und die Wirksamkeit der Deutschen Christentumsgesellschaft im 19. Jahrhundert"; Benrath, "Die Erweckung innerhalb der deutschen Landeskirchen 1815–1888. Ein Überblick."

All these developments sparked the wish among the different Pietist traditions in Germany to unify forces to meet the new challenges and to "build the kingdom of God."[12]

UNIFICATION OF PIETIST TRADITIONS: GEMEINSCHAFTSBEWEGUNG

Unification of the Pietist traditions occurred with the organization of the *Deutscher Verband für Gemeinschaftspflege und Evangelisation* (German Association for the Nurture of Fellowship and Evangelism) in 1897, briefly called *Gemeinschaftsbewegung*. This association became the umbrella organization of the different Pietist groups and movements in Germany.[13]

Paul Fleisch describes the beginnings of unification as a direct result of the holiness convention in Oxford in 1874. A group of German pastors and other leaders of Pietist movements were invited to the holiness convention in Oxford, led by Robert Pearsall Smith[14] and his wife Hannah Whitall Smith.[15] After the participants returned they immediately began to set up similar meetings: holiness conventions in various cities in Switzerland and Germany in 1874, which constituted the beginning of the *Heiligungsbewegung* in German-speaking Europe.[16] One of the strongest proponents was

---

12. The term "building the kingdom of God" became a dictum within the Pietist traditions in Germany in the nineteenth century. See Ohlemacher, *Reich Gottes*.

13. It started out with the Pietist associations from different parts of Germany and grew by adding Pietist youth organizations, various foreign mission associations, theological seminaries and Bible schools, deaconess associations, and organizations reaching out to prisoners, alcoholics, handicapped, and different professional groups, like bakers and railroad workers.

14. Robert Pearsall Smith (1827–1898), American layman, married to Hannah Whitall Smith (1832–1911), was the main speaker at the holiness conferences in Oxford (1874) and Brighton (1875). Before the conference in Brighton Smith also visited Germany and Switzerland and spoke at conferences in different cities in April and May 1875. This time has been called "triumphant journey" by some of his critics, and marked the beginning of the *Heiligungsbewegung* in Germany and Switzerland. His small book, *Holiness through Faith* influenced Jellinghaus and others, who translated it and published it in German, *Die Heiligung durch den Glauben*. Literature on Smith: Möller, *R. Pearsall Smith*; Logan Smith, *Unforgotten Years*; Parker, *The Transatlantic Smiths*; Ekholm, *Theological Roots of the Keswick Movement*; Voigt, *Heiligungsbewegung*.

15. Hannah Tatum Whitall Smith (1832–1911), lay speaker in the holiness movement in the United States, England and other European countries. The most popular book she wrote was, *The Christian's Secret of a Happy Life*.

16. Voigt, *Heiligungsbewegung*.

Theodor Jellinghaus. A more detailed history, especially relating to the involvement of Jellinghaus will be given later.[17]

As Jörg Ohlemacher pointed out, a first initiative for a "conference of Christian men from all of Germany" with the goal of unifying the Pietist groups was planned by three laymen with aristocratic background, Eduard von Pückler (1833–1893), Jasper von Oertzen (1853–1924), and Andreas von Bernstorff (1844–1907).[18] They wanted to return to the "basic principles of the reformation and the praxis of the apostolic church."[19] This meeting was planned to take place in Berlin in 1887. They intended to invite "all Christian men, who were serious that the kingdom of God would be built in peace in Germany" and emphasized three topics: 1) The entitlement, the necessity and the limits of lay involvement; 2) The blessing of fellowship and confraternity and the necessary organization of such in city and country; 3) Discussion of the question: What does Holy Scripture teach about sanctification?[20] The presence and influence of the *Heiligungsbewegung* in Germany between 1874 and 1887 becomes apparent especially in the third topic.

The plans were not realized, nevertheless, they were taken up at the next meeting of the *Deutscher Evangelisationsverein* (German Evangelism Association)[21] in April 1887 and the list of invitees was expanded. The meeting was aimed to take place on Pentecost weekend from May 22–24, 1888 in Gnadau, a little town with a Moravian settlement close to Magdeburg. The topics were the same as planned for the original meeting. Forty-five persons, all members of the German Protestant State Churches, signed the invitation.[22] The meeting was a great success as defined by its initiators: 148 persons came together: pastors, teachers, members of the aristocracy, civil servants, one factory owner and a lawyer.[23] One of the attenders was Theodor Jellinghaus.[24]

The following general features of the *Gemeinschaftsbewegung* can be identified. First, it became something like a repository for the various Pietist

17. Some information will be found later in this chapter, but most details will be discussed in chapter three on the life of Jellinghaus.

18. Ohlemacher, *Gemeinschaftschristentum*, 399.

19. Ibid.

20. Ibid., 400.

21. The *Deutscher Evangelisationsverein* was the first organized association of Pietist leaders in Germany who focused on evangelism within the Protestant State Churches. It became the forerunner organisation for the *Gemeinschaftsbewegung*.

22. Ohlemacher, *Reich Gottes*, 35–60.

23. Pfleiderer, *Verhandlungen*; Ohlemacher, *Gemeinschaftsbewegung*, 26–34.

24. Pfleiderer, *Verhandlungen*, 17.

groups from within the Lutheran, Reformed, and Unified state churches (in some German states Lutheran and Reformed traditions had unified to a single Protestant state church). Second, the *Gemeinschaftsbewegung* was greatly influenced by Anglo-American movements in the areas of evangelism with an emphasis on immediate conversion decisions and mass rallies to reach especially unchurched people and those who were alienated from traditional Christianity. Part of that influence was also a new form of gathering, conferences and conventions, modelled after the holiness conventions in England and America. Third, it was characterized by various individuals, mostly from the aristocracy or the higher social ranks, which gave them a certain financial independence in their religious engagements. Fourth, there was certain distrust in academic theology. Many of the early leaders were lay people. Fifth, there was an emphasis on educating and training *Reichsgottesarbeiter* (workers in the kingdom of God) independent from academic university education. Various schools for evangelists, lay preachers, and deaconesses were started. Sixth, Pietist groups reached out to the fringes of society, especially in the cities. Homes and societies for the homeless, alcoholics, prostitutes, orphans and unwed mothers were organized. Seventh, like in America and the United Kingdom different youth and student organizations were founded, like the *Christlicher Verein Junger Männer (CVJM)*, the German branch of the Young Men's Christian Association in 1883 in Berlin, the *Jugendbund für Entschiedenes Christentum (EC)*, after the model of the Christian Endeavour Society in 1894, and in 1897 the *Deutsche Christliche Studenten-Vereinigung* (German Christian Student Association). Eighth and lastly in this listing, new organizations to support Christian mission to foreign countries were formed. Among them the German branch of the China Inland Mission in 1897, the *Deutscher Hilfsbund für christliches Liebeswerk im Orient* (German Supporting Association for Christian Love Work in the Orient) in 1896 and the *Deutsche Orientmission* (German Orient Mission) in 1896.[25]

The *Gemeinschaftsbewegung* experienced a deep crisis in the years 1903–1909. The crisis was connected to the occurrence of the so called *Zungenbewegung* (Tongues Movement) or *Pfingstbewegung* (Pentecostal Movement) in Germany which came to Germany via Norway. Many of the fellowships were affected as they believed that this movement was a sign of the last times. The *Gemeinschaftsbewegung* was split over the manifestations like speaking in tongues and various physical occurrences. Some of the influential leaders of the movement tried to put an end to it by drawing up the so-called *Berliner Erklärung* in 1909 (Berlin Declaration) where (among

---

25. Ohlemacher, *Gemeinschaftschristentum*, 393–98, 413–25.

other things) they rejected any subsequent works of grace following justification. It also stated that all physical manifestations were "from below," i.e. of demonic origin and not from God. The result was that the *Gemeinschaftsbewegung* was split.[26]

Theodor Jellinghaus was caught up in the middle of this conflict, because he was connected to different groups and fellowships and had friends on both sides. In addition, he became ill and actually had to be in different psychiatric hospitals from 1906–1911. This point will be discussed in more detail later.[27] After the climax of the crisis following the *Berliner Erklärung*, Jellinghaus felt that his teachings had caused the split. Therefore he wrote (with the help of some of the critics of the *Pfingstbewegung*) a recantation of his teachings.[28]

HISTORICAL SURVEY OF THE HOLINESS MOVEMENT

This historical survey of the holiness movement will give a basic overview of the development of a theological tradition which would eventually influence Theodor Jellinghaus's teaching of sanctification. It is clear that a full historical survey is not possible at this point; therefore, an outline of the main characters, movements and their theological convictions will be presented.

The survey begins with the origins of the holiness movement in John Wesley's doctrine of Christian perfection. After that the development in the United States will be briefly examined. Especially during the years between 1835 and 1875 the holiness movement in the United States of America experienced strong expansion inside and outside of Methodism, which itself developed to become the strongest denomination in America.[29] The common characteristic among all groups within the nineteenth-century holiness movement was the conviction that next to the crisis experience of conversion, the crisis experience of sanctification was necessary in the Christian life. The original doctrine of John Wesley was differently interpreted and developed in the various traditions of the holiness movement.

The survey of the holiness movement in the United States will start with Phoebe Palmer's interpretation of the doctrine and go on with the Oberlin expression of sanctification as represented by Asa Mahan and Charles

---

26. Ibid., 426–43.

27. The details of his illness will be discussed in more detail in chapters 3 (his life) and 7 (recantation).

28. This will be dealt with in more detail in chapter 7.

29. Smith, *Revivalism*, 20–22.

Finney. These theological developments would influence the teaching (e.g., theological terminology) of the holiness camp meetings. Quite interesting and fascinating was the passage of the movement and teaching from the United States to Europe in the last quarter of the nineteenth century and how it was adapted in the Keswick movement, especially as it emerged in the United Kingdom under the influence of William Boardman[30] and Robert Pearsall Smith and his wife Hannah Whitall Smith.

Origins of the Holiness Movement: John Wesley

The approach taken in this part of the survey is to examine the relationship of John Wesley's doctrines of justification and sanctification. There are two reasons for that. First, one cannot be understood without the other in Wesley. It could even be said that the definition of one determines the definition of the other. Second, Theodor Jellinghaus emphasized strongly the relationship between justification and sanctification; this will be demonstrated in chapter five.

In order to understand justification in Wesley one must grasp his doctrine of original sin and free grace. In his doctrine of original sin Wesley basically followed Paul, Augustine and the Reformers that humanity was fallen and totally depraved from what the human race was intended to be. Sin for Wesley was basically unbelief and pride, humanity's attempt to "be like God."[31] For him, humankind was created in the threefold image of God: the natural image (as spiritual being, immortal, free, and understanding); the political image (as governor of this lower world, having dominion over all the earth); and the moral image (righteousness and true holiness).[32] In the Fall humanity lost the moral image, while the natural image and political image were retained; however, they were distorted.[33] The state of fallen humankind was depravity. Humanity was totally corrupt and therefore was fleshly (separated from God) rather than spiritual (rightly related to God). Adam represented all of humanity in his spiritual death and separation from God. Thus spiritual death (temporal and eternal) came upon all of humanity

---

30. William E. Boardman (1810–1886), American preacher, exponent of the holiness movement who influenced Robert Pearsall Smith, especially through his book, *The Higher Christian Life*, and worked with him at the conference in Oxford. He also influenced Jellinghaus and other representatives of the German *Heiligungsbewegung*. Literature on Boardman: Boardman, *Life and Labors of the Rev. W. E. Boardman*; Ekholm, *Theological Roots*.

31. Wesley, *Works (BE)*, 2:189–90, "Sermons II, 45. The New Birth."

32. Ibid., 2:188.

33. Ibid., 2:189–90.

and guilt was attached to the corrupt hearts of humanity.[34] From this fallen nature flow all corruptions and evil tendencies of humankind.

Humanity, left alone in this lost state, could not choose God. For Wesley as for the Reformers salvation was the entire work of God (whole and sole work of God). Therefore, salvation was by grace (God's unmerited favor). Grace for Wesley was always saving grace. He looked at saving grace from different angles. First, it was atoning grace of God in Jesus Christ. By it humanity was rescued from the sentence of death executed upon Adam, and it was the basis for the believers' resurrection and eternal life.[35] Atoning grace thus encountered sin on the one hand as an objective factor, which had destroyed humanity's relationship to God, and on the other hand as subjective factor, which had disturbed humanity's relationship to themselves.[36] Atoning grace also cancelled the guilt attached to original sin.[37] Second, Wesley saw it as prevenient or preventing grace. This was closely related to atoning grace; it was just another viewpoint of the one grace. As prevenient grace it was free for all (universal) and free in all.[38] That meant that Wesley believed that each person received God's gift of prevenient grace. Prevenient grace in the proper sense restored a measure of freedom humanity lacked in the bondage of original sin.[39] The end or purpose of prevenient grace was to bring humanity to Christ for justification.[40] That happened through a radical self knowledge, a conviction of sin and helplessness (human beings cannot save themselves) which would drive humanity to despair so that God could have "full course" in the life of a human being.[41] In summary, through prevenient grace the guilt of original sin was removed, a degree of freedom was restored to every human being, a beginning of divine light was present in every soul, and all of humanity was made "salvable."[42]

As humanity despaired in their helplessness they would come to a point of total self-knowledge of their sinfulness which would lead to their

---

34. Ibid. Cox, *John Wesley's Concept of Perfection*, 156; Maddox, *Responsible Grace*, 74–75; Collins, *The Scripture Way of Salvation*, 34–38.

35. Wesley, *Works (Jackson)*, VIII:277–78, "Addresses, Essays, Letters. VI. Minutes of some late Conversations between the Rev. Mr. Wesley and others, in 1744. Conversation I. Monday, June 25th, 1744."

36. *Works (BE)*, 2:190; 12:465–66.

37. *Works (Jackson)*, 8:277.

38. *Works (BE)*, 3:482; 4:163; 3:544–45.

39. Ibid., 11:112, where Wesley quoted Article X of the Book of Common Prayer of the Church of England; ibid., 12:254, 257, 279; 13:287.

40. Ibid., 9:64.

41. Ibid.

42. Cox, *John Wesley's Concept of Perfection*, 155.

repentance. Repentance for Wesley was prior to justification. As the Holy Spirit through prevenient grace awakened the sinner (through law and gospel) he or she would begin to turn from his or her sins to God, doing works meet for repentance (i.e., forgiving brother or sister, ceasing from evil, doing good, using the ordinances of God, and in general obeying God according to the measure of grace received). Since these works were done by prevenient grace which God gave to all human beings, these works were good. Nevertheless, Wesley held that it was faith alone which justified. Repentance and fruits meet for repentance were preparing justification and therefore in some sense (although not in the same sense) necessary to salvation.[43]

Wesley's view of repentance is made clearer in light of his distinction between repentance faith (faith of a servant) and justifying faith (faith of a son). By faith of a servant he meant "a species of faith" prior to justification.[44] God worked in the heart producing a sense of sin and need so that a person would be waiting for justifying faith. Humans, by acting under the conviction of prevenient grace, would amend their ways and turn to God. This would then lead to forgiveness of sins and declaration of righteousness (justification by faith). By faith of a son Wesley spoke of the gift of God by which a person became aware that salvation comes by faith alone and not by works of repentance. This was the point of readiness where the person would allow Christ to work within. God gave it to the believer not because of his works, but he gave it for Christ's sake.[45] Justification, therefore, had usually two movements for Wesley: first, repentance faith (free response to God's prevenient grace and sincere desire to please him) and second, justifying faith proper (a sure trust and confidence in Christ and the forgiveness of sins). For Wesley it was faith alone (based on God's grace alone) which justified the sinner.[46] For Wesley justification was primarily pardon, "the forgiveness of sins . . . for the sake of the propitiation made by the blood of His Son. . . . It is the act of God the Father, whereby, for the sake of the propitiation made by the blood of His Son, He 'showeth forth his righteousness' (or mercy) 'by the remission of sins that are past.'"[47]

While justification in Wesley negatively meant the non-imputation of sins positively it meant to be received into God's favor. The believers were "accepted through the Beloved" and "reconciled to God through His

---

43. *Works (Jackson)*, 8:283; Lindström, *Wesley and Sanctification*, 113–14; Collins, *The Scripture Way of Salvation*, 62–68.

44. Maddox, *Responsible Grace*, 174.

45. *Works (BE)*, 11:47–48.

46. *Works (Jackson)*, 10:345; Maddox, *Responsible Grace*, 172–76; Collins, *The Scripture Way of Salvation*, 94–100.

47. *Works (BE)*, 1:189.

blood."[48] Thus humans were reconciled to God (renewal of broken relationship) and adopted as children.

When it comes to the relationship of justification and sanctification in Wesley's theology, it was Harald Lindström who stated that justification in Wesley denoted what God does for the believers through his Son (forgiveness of sins) and thus represented a relative and objective change in which persons were delivered from the guilt of sin and thus restored to the favor of God. Sanctification, on the other hand, denoted what God did by his Holy Spirit, a renewal of the persons, liberation from the power and root of sin, and thus represented a real and subjective change.[49] Justification for Wesley was prior to sanctification in two respects. First, logically justification must precede sanctification, for only the justified persons can be sanctified. Second, the distinction between justification and sanctification took on temporal quality as well in the sense that sanctification was continuous in its process, while justification was complete in the believers' forgiveness and acceptance by God.[50]

In his teaching of sanctification, Wesley first of all highlighted regeneration or new birth which for him was an instantaneous act of God by which he imparted the righteousness of Christ in the believers' hearts and enabled them not to commit actual sins and to love God and neighbor.[51] In relation to justification, it took place chronologically at the same time, yet must be logically distinguished because it denoted primarily the work of God in the believers (subjective) while the former was primarily God's work for the believers (objective). In relation to sanctification, regeneration was the beginning of the process of sanctification; yet must be distinguished, because it is an instantaneous act of God and complete in that new life began, while sanctification denoted a process.[52]

Through justification and regeneration believers had power over outward sin; they did not have to commit sin. Yet, for Wesley, believers were not completely sanctified at that point, for there was latent within them dispositions which would trouble them (inward sin) which furnish the occasion of their possible falling back again into sin.[53] Sanctification had to do with the

---

48. *Works (Jackson)*, 8:275.
49. Lindström, *Wesley and Sanctification*, 84–85.
50. Ibid., 86.
51. Collins, *The Scripture Way of Salvation*, 105.
52. Cox, *John Wesley's Concept of Perfection*, 156; Collins, *The Scripture Way of Salvation*, 111.
53. *Works (BE)*, 13:148–49.

believers' internal disposition (inward sin), "our present deliverance by God from the *plague* of sin, not just from its *penalty*."[54]

At this point it is necessary to briefly look at Wesley's view of sin. First of all it needs to be stated that Wesley believed that sin was sin, meaning that there were no degrees of sin. However, he viewed sin from different perspectives in order to capture the comprehensiveness of its manifestations. On the one hand, Wesley spoke of outward sin. By this he meant "a voluntary transgression of the known law of God."[55] On the other hand, he also believed in inward sin. This was the sin that remains after justification and regeneration as an inward corruption of the affections (pride, self-will, love of the world, lust, etc.). It could be described as sin in believers. In the process of sanctification (the Holy Spirit's work within the believers) humans would be convicted of the remaining sin in their hearts, they would be convicted that sin was still cleaving to their words and actions, and they would be convicted of their helplessness. This Wesley called the repentance of believers. In this sense even Wesley believed in *simul iustus et peccator*, however, it is to be distinguished from the Reformers' understanding of the term.[56]

Here we come to the heart of Wesley's theology and his great contribution to the thought of Christian doctrine. Sanctification for Wesley was the inward work of the Holy Spirit in the believer, the cleansing of original sin. This was certainly not new, but new was his "claim that the specific transition to this dynamic level of Christian life is an instantaneous one, however much gradual growth there may be before or after it."[57] The cleansing of the believer's heart from remaining sin began at regeneration and continued in the believer until by faith the Holy Spirit finished the cleansing he began (entire sanctification). It could be stated that this was the negative aspect of entire sanctification. The positive aspect was described by Wesley as the believer's heart perfected in love. Both aspects took place at the same time and were only two expressions of the same event. "Entire sanctification . . . is neither more nor less than pure love—love expelling sin and governing both heart and life."[58] "It is love excluding sin; love fulfilling the heart, taking up the whole capacity of the soul. . . . For as long as love takes up the whole heart, what room is there for sin therein?"[59]

54. Maddox, *Responsible Grace*, 176.
55. Cox, *John Wesley's Concept of Perfection*, 156.
56. Dicker, *Concept of Simul Iustus et Peccator*, 75–96.
57. Maddox, *Responsible Grace*, 188.
58. *Works (Jackson)*, 12:432.
59. *Works (BE)*, 2:160.

Wesley called this phase of the Christian life Christian perfection. Because the term perfection had always been ambiguous, he distinguished two kinds of perfection. On the one hand, there was Christian perfection (Wesley refers to that), which was attained when the heart of the believer was made pure and love alone reigned (perfect love) and the believer was fully restored to the moral likeness of God.[60] Yet, Wesley believed that there remained such imperfection which was inseparable from human life. Here he spoke of the perfection which was ever ahead of the Christian and could not be attained in this life because of the believer's limitedness and ignorance which were side-effects of original sin which would always remain with human beings as long as they were in the human body (although the body was not intrinsically evil).[61]

Because of the distinction between the two kinds of perfection, Wesley distinguished between two kinds of sin. On the one side Wesley spoke about sin which was cleansed in entire sanctification (inward sin, moral depravity, a wrong disposition of the will, evil temper, self-will, evil moral desire, all of which are opposed to love of God and neighbor). On the other side, he believed that there were human limits by which humanity, as fallen, was pressed down by a corruptible body and acted through a faulty mind. Although a human being may not deviate from the law of love he or she would deviate from the perfect law given to Adam. Here Wesley agreed with the Reformers that even these deviations were sins, yet not sin properly so called (which were willful transgressions of the known law of God). Therefore, Wesley taught that these sins needed the atoning blood of Christ and daily forgiveness.[62] In summary, it could be said that Wesley did not teach perfect performance but rather pure intention.[63] One demonstration of John Wesley's understanding of Christian Perfection is found in his own eleven-point-summary in the closing pages of his *Plain Account of Christian Perfection*.[64]

60. Lindström, *Wesley and Sanctification*, 118.
61. Cox, *John Wesley's Concept of Perfection*, 157.
62. Ibid., 157–58.
63. Ibid.
64. *Works (BE)*, 13:187–88:

> 1. There is such a thing as perfection; for it is again and again mentioned in the Scripture. 2. It is not so early as justification; for justified persons are 'to go on to perfection' (Heb.vi.1). 3. It is not so late as death; for St. Paul speaks of living men that were perfect (Phil.iii.15). 4. It is not absolute. Absolute perfection belongs not to man, nor to angels, but to God alone. 5. It does not make a man infallible: None is infallible, while he remains in the body. 6. Is it sinless? It is not worthwhile to contend for a term. It is 'salvation from sin'. 7. It is 'perfect love' (1.John iv.18). This is the essence of it; its properties,

Wesley's doctrine of justification could be described as the gate of religion, while religion itself was the life of holiness, the loving of God and neighbor. "The real purpose of the imputation of the righteousness of Christ is thus to be declared the sanctification of man."[65] Even faith was not an end in itself but only a means, the end of all things was love.[66] Salvation for Wesley, therefore, was not merely deliverance from hell, or going to heaven; but it was a present deliverance from sin, a restoration and renewal of humanity in the image of God, in righteousness and true holiness, in justice, mercy, and truth.[67]

John Wesley's teaching of Christian perfection must be viewed in the whole scope of God's story with humanity and creation. It was part of God's renewal of creation, of humanity's relation to God, to each other and to the rest of creation. That is an important point because later developments (which we will consider below) seem to have narrowed it down to the subjective experience of victory over sin or a happy Christian life and much of its wider impact was neglected. This did not strengthen the original teaching but rather weakened it, because the heart of Wesley's teaching of love (in relationship to God, other human beings and the rest of creation), i.e., its ethical and moral impact in the widest sense, was torn out and left was a teaching of primarily subjective experiences.

Phoebe Palmer's Shorter Way

Phoebe (Worrall) Palmer (1807–1874)[68] was born and raised in a Methodist family. Her father emigrated from England to the United States. In

---

or inseparable fruits, are, rejoicing evermore, praying without ceasing, and in everything giving thanks (1.Thess.v.16&c.). 8. It is improvable. It is so far from lying in an indivisible point, from being incapable of increase, that one perfected in love may grow in grace far swifter than he did before. 9. It is amissible, capable of being lost; of which we have numerous instances . . . 10. It is constantly both preceded and followed by gradual work. 11. But is it in itself instantaneous or not? . . . It is often difficult to perceive the instant when a man dies: yet there is an instant when life ceases. And if ever sin ceases, there must be a last moment of its existence, and a first moment of our deliverance from it.

65. Lindström, *Wesley and Sanctification*, 101.
66. *Works (BE)*, 9:228–29.
67. Ibid., 9:229.
68. For more detailed information on Phoebe Palmer, see the following resources: Heath, *Naked Faith*; Raser, *Phoebe Palmer*; Oden, *In Her Own Words*; Oden, *Phoebe Palmer*; White, *The Beauty of Holiness*; Reuther and Keller, *Women and Religion in America*; Taylor, ed., *Handbook of Women Biblical Interpreters*.

England he had a conversion experience under the influence of John Wesley and remained faithful to the Methodists in the new world. In 1827 Phoebe married the physician Dr. Walter Clarke Palmer, an influential lay worker in the Episcopal Methodist Church.[69] Although she claimed that the main influence for her thinking originated in the Bible, it is unquestionable that she was influenced heavily by Methodist preachers and theologians, the strongest of which were John Wesley, John Fletcher, and Adam Clarke.[70] The influence of John Wesley was obvious. Palmer wanted to reassure her audience that her teachings were based on the doctrines of Wesley; and she quoted from his sermons, journal and letters to show that she was faithful to the old Methodist teachings.[71]

Phoebe Palmer followed John Fletcher[72] (1729–1785), designated successor of John Wesley who preceded him in death, by identifying entire sanctification with receiving the Holy Spirit or the "baptism with the Holy Spirit and fire."[73] She modified some of his thoughts and developed them further. Another thought of Fletcher was further developed by Hester Ann Roe-Rogers (1756–1794)[74] and adopted by Phoebe Palmer, namely the understanding of faith as apprehending of God's promises. Regarding sanctification, the promise of God was not to be understood as a general impersonal aptitude, but as trusting in God's word.[75]

Adam Clarke[76] (1760/1/62–1832), Methodist theologian and biblical interpreter, influenced Phoebe Palmer in two areas. First, Clarke remarked extensively in his Bible commentaries (see Romans 12:1–2, Hebrews 13:10 and Exodus 29:37) that believers should make themselves available as living sacrifices to God by putting themselves on the altar.[77] Here Palmer found the basic arguments and language for her own so-called altar theol-

---

69. Dieter, *19th-Century Holiness Movement*, 130.

70. White, *The Beauty of Holiness*, 120.

71. Ibid., 122.

72. For more information on John Fletcher, see the following sources: Knight, *John William Fletcher*; Streiff, *Reluctant Saint*; Forsaith, *Unexampled Labors*; Wood, *The Meaning of Pentecost*.

73. White, *The Beauty of Holiness*, 122.

74. Hester Ann Roe-Rogers (1756–1794) met John Wesley in 1776 and became leader of a class meeting. She and her husband worked in Dublin and Cork. Until John Wesley's death in 1791 she stayed in contact with him. Her book *Life of Faith Exemplified or Extracts from the Journal of Mrs. Hester Ann Rogers* became a classic in Methodism. Schmid, *Heiligungskonferenzen von Oxford*, 92.

75. White, *The Beauty of Holiness*, 123.

76. For more information on Adam Clarke see the following sources: Sellers, *Adam Clarke*. Tracy, *When Adam Clarke Preached, People Listened*.

77. White, *The Beauty of Holiness*, 123.

ogy. Second, according to Charles White, Clarke's understanding of entire sanctification contained four elements. He first of all taught instantaneous sanctification. While Wesley and Fletcher seemed to have kept a tension between process and moment in the experience of entire sanctification, Clarke emphasized more the instantaneous moment.[78] Second, Clarke taught that entire sanctification is neither the culmination nor the goal of growth in Christian life, but rather the condition.[79] Third, Clarke put more emphasis on a methodological presentation for achieving Christian perfection than Wesley and Fletcher had. While the latter two encouraged believers to seek entire sanctification as a goal, Clarke criticized those that had not attained Christian perfection because they had not been looking for it in the right way.[80] Fourth, Clarke put more emphasis on the relationship of sanctification and power than Wesley and Fletcher did.[81] Phoebe Palmer followed Clarke's interpretation of the holy life more closely than she did Wesley and Fletcher and found arguments and connecting factors to her own teaching of the so-called shorter way.

Another important influence on Palmer was the Methodist minister and editor of the magazine *Guide to Christian Perfection*, Timothy Merritt. He influenced her with his understanding of a personal covenant between the believer and God as a step to attain entire sanctification.[82] As Charles White has pointed out, Phoebe Palmer modified John Wesley's original doctrine of entire sanctification in at least six points.[83] First, she identified entire sanctification with the baptism of the Holy Spirit (influenced by Fletcher). Second, she linked sanctification with empowerment (influenced by Clarke). Third, she emphasized instantaneous sanctification (influenced by Clarke). Fourth, entire sanctification was not the goal of a fulfilled Christian life but rather its condition (influenced by Clarke). Fifth, through her altar theology she simplified the process of entire sanctification to a three-step progression. And sixth, the assurance of entire sanctification was given by the biblical text which believers must trust.[84]

---

78. Ibid.
79. Ibid.
80. Ibid., 124.
81. Ibid.
82. Ibid.
83. Ibid. On a discussion about the differences between John Wesley and Phoebe Palmer on entire sanctification, see also Jones, *Perfectionist Persuasion*, 4–5.
84. White, *The Beauty of Holiness*, 125–26.

Phoebe Palmer believed that there was a shorter way to holiness and that it was available to everyone who believed it.[85] "Certainly you may look for it now, if you believe it is by faith."[86] This shorter way consisted of three steps. First, full surrender with all your will, heart and soul was essential.[87] Second, faith was necessary to receive and to remain in the experience of entire sanctification.[88] Third, to give witness about the experience with thankfulness to God with the aim to help others to the experience was the last step.[89] Key in this shorter way was her so-called altar theology. Palmer challenged believers to present themselves to Christ as living sacrifices. Christ himself was the altar on which the sacrifice was to be placed. The sacrifice was the believer himself or herself and he or she must place everything on the altar and leave it on the altar. Because everything that touched the altar was sanctified, the believer was sanctified. Therefore, the full surrender guaranteed entire sanctification.[90] The basic ingredients of a life of holiness were Bible reading, prayer, observing the Sabbath and fellowship.[91] On the other hand, hindrances to a life of holiness were extravagant clothing, pious amusements, lofty worship services and money.[92]

Phoebe Palmer's understanding of holiness became quite influential for the holiness movement in the United States of America. The founding and growth of the National Camp Meeting Association (NCMA) institutionalized Palmer's teaching. These camp meetings became popular and the holiness preaching and teaching was spread by tracts, magazines and hymnals.[93] Her theology also played an important role in the emergence of holiness groups, churches and denominations.[94]

Oberlin Perfectionism

A different yet not totally unrelated development found its expression at Oberlin College in Ohio through the teachings of Charles Grandison

---

85. Palmer, *Way of Holiness*, 17–18.
86. Ibid., 100.
87. White, *The Beauty of Holiness*, 135–36.
88. Ibid., 137–38.
89. Ibid., 138.
90. Ibid., 140; and Palmer, *Way of Holiness*, 62–67.
91. White, *The Beauty of Holiness*, 147–49.
92. Ibid., 150–53.
93. Ibid., 157.
94. Ibid., 158.

Finney (1792–1875)⁹⁵ and Asa Mahan (1799–1889),⁹⁶ which became known as Oberlin Perfectionism. Both men and the school were part of the Reformed tradition and had a great influence on non-Methodist groups and churches. Since Oberlin was an academic institution which also educated ministers, the theological development and prominence of holiness teaching influenced pastors stronger than in the primarily lay-movement of Phoebe Palmer. In addition, because Oberlin was also known for promoting co-education, abolition of slavery and prohibition, the holiness movement became influential in American society. It seems that in Oberlin Perfectionism there is a certain synthesis of New School Calvinism and the Wesleyan doctrine of entire sanctification. This might have helped those persons that were reached for the holiness movement through the new revivalist events who came from a non-Methodist background.⁹⁷

Greathouse argues that a new emphasis found expression in the Oberlin teaching, namely that entire sanctification was accomplished by a personal baptism with the Holy Spirit as modelled by the early church on the Day of Pentecost in the Book of Acts.⁹⁸ This modification of Wesley's original doctrine would have an impact and be generally accepted by the later holiness movement. White claimed that there were cultural and theological reasons for the emergence of Pentecostal language. In the mid-nineteenth century in the United States society was not as optimistic as a couple of decades earlier (during the time of the Second Awakening), which was due to massive immigration, urbanization and industrialization. Instead of looking forward society tended to look backward. Terms like Christian perfection pointed into the future, while Pentecostal language idealized God's great and wonderful intervention in a difficult situation for the early Christians when he cleansed them and empowered them to change the world.⁹⁹ Theologically it seemed that the doctrine of entire sanctification could be presented more plainly in Pentecostal language rather than in perfectionistic language. The latter needed additional explanation, especially to other

---

95. Charles G. Finney was a Presbyterian minister, evangelist, social activist, professor, and later president at Oberlin College in Ohio (USA). See Hardman, *Charles Grandison Finney*; Hambrick-Stowe, *Charles G. Finney*.

96. Asa Mahan, Presbyterian minister, was an educator, writer, theologian of the holiness movement, and first president at Oberlin College in Ohio. See Brown Zikmund, *Asa Mahan and Oberlin Perfectionism*; Madden and Hamilton, *Freedom and Grace*.

97. Bassett and Greathouse, *Exploring Christian Holiness*, 302.

98. Ibid. See especially Mahan, *Baptism of the Holy Ghost*.

99. White, *The Beauty of Holiness*, 127.

theological traditions. Pentecostal language bridged the differences between the different traditions more easily.[100]

Asa Mahan's book, *Baptism of the Holy Ghost*, was not only the first full-length book on the subject but also defined both the pattern and method of the experience of sanctification.[101] The method is the "baptism of the Holy Ghost, to be sought and received by faith in God's word of promise, on the part of the believer, after he has believed."[102] He went on to describe the pattern and method by stating: "In this baptism of power, this sealing and earnest of the Spirit, which is always given, not in conversion, but after we have believed, the promise of the Spirit is fulfilled."[103] Mahan taught that there were two classes of believers. First the ones who were converted by repentance and received by faith pardon and eternal life, and second those who after their conversion experienced receiving the Holy Ghost.[104] The difference between the two groups was that the former have "a measure of assurance that God is their Father, but this is mixed with doubts and fears; their spiritual life is weak and best portrayed in the seventh chapter of Romans."[105] The latter group, on the other side, enjoys "absolute assurance and hope" and experience "fellowship with the Father, and with his Son Jesus Christ."[106]

Charles Finney agreed with much of the teaching of Asa Mahan on entire sanctification. One of his contributions has been the connection of the baptism with the Holy Spirit and the empowerment of the believers for service. This need for the power for service was twofold: first, to enable the Church to fulfill the Great Commission given by Christ; and second to establish in "permanent sanctification" the believers in the Lord Jesus Christ.[107] As Greathouse pointed out, permanent sanctification was another term for entire sanctification and was viewed by Finney as "the elimination of selfishness to which we are voluntarily committed as free agents."[108]

---

100. Ibid.

101. Bassett and Greathouse, *Exploring Christian Holiness*, 305.

102. Mahan, *Baptism of the Holy Ghost*, 13, as quoted in Bassett and Greathouse, *Exploring Christian Holiness*, 306.

103. Mahan, *Baptism of the Holy Ghost*, 38, as quoted in Bassett and Greathouse, *Exploring Christian Holiness*, 306.

104. Bassett and Greathouse, *Exploring Christian Holiness*, 306.

105. Ibid.

106. Mahan, *Baptism of the Holy Ghost*, 54, as quoted in Bassett and Greathouse, *Exploring Christian Holiness*, 306.

107. Finney, *Power from On High*, 5 and 39, as quoted in Bassett and Greathouse, *Exploring Christian Holiness*, 310.

108. Bassett and Greathouse, *Exploring Christian Holiness*, 311.

However, it must be stated that Finney did not mean the same as Wesley by entire sanctification. He did not believe in the cleansing of original sin, but rather in "keeping under" the "flesh," which was later adopted by many, especially in the United Kingdom and the Keswick teaching of holiness.[109] Finney's teaching became accepted by the Calvinistic tradition of the movement. The baptism with the Holy Spirit was not for cleansing but rather empowering for victorious living and effective witness.[110]

The modification of Wesley's original teaching happened both within the Methodist tradition (the climax of which was Phoebe Palmer's so-called shorter way) and in the wider evangelical circles of which the Oberlin perfectionism became the most influential tradition. Both developments would meet and mingle and be popularized through the camp meetings of the holiness movement.

Holiness Camp Meetings in the United States

Another important catalyst in the development of the holiness movement in the United States became the so-called camp meetings. Camp meetings were an American frontier phenomenon in the early nineteenth century to gather Christians who lived miles away from each other for Christian services and fellowship for a period of time.[111] These camp meetings were organized by different denominations and followed detailed daily schedules. People lived in tents and the Christian meetings were carried out in larger tents or in the open. The speaker was usually placed in the middle of the meeting place and the audience gathered around the platform.[112]

The holiness movement adopted the method of camp meetings for the proclamation of the message of holiness. In July 1867 the first holiness camp meeting took place in Vineland, New Jersey with apparently 10,000 participants.[113] The following year the meeting took place near Manheim, Pennsylvania with "more than 300 ministers and 25,000 other attendants crowded into the camp area."[114] Dieter noted that this meeting "was significant to

---

109. Theodor Jellinghaus followed this thought as well, as will be demonstrated in chapter 5.
110. Bassett and Greathouse, *Exploring Christian Holiness*, 312.
111. Finke and Stark, *The Churching of America*, 96.
112. Ibid., 103.
113. Dieter, *Holiness Revival*, 106.
114. Ibid., 107.

the American holiness revival, not only because of the large crowds who gathered there, but also because of the interdenominational influences."[115]

The camp meetings were organized by the National Camp Meeting Association (NCMA) of which John Inskip was the leader for many years. The camp meetings became the most dominant force for the holiness movement. The message of sanctification followed the basic teachings of Phoebe Palmer and the Oberlin School. The center of the message was the instantaneous experience of the baptism with the Holy Spirit with the empowerment for service with the goal of "reviving the doctrine and experience of 'holiness of heart and life.'"[116]

The history of the holiness movement in the United States before the conferences in Oxford and Brighton (1874 and 1875) were characterized by rapid growth of the Methodist Episcopal Church as well as the movement in general. The sphere of influence of the holiness movement went well beyond the Methodist movement founded by John Wesley. The non-Wesleyan denominations, mostly in the Calvinistic tradition, are described as being Arminianised, i.e., they adopted with the holiness movement much of Wesleyan Arminianism.[117] However, the American holiness movement was neither a unified body nor uncontroversial. Developments were taking place in methodology and theology which would lead the adherents of the holiness movement into different groups and cause separation and schism. This can be observed especially in the development of different holiness denominations.

Conferences in England and Keswick Convention

At the center of the holiness conferences in Oxford (1874) and Brighton (1875) stood the American lay preachers Robert Pearsall Smith, his wife Hannah Whitall Smith, and William E. Boardman who were influenced by the holiness movement in the United States of America. When the American

---

115. Ibid., 107–8. Denominations represented were Presbyterians, Methodists, Baptists, Dutch Reformed, Congregationalists, and Quakers according to Dieter.

116. Bassett, "Holiness Movement."

117. The term "Arminianism" goes back to the Dutch theologian Jacobus Arminius (1560–1609), professor of theology in Leiden (Netherlands). He criticized rigorous Calvinism. John Wesley adapted Arminian teaching into his own theological system. He even called his regular publication *Arminian Magazine*. Especially in regard to original sin, John Wesley did not fully accept Arminian teaching. The main points of his "Arminianism" were human responsibility, conditional election, general atonement, resistible grace, and possible falling from grace. See Greschat, *Gestalten der Kirchengeschichte*, 7:51–64.

holiness movement experienced its climax[118] this energetic couple was instrumental in the breakthrough of the movement in Europe. However, they were not original thinkers. They actually transported both the methodology and content of what they experienced in the holiness movement in the United States in their publications and public addresses in England, France, Germany and Switzerland. The first holiness conference with Robert Pearsall Smith and his wife in Oxford came to be a success with 1,500 participants from the United Kingdom and continental Europe.[119] Two questions arise at this point: First, why did England become the bridgehead of the American development of the holiness movement? Second, why did Christians from all over Europe participate at the Oxford conference?

Urs Schmid argues that England became the most important platform in the transatlantic network of evangelicals. This was due to the geographical position and the historical ties between the two countries.[120] In addition the common language made communication and publications in both countries easier. Many of the popular speakers and teachers of the holiness movement visited England; among them Charles Finney, Asa Mahan and even Phoebe Palmer; later William E. Boardman and the Smiths did the same. Many of their publications were widely spread in England.[121] The news of revivals in the United States fell on fertile ground with evangelicals in England who were longing for spiritual renewal and awakening.[122] The enthusiastic reports of the holiness camp meetings from 1867 on seemed to have been received readily in England. Since January 1872 Cuthbert Bainbridge published the magazine *King's Highway* which would play a similar role for the holiness movement in England as did Merritt's *Guide to Holiness* in the United States.[123] Boardman's book *The Higher Christian Life* (1858) became a bestseller so that when Boardman visited England in 1869 for business reasons, he was invited to speak at different events.[124] This shows that both Boardman and later the Smiths could build on relationships and developments that had happened before their presence in England and which had laid the groundwork for their ministry.

---

118. Dieter believes that the climax of the American holiness movement is found in the decade following the American Civil War from 1867 until 1877. Dieter, *Holiness Revival*, 79–116.

119. Ibid., 167.

120. Schmid, *Heiligungskonferenzen von Oxford*, 156.

121. Ibid., 157.

122. Ibid.

123. Ibid.

124. Ekholm, *Theological Roots*, 26.

Connections between the evangelicals in England and the European continent were happening on various levels, among which were missionary agencies, Bible societies, and especially influential European leaders who had lived and ministered in England. Out of these connections networks developed in the mid-nineteenth century among which the Mildmay conferences of William Pennefather and the Evangelical Alliance were probably the two outstanding organizations.[125] It was primarily in England where leading evangelicals of the United Kingdom and Pietists of the European continent got into contact with the message and methodologies of the American holiness movement. William Boardman and Robert Pearsall Smith and his wife Hannah Whitall Smith made use of these networks which set the stage for the relatively quick success of the holiness movement in Europe.

Robert Pearsall Smith came to England in 1873 without his wife and the family. Before he and Boardman spoke at the first holiness conference in Oxford,[126] they promoted the holiness message primarily in informal meetings and with individuals.[127] In 1874, especially with the arrival of Hannah Whitall Smith and their children, activities intensified. In February of that year, the holiness magazine *The Christian Pathway to Power* was founded by Smith.[128] They spoke at conferences and travelled to France. In Paris, where they spoke to 150 persons, they met the French pastor Théodore Monod,[129]

---

125. More detailed information on the individuals involved, the organizations, and the networks that developed can be found both in Ekholm's and Schmid's dissertations.

126. The meeting was called Union Meeting for the Promotion of Scriptural Holiness.

127. Schmid gathered information on where R. P. Smith and Boardman spoke in the summer and autumn of 1873 and who they met, some of whom became supporters for their ministry. Schmid, 166.

128. The opening article gives good insight into the message of Smith. "On introducing to the Christians of Great Britain a periodical devoted to the subject of personal Consecration and Power for Service, it may be well to state briefly what we conceive to be the practical possibilities of faith. We believe the Word of God teaches that the *normal* Christian life is one of uniform sustained victory over known sin; and that no temptation is permitted to happen to us without a way of escape being provided by God, so that we may be able to bear it. We believe that the cross of Christ, which has effectually separated us from the penalty or consequences of our sins, is also the means by which we become separated from their power; and the only true way of overcoming the evil within us, is by recognizing our position as those that 'have crucified the flesh with the affections and lusts;' that the reckoning of ourselves to be dead indeed unto sin, is the great duty of faith, and the secret of a life of abiding communion with God." *The Christians Pathway of Power* 1, no. 1 (1874) 1, as quoted in Schmid, *Heiligungskonferenzen von Oxford*, 166.

129. Théodore Monod (1836–1921), nephew of the French evangelist Adolphe Monod. He studied law and during a trip to the United States in 1858 was awakened to the Christian message and returned to France and became a preacher. From 1860 he

who was won for the holiness movement and became a well-known speaker at holiness conferences in England, France and Switzerland.[130]

If the holiness conference in Oxford in 1874 can be seen as the initiating event of the Keswick Convention,[131] then the Broadlands Conference (July 17–23, 1874) was the initiator of the Oxford conference.[132] The Cowper Temple family invited the Smiths and about 150 persons to their private estate in the Broadlands. Schmid argues that the personal friendship between Mr. and Mrs. Cowper Temple and Mr. and Mrs. Smith strengthened the position and influence of the latter couple in the holiness movement in England and set the stage for the conference in Oxford and the later "triumphant journey"[133] through Germany and Switzerland.[134] Both the content of the messages and the methodology, even the daily plan, followed basically that of the camp meetings of the NCMA.[135] An additional characteristic of the Broadlands conference seems to have been its ecumenical character. Participants from different confessional and denominational backgrounds and even nationalities enjoyed these times and expressed their experiences in enthusiastic reports.[136] Because of these experiences and the positive atmosphere, the decision was made to have another similar conference which should even be planned on a broader basis, a conference in Oxford.[137]

The participants from different European countries (among them also Theodor Jellinghaus) experienced for the first time a Christian conference that followed the model of the camp meetings in the United States. Typical elements of the meeting in Oxford were new and simple songs (many of which were later translated into German), a new form of free preaching with an invitation to react after the service, open and lively prayer times, optimistic promises about the work of God for new power and a life in victory

---

worked as pastor in Paris and was influenced by Robert Pearsall Smith during a visit in Paris and became part of the holiness movement. Literature: Monod, "Um was es sich handelt"; and Monod, *Looking unto Jesus* and *Gift of God*. Through him the holiness movement gained reputation, not only in France, but also in Switzerland and Germany. Schmid, *Heiligungskonferenzen von Oxford*, 120.

130. Ibid., 168.

131. Barabas, *So Great Salvation*, 15–23.

132. Ibid.

133. The term "triumphant journey" had been coined by some of Smith's critics, and marked the beginning of the *Heiligungsbewegung* in Germany and Switzerland. See Voigt, *Heiligungsbewegung*.

134. Schmid, *Heiligungskonferenzen von Oxford*, 170.

135. Ekholm, *Theological Roots*, 79.

136. Schmid, *Heiligungskonferenzen von Oxford*, 171.

137. Ibid. About 1,500 persons participated in this conference.

through faith, and public sharing of personal testimonies. Many German participants experienced these days as "days of blessing."[138] In summary, it can be said that the conference in Oxford marked the breakthrough of the American holiness movement in the old world. Following the examples of the holiness camp meetings in the United States in message and methodology, a ten day conference was held with 1,500 participants from all over Europe.[139] The positive experience inspired the participants from Europe to hold similar meetings on the continent and the United Kingdom.[140]

In the following year, the conference in Oxford was followed by a second, even larger holiness conference in England, namely in Brighton (May 29 to June 7, 1875), right after Smith's journey through Germany and Switzerland with about 8,000 participants.[141] Soon after the Brighton convention Robert Pearsall Smith and his wife returned to the United States due to a scandal. Rumors regarding inappropriate behavior circulated quickly. Apparently Smith met with a young lady, Hattie Hamilton, for private counselling. It is not clear whether this was a case of indecent actions or incautious conduct of being alone with a young lady in a room. However, since it was talked about and not all questions were answered, Smith could not continue his ministry. One of the reasons given was that because of overexertion in the last year, Smith's headaches had come back and it was felt best for them to return to their home country.[142] After the Brighton conference, the holiness movement in Europe developed more independently from the United States. The development in the German-speaking areas of Europe (western France, Switzerland and Germany) will be portrayed in the next chapter. In England, the Keswick Convention became the primary bearer of the movement.

---

138. Warneck, *Segenstage*. More on the influences of this new style of Christian conferences on the Christian life in Germany, see Fleisch, *Heiligungsbewegung*, Ohlemacher, "Evangelikalismus und Heiligungsbewegung im 19. Jahrhundert"; Holthaus, *Heil—Heilung—Heiligung*.

139. Schmid, *Heiligungskonferenzen von Oxford*, 185.

140. This can be clearly seen in the report of the meetings in Oxford: *Account of the Union Meeting for the Promotion of Scriptural Holiness, held at Oxford, August 29th to September 7th, 1874*. The report was also translated into German: *Die Segenstage in Oxford. Reden gehalten bei den Versammlungen vom 29. Aug. bis 7. Sept. 1874*.

141. Two German participants summarized their experience and published them: Wangemann, *Pearsall Smith und die Versammlungen zu Brighton*; Warneck, *Briefe über die Versammlungen zu Brighton*.

142. Jellinghaus writes about the situation quite extensively in the first edition of his book, *Das völlige Heil*, 39–53. See also Barabas, *So Great Salvation*, 25–26. Pollock and Randall, *The Keswick Story*, 41–50. Schmid, *Heiligungskonferenzen von Oxford*, 281–87; Ekholm, *Theological Roots*; Krause, "Robert Pearsall Smith."

Meetings of the Keswick Convention began in 1875 after the meetings in Brighton. The early leaders were T.D. Harford-Battersby and Robert Wilson. The name of the Convention was chosen after the first meeting place, Keswick, in the northwest of England.[143] In contrast to the beginnings in Oxford and Brighton, the Keswick Convention began to reflect the doctrine of sanctification theologically. The outstanding theological leaders of the early years were Evan H. Hopkins, J.W. Webb-Peploe and especially H.C.G. Moule, who later became Bishop of Durham.[144] Other prominent representatives included Andrew Murray, F.B. Meyer, Hudson Taylor and Amy Carmichael.[145]

Barabas suggested that the teaching of the Keswick Convention is best reflected in the weekly schedule of the meetings:

> Day 1: Careful diagnosis of the spiritual ills is made so that Christians will know where they stand.
>
> Day 2: Teaching the provision God has made in Christ for the problem of sin.
>
> Day 3: Teaching on consecration: Man's response to God's call for complete abandonment and surrender to Him—at once a crisis and a process.
>
> Day 4: Teaching on the Spirit-filled life: To be completely controlled by the Spirit.
>
> Day 5: Christian Service because sanctification, the life in the Spirit, is not an end in itself, it is rather equipment for life and service.[146]

The doctrine of sanctification in the Keswick Convention followed the pattern of the Smiths' and Boardman's teachings and adapted them to the English setting.[147] The convention and its teachings would become a major influence in the evangelical circles in England and the United Kingdom.[148]

---

143. The detailed history of the Keswick Convention can be found in the following sources: Harford, *The Keswick Convention*; Sloan, *These Sixty Years*; Barabas, *So Great Salvation*; Pollock, *The Keswick Story*; Pollock and Randall, *The Keswick Story*; Price and Randall, *Transforming Keswick*.

144. Schmid, *Heiligungskonferenzen von Oxford*, 230.

145. Naselli, *Keswick Theology*.

146. Barabas, *So Great Salvation*, 148–49.

147. For critical reflections on the teaching of the Keswick Convention, see especially two publications: Packer, *Keep in Step*, 145–64; Bebbington, *Evangelicalism in Modern Britain*, 151–80.

148. This is argued especially in the works of Bebbington and Packer.

SUMMARY AND FUNCTION OF SURVEYING THE HISTORICAL-THEOLOGICAL SETTING

The life and work of Theodor Jellinghaus must be examined in its context. The survey of the historical-theological setting presented in this chapter helps to gain a broad overview of this context. It was the intention to begin with the broadest context and narrow it down to the immediate framework which influenced Jellinghaus. The impacts will become apparent in the portrayal of the life and teachings of Jellinghaus in chapters three, four, five, and six.

The broadest context (historical-theological setting in Germany in the nineteenth century) influenced especially his doctrine of reconciliation. An influence of Schleiermacher and theologians of the Erlangen school will be demonstrated in chapter four. The Pietist tradition had the strongest influence on Jellinghaus's basic doctrine of redemption (see chapter five) as well as his practical ministry (chapters three and six).

The next layer in the historical-theological setting constituted the unification of the Pietist tradition in the *Gemeinschaftsbewegung* in the last quarter of the nineteenth century. Jellinghaus was personally involved in the unification and participated actively in the development of the *Gemeinschaftsbewegung*. His life and work cannot be understood without his involvement in and conflicts with the *Gemeinschaftsbewegung*. This will be examined and assessed in chapter three.

The immediate setting is represented by the holiness movement. Since the holiness movement had its theological and methodological roots outside of Germany, the movement was surveyed historically in broad strokes. The question must be asked if there was any direct influence of John Wesley's theology on Theodor Jellinghaus.[149] In light of the summary of Wesley's teaching, it becomes clear that Jellinghaus did not follow his thinking, but rather the ideas of later representatives of the holiness movement. How the doctrine developed until Jellinghaus heard it in Oxford has been portrayed in the surveys of the teachings of Phoebe Palmer, Oberlin Perfectionism and the camp meetings of the holiness movement in the United States of America. Jellinghaus basically adopted and adapted what he had heard in Oxford and incorporated it into his own theological system. How and what he did in this regard will be reviewed and assessed in the following chapters.

---

149. Jellinghaus refers to reading in John Wesley's *Works* after his return from missionary service in India (probably sometime between 1870 and 1877) in *MadB* 17:10. However, he only mentions the fact that he read in Wesley's *Works*, but does not give any information on what he read.

3

Life of Theodor Jellinghaus

FAMILY, CHILDHOOD, EDUCATION

THEODOR GERHARD JELLINGHAUS[1] WAS born on June 21, 1841[2] at 9:00 am in Schlüsselburg/Westphalia as one of seven children into the family of a Lutheran minister.[3] Many of his ancestors since the Reformation had been ministers.[4] During the years of his childhood and youth the family lived in Wallenbrück/Westphalia, where his father, Karl Heinrich Franz Florens Jellinghaus (1799–1876) served as pastor of the Lutheran church. He went to school at the *Evangelisches Gymnasium* in Gütersloh and finished with the university entrance diploma (*Abitur*) in 1861.[5]

---

1. A biographical timeline of Theodor Jellinghaus is found in the appendix.

2. He was baptized by his father on July 30, 1841 according to the archives of the Evangelisches Pfarramt Schlüsselburg.

3. Of the seven children, two died in infancy according to the archives of the Evangelisches Pfarramt Schlüsselburg. His father and grandfather were part of the Pietist movement in northwest Germany. This is mentioned by Paul Jellinghaus (Theodor's son) in a printed memorial sermon after the death of Theodor Jellinghaus in *MadB* 49:6–13.

4. Bauks, *Die evangelischen Pfarrer in Westfalen*, 232; and Fischer, *Evangelisches Pfarrerbuch*, 1:379. There were also pastors in the family of his mother. Additional information about his ancestors can be found in a recollection of his family history in *MadB* 6:3.

5. Information on his childhood and other family memorabilia can be found in the Jellinghaus family archives of Sigmar Jellinghaus in Heidelberg, Germany.

On the occasion of his sixtieth birthday, Theodor Jellinghaus mentioned his childhood in an article in the *Mitteilungen aus der Bibelschule*, where he wrote: "I am thankful for the grace of God which has led me to the Redeemer, protected me from evil ways, and has prepared me all of my life for the Christian ministry. From the time of early youth I was filled with the assurance that I should become a missionary to the heathen."[6]

Like his father and his two older brothers, Jellinghaus began his theological studies in Halle (1861–1862).[7] He continued his studies in Erlangen (1862–1864)[8] and sat his two theological exams at the Royal Consistory in Münster (1864 and 1865).[9]

Theodor Jellinghaus was married twice and had altogether seven children, three of whom died in infancy. One of his daughters passed away 26 months before his own death. His first wife was Mary Prochnow (1840–1870),[10] whom he married in November 1867 in India where both of them served as missionaries. Two children were born, Emil (1868) and Martha (1870). Owing to illness both children and the mother passed away within a couple of weeks in 1870. After this tragedy Jellinghaus returned to Germany.[11] Three years after his return to Germany Theodor Jellinghaus married Caroline Sluyterman van Langeweyde (1840–1928)[12] in April

---

6. *MadB* 8:1.

7. Student records in the archives of the Martin-Luther University Halle-Wittenberg in Halle. Jellinghaus studied with the following professors (among others): Willibald Beyschlag (1823–1900) and Friedrich August Gottreu Tholuck (1799–1877).

8. The following professors taught at the Protestant faculty in Erlangen during this time period: Theodosius Harnack (1817–1889), Gottfried Thomasius (1802–1875), Johann Christian Konrad von Hofmann (1810–1877), Franz Delitzsch (1813–1890), Franz Hermann Reinhold Frank (1827–1894), and the private lecturer (who later became professor in Erlangen) August Köhler (1835–1897).

9. Records in the archives of the Evangelische Kirche von Westfalen in Bielefeld.

10. Mary Prochnow was the daughter of Rev. Dr. Johann Prochnow (1814–1888) who served as missionary in India and for some time was the chairman of the Gossner Mission Association. She was born and raised in India before she returned at the age of eighteen with her parents to Germany.

11. Most of this information comes from the family archives of Sigmar Jellinghaus. More details on the India experience will follow later.

12. She was the daughter of the Dutch landholder Johann Cyprian Sluyterman van Langeweyde and his wife Anne Sophie Alwine (née Funk or Funke).

1873. They had five children: Martin (1874), Frieda (1875–1921),[13] Paul (1876–1960),[14] Anna (1879–1911), and Hilda (1884–1959).[15]

FIRST MINISTRY PERIOD: MISSIONARY TO INDIA AND RETURN TO GERMANY

After being ordained as Lutheran minister at the St. Matthäikirche in Berlin on September 24, 1865, Jellinghaus was sent as a missionary of the Gossner Mission Association to India on October 7, 1865.[16] It is not clear how exactly Jellinghaus came into contact with the Gossner Mission Association. We only know of his desire early in his youth to become a "missionary to the heathen."[17] On October 9, 1865 he embarked a ship from Hamburg to Portsmouth. There he changed ships and on October 19, 1865 he boarded the Marborough that took him and the other passengers to Calcutta, where they arrived on February 18, 1866.[18] From February 1866 until May 1870 Theodor Jellinghaus worked as missionary in the Chotanagpur region in India among the Adivasi,[19] especially in Ranchi (modern capital city of the Indian state of Jharkhand) and smaller surrounding towns. Jellinghaus

---

13. In 1895 she married Rev Richard Horst. In his pastorate in Mansbach (near Hersfeld/ Hessen), he also propagated the message of the *Heiligungsbewegung*. Horst even wrote a small book (45 pages), *Jesus unsere Heiligung* (Jesus Our Sanctification) (Kassel, no date).

14. Dr. phil. Paul Max Jellinghaus studied in Edinburgh, Geneva, Berlin, and Münster. He graduated with a doctorate in philology from the university in Münster, but also had taken philosophical and theological courses. He later became the closest co-worker to his father and eventually his successor in leading the Bible seminary in Berlin. Information on him and his family is found in the family archives of Sigmar Jellinghaus as well as in *MadB* 49:6–13 and Fischer, *Evangelisches Pfarrerbuch*, 379.

15. Hilda Jellinghaus married late in life (1931) when she became the second wife of Rev Asmus Christiansen, pastor in the Protestant church and a leader in the *Gemeinschaftsbewegung*. Rev Christiansen also played a role in Theodor Jellinghaus's recantation in 1911/1912.

16. Fischer, *Evangelisches Pfarrerbuch*, 379

17. *MadB* 8:1–2. In this article he also confesses, that his way to the mission field had not been one of enthusiasm, but rather one of obedience. He was afraid of sufferings and failure as missionary.

18. Information from the family archives of Sigmar Jellinghaus.

19. Adivasi is the term used by this Indian indigenous group to designate their own tribe. European missionaries at the time used the term "Kol" or "Kolh," which was used by the majority Hindu population, but which was a rather racist term. An important source for the work of the Gossner Mission Association among the Adivasi is Roeber, "Gossner Mission," 45–54.

served primarily as teacher and principal of a seminary for ministers and evangelists.

Few details are known of the ministry of Jellinghaus in India. He mentioned especially one period which seemed to have been a crisis in the Gossner Mission Association in India.[20] Apparently there was a split among the missionaries of the Gossner Mission Association. The headquarters in Berlin planned various organizational changes which included the cut of privileges for tenured missionaries. This was received as an affront by those who had been serving for some time in India and caused some of them to leave the association and together with the Society for the Propagation of the Gospel (SPG) start a separate work among the Adivasi. This in turn led to frictions with the British mission organization and apparently even the British Indian government. All of this seemed to have come to an end after a longer correspondence between the parties involved in April 1870. Jellinghaus was among the younger missionaries and was quite upset about the whole development. He experienced this time as "heavy, dreary time of battle" where a "heavy disposition of spirit" dominated the work and relationships.[21]

Toward the end of this time of crisis an epidemic of cholera occurred. Among others the Jellinghaus family was affected heavily. First of all, his eighteen-month-old son Emil passed away on March 20, 1870. Two days later a second child, Martha was born. However, Mary Jellinghaus was so weak that she died within five days after giving birth to her daughter. Theodor Jellinghaus, physically weakened himself, experienced a nervous breakdown. The doctors advised him to return to Germany with the newborn daughter. Shortly before embarking the ship the little girl died as well on April 24, 1870. After burying his wife and two children, Theodor Jellinghaus boarded a ship to return to Germany in May 1870.[22]

Originally Jellinghaus planned to return to Westphalia where his family lived. He wanted to be close to his parents and some Pietist-minded people planned to call him to a Lutheran church in the Ravensberg Land. The church consistory and superintendent were hesitant because of his close ties to his father-in-law (Johann Dettloff Prochnow), who was well-known as a "unionist."[23] Jellinghaus was disappointed, not only personally but also

20. Jellinghaus, *Kolhsmission*, 10–11. The periodical of the Gossner Mission Association, *Der Berliner Hülfsverein für die Evangelische Mission unter den Kolhs an seine Freunde*, vol. 8, 35.

21. Ibid., 10–11.

22. Besides information in the family archives, see also *MadB* 49:2.

23. The term refers to the decreed union between Lutheran and Reformed churches in Prussia. At the beginning of the nineteenth century the Prussian king, Wilhelm

because he felt that this separatist thinking should be overcome within the Protestant church. As a result he withdrew his name from nomination and moved to Berlin to work closely with his father-in-law. This would prove to be a wise move in light of later developments in his life. In Berlin he was able to make more contacts with people and movements within the church and the Pietist movement. After Jellinghaus moved to Berlin, he worked as curate with Prochnow at the *Johannes-Kirche* in Berlin-Moabit, the *Nikolai-Kirche* in Potsdam and various hospitals.[24]

Another important part of his early years in Berlin was the publication of articles and books about the missionary work in India.[25] He also took time for personal studies. During this time he read for the first time in the works of John Wesley.[26] Almost three years after he had left India, Theodor Jellinghaus married in April 1873 his second wife, Caroline Sluyterman van Langeweyde and began his first pastoral assignment in the little parish church at Rädnitz (close to Crossen at the Oder River).[27]

SECOND MINISTRY PERIOD: PASTOR IN RÄDNITZ AND GÜTERGOTZ

Theodor Jellinghaus served for twenty-one years as a pastor (1873–1894). Although it is a long time-span, not much is known about his pastoral ministry. That is due to the fact that he did not report much himself about this time. He started his first pastorate in 1873 in Rädnitz and served there for 9 years. Because it was a small parish, Jellinghaus could continue his literary work, especially his work on the missionary work among the Adivasi in India.[28] One year after taking on the small parish a son, Martin, was born to

---

III, established by decree the union of Lutheran and Reformed churches to form one Protestant state church on Prussian territory. This caused quite some upheaval in the different churches (Lutherans were in the majority and the king and his family had been Reformed). This union was primarily an organizational union. Most of the churches kept their different confessions. But even this would change over time. Foerster, *Die Entstehung der Preußischen Landeskirche*.

24. Information from the family archives of Sigmar Jellinghaus.

25. Jellinghaus, *Sagen, Sitten und Gebräuche*; and Jellinghaus, *Die deutsche Kohlsmission*; and Jellinghaus, "Die Kolhs in Ostindien und ihre Christianisierung" in *AMZ*, vol. 1, 24–35, 104–12, 167–84, 203–14, 253–70, 290–95, 341–50; and Jellinghaus, "Die Missions-Conferenz in Allahabad" in *AMZ*, vol. 2, 433–38, 481–94.

26. Jellinghaus refers to that in *MadB* 17 (1904) 10.

27. Fischer, *Evangelisches Pfarrerbuch*, 379.

28. His book, *Kolhsmission* and the articles in the *AMZ* were written in the first two years of his ministry in Rädnitz.

Theodor and Caroline Jellinghaus in 1874. However, within fourteen weeks the baby died, which left the young family in shock.

Two months later he travelled with his first father-in-law, Dr. Prochnow, and other theologians and lay people to England to participate at the Union Meeting for the Promotion of Scriptural Holiness in Oxford (August 29 until September 7, 1874). In this conference the roots and beginnings of the third ministry period for Jellinghaus were planted, because in the following years he became a leader in the *Heiligungsbewegung* in Germany. The next section will explore that in more detail. After returning to Germany, Jellinghaus's literary work began to concentrate on the *Heiligungsbewegung*. Besides writing articles in Pietist magazines in Germany, he published the first edition of his major work in 1880, *Das völlige, gegenwärtige Heil in Christum*. Jellinghaus also participated in various meetings and conferences of the new *Heiligungsbewegung* in Germany. Of these the so-called triumphant journey of Robert Pearsall Smith in 1875 was the most important one. The next section will look into this development. It is important to note that it seems that there was no conflict either in time or interest with his pastoral work in Rädnitz; at least nothing has been reported.

In 1882 the family moved to a small town southwest of Berlin and Theodor Jellinghaus began his ministry at his second parish, in Gütergotz (close to Potsdam). This parish was even smaller than the one in Rädnitz, but it was much closer to Berlin and the developments of the *Gemeinschaftsbewegung* there. The highlight of his time at Gütergotz was that Jellinghaus began his Bible school there. From 1885 until his early retirement in 1894 he conducted courses in the manse from January to March of each year. These courses were for lay people to receive some basic training for leading Bible studies and prayer meetings. This work must have affected his pastoral responsibilities, because for three months of the year he met daily with his students and also had to plan room and board and the finances for this endeavor. His early retirement in 1894 could be related to being overworked.

It seems difficult to assess the second period of his ministry, because not much is known about it. However, the fact that he did not report much about it is significant. The following conclusions for this period of his ministry could be proposed. First, it appears that his pastoral ministry did not seem to have given him the personal fulfillment he looked for in his work for the kingdom of God.[29] As he reflected on his ministry, he stated that the highlight of his work for God was his time as a teacher at the Bible school.[30]

---

29. Theodor Jellinghaus's understanding of the kingdom of God will be further explained in chapter 6.

30. *MadB* 8:3–4 and *MadB* 18:8.

Second, it seems that the parishes were too small for him. Jellinghaus felt that his field of work was the kingdom of God. Because of his missionary experience as well as his involvement in the *Heiligungsbewegung* he looked beyond his parishes. This view seems to have been motivational for his ministry. Third, Jellinghaus's theological convictions played a role as well. At the heart of his ministry was the regeneration of the believer, which he viewed to be an act of will by faith in Jesus Christ. This good news, the gospel as he understood it, needed to be preached everywhere. In the context of his small parishes he could not share this doctrine as far as he felt it needed to be spread. Fourth, Jellinghaus appears to have been a free spirit. He needed a certain independence to fulfill his calling (as he understood it) and to be able to propagate his theological convictions fully. The pastoral work did not serve this purpose completely and restricted his freedom. Fifth and last, it looks as if the second period of his ministry was a transitional period. That was important especially in view of his dramatic experiences at the end of his missionary service in India and the start of a new family in Germany. It also gave him a guaranteed income. The two locations seem to have been important as well. Rädnitz was connected to eastern Germany. Here he made contacts which would prove important for the future. The second location was close to Berlin, where he renewed contacts to people who would be instrumental in the *Gemeinschaftsbewegung* in Berlin as well as in the *Evangelische Allianz* (Evangelical Alliance)[31] later on. Therefore, it was no coincidence that after his early retirement he moved back to Berlin and continued with his Bible school in the capital city of Germany.

Nevertheless, Jellinghaus always understood himself as a minister in the Protestant church. That was important to him, personally as well as for his theological convictions. He felt that the *Gemeinschaftsbewegung* had been given the mandate to renew the Protestant church in Germany; and by remaining in both he could be effective in both. That becomes apparent also by the fact that the third period of his ministry ran parallel to the second period for many years.

THIRD MINISTRY PERIOD: LEADER IN HEILIGUNGSBEWEGUNG

The third and most important period of his ministry can be divided into three phases. First, the holiness conference in Oxford and its impact on his

---

31. The German term *Evangelische Allianz* will be used when it refers to the movement in German speaking countries. The English term will be used for the movement in the United Kingdom.

life and ministry (1874–1885); second, the work of Theodor Jellinghaus in the *Heiligungsbewegung* through his Bible school and Bible courses (1885–1906); and third, the time of his illness and death (1906–1913).

First Phase: Holiness Conference in Oxford and Its Impact on Life and Work of Theodor Jellinghaus (1874–1885)

The holiness conference in Oxford, described in the previous chapter, was a catalyst for the holiness movement to reach the European continent. Jellinghaus wrote that he received a "new stream of light and power in Jesus and a life-task" during these days.[32] This assessment has to be related to both his personal life and his theological convictions.[33] He was especially touched by the lectures and sermons of Robert Pearsall Smith, William E. Boardman, and Théodore Monod.

Jellinghaus's first reaction in the letter to his parents emphasizes three teachings which would become part of his own convictions: First, he spoke about a personal experience of "abiding victory."[34] Second, the emphasis on "Jesus saves me now"[35] would become important for his own exposition of the holiness doctrine. Third, he was enthusiastic about the international and interdenominational character of the conference. Nationality and different church backgrounds were not experienced as boundaries. On the contrary, the fellowship and joyful community was something that he and the other participants had not experienced before.[36] This would have an influence on his future ministry in his involvement in the *Evangelische Allianz* and his conviction that his Bible school should "not serve only one church but the kingdom of God."[37]

The impact of this conference for the *Heiligungsbewegung* would only become evident in the following months. After returning from England it was primarily the Swiss pastor Carl Heinrich Rappard[38] who started

32. *MadB* 8:2.

33. This is clearly expressed in a letter he wrote from Oxford to his parents on September 8, 1874. Letter is part of the family archives.

34. Ibid.

35. Ibid.

36. Ibid.

37. P. Jellinghaus, *Bibelschule*, 21–22.

38. Carl Heinrich Rappard (1837–1909) studied theology in Switzerland and Scotland and spent some time in England. After that he served as missionary in Egypt. From 1868 until his death in 1909 he served with the Pilgermission St. Chrischona near Basel, Switzerland. He was a popular speaker at holiness conferences in Switzerland and Germany. In addition, together with his brother-in-law, Paul Kober-Gobat, who

similar conferences at the end of 1874 and beginning of 1875, especially in Switzerland and Alsace.[39] The highlight of these events was the so-called triumphant journey by Robert Pearsall Smith, American lay preacher and main speaker at the conference in Oxford, from April 1 until May 3, 1875 in Germany and Switzerland.[40] The initiation of the journey was in Berlin (April 1–5, 1875)[41] where the court chaplain and future general superintendent Wilhelm Baur had invited Smith personally.[42] Jellinghaus was present in Berlin and participated in meetings. On Thursday (April 1, 1875) during a meeting for ministers, Jellinghaus and Johannes de le Roi[43] spoke about the "blessings they had received in Oxford."[44]

The journey continued to Basel, Zurich, Karlsruhe, Korntal, Stuttgart, Frankfurt/Main, Heidelberg and ended in Barmen and Elberfeld on May 3, 1875.[45] The situation was different in each city. Smith preached and reported about the holiness movement in England and the United States and gave testimony to his own experiences. Sometimes there were several events on the same day. In addition he had various personal meetings and conversations with individuals. It was totally unexpected that thousands in

---

was a publisher in Basel, he edited the first German speaking holiness magazine, *Des Christen Glaubensweg—Blätter zur Weckung und Förderung des christlichen Lebens* (The Christian Walk of Faith). Together with his wife, Dora, who also was a prolific writer and speaker at conferences, he translated songs from English into German. Rappard, *C. H. Rappard, Inspektor*.

39. Rappard, *C. H. Rappard, Inspektor*, 99–114; Voigt, *Heiligungsbewegung*, 196.

40. The most comprehensive work regarding the "triumphant journey" of Robert Pearsall Smith has been written by Voigt, *Heiligungsbewegung*; and Schmid, *Heiligungskonferenzen von Oxford*. The term "triumphant journey" was chosen because this tour in Germany and Switzerland was a triumph for the *Heiligungsbewegung* in terms of numbers of participants and impact on the Pietist circles. It seemed that Germany and Switzerland had not experienced anything like it before.

41. Baur, *R. Pearsall Smith in Berlin*; Fleisch, *Gemeinschaftsbewegung 1*, 21–23. Weyer, 100–101; Voigt, *Heiligungsbewegung*, 41–86.

42. Letter of R. P. Smith to Wilhelm Baur from March 12, 1875, reprinted in Voigt, *Heiligungsbewegung*, 10. See also the comment by Jellinghaus that Smith was not invited by the Berlin delegation in Oxford but rather by Wilhelm Baur (Jellinghaus, *Das völlige Heil*, v).

43. Johannes de le Roi (1835–1919) was of Huguenot descent and studied theology in Halle, Tübingen, and Erlangen. After some years in pastoral ministry he served from 1866–1883 as preacher at the Israel-Mission in London. From 1884–1895 he was pastor at the Lutheran Church in Elberfeld. J. De le Roi participated at the conference in Oxford and Smith's visit in Berlin. Jung, *Kampf der Väter*, 278.

44. See Fleisch, *Gemeinschaftsbewegung 1*, 21; and Voigt, *Heiligungsbewegung*, 57–58.

45. Fleisch, *Gemeinschaftsbewegung 1*, 21–23; Weyer, 100–101; Voigt, *Heiligungsbewegung*, 87–131.

Germany and Switzerland would come to hear him in churches, meeting rooms of Pietist groups and even secular halls. Karl Heinz Voigt points out a significant side effect. In some cities (Zurich, Frankfurt/Main and Wuppertal) these events brought together participants from different denominations for a common occasion, which had not happened before.[46] Through this triumphant journey the holiness movement had reached Germany and Switzerland. In the same month Smith led the next holiness conference in England. The Convention for the Promotion of Scriptural Holiness met in Brighton from May 29 to June 7, 1875 and many theologians and lay people from continental Europe were present. However, there is no indication that Theodor Jellinghaus participated in this event.[47]

In late summer of the same year Baron Julius von Gemmingen[48] issued an invitation for a holiness meeting in Gernsbach/Baden, which marked the beginning of a series of similar events in that town for several years. Although there is no evidence that Jellinghaus participated in the first meeting, it is clear that he was one of the main speakers in later events (1878 and 1879) and that he kept close ties with the baron in the *Heiligungsbewegung*.[49] It was also in this year (1875) that Theodor Jellinghaus came to the conclusion that he should write a book about the doctrine of the *Heiligungsbewegung*. However, it took another five years until the first edition was published.[50]

---

46. Voigt, *Heiligungsbewegung*, 131–32.

47. Jellinghaus himself does not report a participation in Brighton. Other sources do not mention him. See Warneck, *Briefe*. The name Theodor Jellinghaus does not appear on the participants' list "Addresses of Foreign Visitors to the Brighton Convention" (in Schmid, *Heiligungskonferenzen von Oxford*, appendix, document 1, 357–61).

48. Baron Julius von Gemmingen (1838–1912) was chairman of the Christian colportage association in Baden and editor of the Christian magazines *Ölblatt* and *Beröa*. He was a leading figure of the *Heiligungsbewegung* in southern Germany and was leading the holiness meetings in Gernsbach in Baden. He was also involved in various compassionate ministries. One of his aunts (Mathilde von Gemmingen) was married to August von Tholuck, professor of theology at the University of Halle. See Holthaus, "Baron Julius von Gemmingen d.J. (1838–1912): Publizist und Sozialreformer der Heiligungsbewegung," in *Mission und Diakonie, Kultur und Politik*, 217–32. Jung, *Kampf der Väter*, 266.

49. See the following publications by Jellinghaus, *Rede bei den Oktober-Versammlungen* and *Heiligungskraft*; and Jellinghaus, *Erst Glaube, dann Erfahrung*. Regarding the meeting in 1879 see *MadB* 2:4. In this publication Jellinghaus writes on page 4 that similar meetings were held in Stuttgart, Züllichau and Königsberg. Other speakers in the early holiness meetings included Otto Stockmayer (1838–1917) and Dr. Friedrich Wilhelm Baedeker (1823–1906), who had served as translator for Smith on his "triumphant journey" in 1875.

50. *MadB* 8. In this article Jellinghaus reports that he felt the need to publish a book on sanctification based on a sound biblical foundation. It also should demonstrate the

From 1875 until 1877 Jellinghaus worked as contributor to a German-speaking monthly holiness magazine (*Des Christen Glaubensweg*), edited and published by Carl Heinrich Rappard and Paul Kober-Gobat in Basel. The magazine was published from 1875 until 1878 with a circulation of about eight thousand issues and later was integrated into the magazine *Der Glaubensbote*.[51]

It was in these beginning years of the third ministry period that Jellinghaus came to the conclusion that the "old Anselmic ecclesiastic doctrine of the atonement"[52] was "not maintainable anymore."[53] He felt that it was his duty to develop his own "biblical doctrine of reconciliation" in which "forgiveness of sins, justification, regeneration, sanctification and adoption into the kingdom of God" must concur.[54] This perception would lay ground for one of his basic doctrines which would determine his *heilistisches System*. In 1880 Jellinghaus published the first edition of his major work, *Das völlige, gegenwärtige Heil durch Christum*. This book went through five editions until 1903. The book was called the textbook or dogmatic theology of the *Heiligungsbewegung*.[55] It can be characterized as Jellinghaus's theological processing of the holiness message which he had received in Oxford. Its primary purpose was to serve as textbook for his Bible school. At the

connection to the doctrines of repentance, faith, justification, regeneration, and assurance of salvation. Because similar terms were used differently he mentioned that he thoroughly reviewed these doctrines in the Lutheran, Reformed, Pietist, and Methodist traditions (pages 2–3). He was also aware of the weakness of overemphasizing experiences over sound doctrine, which he felt was the case with some English and American publications. Therefore he aimed at demonstrating biblically and theologically what agreed with his experience as well (page 3).

51. The full title of the magazine from 1875–1878 was, *Des Christen Glaubensweg. Blätter zur Weckung und Förderung des christlichen Lebens*. See also Krug, "Carl Heinrich Rappard"; and Cochlovius, "Theodor Jellinghaus."

52. Jellinghaus used this term to refer to the penal substitution theory of the atonement based on Anselm's satisfaction theory. It refers to the teaching that Christ's death on the cross was a substitution for all sinners. Because of God's justice and holiness all of humanity (all humans were sinners) had to face death. Christ on the cross died in humanity's place, bearing the penalty for humanity, therefore taking the punishment for sin and making possible justification of humanity. God imputed the guilt of humanity's sins to Christ, making possible forgiveness for sinners without compromising God's holy standard (law) and nature (holiness). For further discussion of Jellinghaus's standpoint, see chapter 4 of this work.

53. Jellinghaus mentioned this in the opening devotional to the first *Eisenacher Konferenz* on May 26, 1902 in Eisenach. See Lepsius, *Erste Eisenacher Konferenz*, 21.

54. Ibid.

55. Theodor Hardeland was probably the first to use these terms in 1898. See also Brandenburg, "Theodor Jellinghaus"; Mirbach, "Theodor Jellinghaus"; Ohlemacher, "Theodor Jellinghaus."

same time it is the highlight of the first phase of the third ministry period (1874–1885). Later theological publications were grounded in *Das völlige Heil*; at least they would trace the same concerns.

It can be concluded that during this first phase of Jellinghaus's third ministry period the basic orientation of both his involvement in the *Heiligungsbewegung* and his theological convictions were developed. The decisive event was the holiness conference in Oxford. He was fascinated by the spirit and atmosphere of the gathering (brotherhood of believers beyond denominational and national boundaries) as well as by the message and the services. The positive message of victory over sin paired with the plain preaching of this message by a charismatic personality intrigued him deeply. Jellinghaus not only experienced victory over sin as personal blessing but felt called by God to theologically process his experience and pass it on in his own German context. This was probably due to his personality but also to life experiences, starting with his upbringing in a Pietist family, his education, his time as missionary in India, his pastoral ministry, participation in the holiness conference in Oxford, being involved in the early developments of the *Gemeinschaftsbewegung* in Germany, and the different contacts with Christians from different denominations and nations. His theological convictions would not only shape his publications and preaching but especially also his ministry involvement. This becomes clear especially in the next phase of his ministry.

Second Phase: Bible School and Relationships with the Gemeinschaftsbewegung(1885–1913)

Bible school[56]

The Bible school not only denotes a phase or a ministry in the life of Theodor Jellinghaus, it also describes his life's work (in relationship to publishing *Das völlige Heil*). He himself described the Bible school ministry as giving him true fulfillment and joy.[57]

---

56. The term "Bible school" (*Bibelschule*) is quite ambiguous in German. It can be understood as a local church ministry (*Gemeindebibelschule*) geared toward lay people as well as an institution for the preparation of ministers (geared toward ministry in local churches or as evangelists or as missionaries). See Becker, "Bibelschule" in *RGG*³ 1:1192–93. Buttler, "Bibelschule" in *RGG*⁴ 1:1486–87. Bärend, "Seminar/Bibelschule" in *ELThG* I, 161. Ohlemacher, "Gemeinschaftschristentum," 418–25.

57. On the occasion of his sixtieth birthday Jellinghaus wrote, "My greatest joy in the past twenty years has been the possibility of teaching in the Bible school. I always had the feeling that I have been born a teacher rather than an evangelist, a prophet or a

Theodor Jellinghaus's Bible school went through different stages:

Stage 1 (1885–1893): Bible school in the manse in Gütergotz. The goal was to equip Christian lay people to lead Bible studies besides their regular work.

Stage 2 (1893–1895): Because of his illness Theodor Jellinghaus could not operate his Bible school for two years.

Stage 3 (1895–1898): Bible school courses in different cities in Germany, because no designated facilities were available for a local school.

Stage 4 (1898–1904): Bible school in Berlin and Bible school courses in different cities in Germany.

Stage 5 (1904–1906): Bible school in Berlin and all-year Bible seminary in Lichtenrade focusing on theological education of eastern European men. Jellinghaus was still holding Bible school courses in different cities in Germany. Because of his illness Theodor Jellinghaus resigned as director of the enterprise in 1906.

Stage 6 (1906–1912): The school moves all programs to Lichtenrade. Dr. Paul Jellinghaus succeeds his father in directing the school and leads the organization according to the changes of 1904. The property and facilities in Lichtenrade were sold in 1912.

Stage 7 (1912–1914): Move to Wilhelmsdorf/Havel with a new focus of Bible school and convalescence home and end of Bible school ministry. This last stage of the Bible school was initiated before the death of Theodor Jellinghaus and directed by his son. However, the elder Jellinghaus was not totally uninvolved. Connected to his recantation of all his teachings in 1912 was the sale of the Lichtenrade campus (which was his personal property) against the will of the leadership of the school (his own son).

STAGE 1 (1885–1893): THE BEGINNINGS

According to his newly developed theological conviction, a victorious sanctified Christian life was not just an individual experience, although the experience was fundamental; it was a way of life for all Christians, an integral part of the gospel. This message must be passed on. Theodor Jellinghaus was wondering why the religious awakenings of the first half of the nineteenth century were only bearing some fruit in particular parts of Germany, like the Siegerland and the Schwäbische Alb. He believed that one of the reasons for that was that there were not enough Christian lay people who could

---

pastor." *MadB* 8:3–4. Four years later he expressed his feelings similarly. "This ministry is still the most lovely and blessed work in my life." *MadB* 18:8.

"interpret God's word and pass on the gospel plainly."[58] The believers were always dependent on ministers, who did not want to encourage lay people to become too self-reliant. The pastors were afraid that this would open doors for false teachings and enthusiasm. They followed the motto: "No Pietism without Orthodoxy and no Orthodoxy without Pietism!"[59] Jellinghaus argued that history has shown that because of this position "first Pietism became threatened and secondly also true Lutheran Orthodoxy began to die off."[60] A different story could be told after the Siegerland awakening in mid-nineteenth century according to Jellinghaus. Pastor Eduard Bernoulli in Freudenberg[61] instructed men to interpret Scripture and pass it on. In this part of Germany, Jellinghaus believed, "the fruits of the awakening remained much longer" than in other areas where this was not happening.[62] Therefore, Jellinghaus came to the conclusion that the *Heiligungsbewegung* in Germany only would bear lasting fruit if lay people became involved in ministry.[63] This became the first impulse to start a Bible school which would give lay people a basic theological training.

Another reason for Jellinghaus to start a Bible school for lay people was the "fact that a far reaching awakening could not be managed effectively in terms of time and money" if only ministers were carrying the burden of biblical instruction.[64] Well trained lay people were needed to help carry the burden. This was not only Jellinghaus's viewpoint; many in the *Gemeinschaftsbewegung* had similar positions.[65]

---

58. Ibid., 1:1.

59. Ibid.

60. Ibid.

61. The Basel minister Eduard Bernoulli served in Freudenberg from 1858–1866, where he collaborated with Tillmann Siebel (1804–1875), another leader of the Siegerland awakening. From 1863 he was editor of the monthly magazine *Der Evangelist aus dem Siegerland*. See Hinrichs, "Tillmann Siebel."

62. *MadB* 18:6; and P. Jellinghaus, *Bibelschule*, 7–8. Theodor Jellinghaus only speaks of the Siegerland here. However Erich Beyreuther argues that the mobilization of laymen became one of the marks of the awakening, although there was no common or even comparable development in the different areas of Germany. See Beyreuther, "Die Erweckungsbewegung" in *KIG*, vol. 4 R, part 1, 7.

63. *MadB* 1:2.

64. P. Jellinghaus, *Bibelschule*, 5–8.

65. In fact this was one of the main points of the *Gnadauer Pfingstkonferenz* in 1888. See Pfleiderer, *Gnadauer Pfingstkonferenz 1888*. One of the topics was called: "Concerning the right for private edification, fellowship, evangelism and involvement of the laity in relation to the ordained ministry" (7–19). See Drechsel, *Gemeindeverständnis*, 25.

A third impulse came from his experience with the Gossner Mission organization. Its founder, Johann Evangelista Gossner,[66] prepared young craftsmen in a three-month training school for mission work in foreign countries. A similar development with a comparable concept could be seen at the Swiss mission organization *Pilgermission St. Chrischona*, with which Jellinghaus was in close contact since 1875. Christian Friedrich Spittler[67] sent out young craftsmen in 1827 from the Basle Youth Association to Austria, France and Belgium. They would work in their trades and be witnesses for Jesus Christ. Because of their experience it was felt that a basic theological training was necessary for such ministry. Therefore, he founded in 1840 in the former pilgrimage church St. Chrischona near Basle the *Pilgermission St. Chrischona* with the goal to train young craftsmen who felt a call to preaching, counselling and missionary service.[68] These two outstanding men and their approach to educating lay people for evangelistic and missionary service served Jellinghaus as effective examples for his Bible school.

Another inspiration for training young lay people came through his missionary service with the Gossner Mission organization in India, where he served as teacher at a Bible school. At the educational institution in India young men received some basic theological training for evangelistic ministries. Jellinghaus discovered that lay people were often more effective evangelists. He felt that the ordinary peasants could witness to their Christian faith better to their fellow countrymen than foreign missionaries. Jellinghaus wondered if this could be a universal principle which was valid independently from country and culture.[69]

Jellinghaus got one more impulse for his idea—and that from a part of society that was not expected. He observed that the rising socialist political

66. Johann Evangelista Gossner (1773–1858) studied Roman Catholic theology and served as priest in various parishes. During this time he had a conversion experience. After serving for some time in St. Petersburg in Russia he joined the Protestant Church in 1826 and later came to Berlin where he served the Bethlehem Church (1829–1846). In 1836 some young men came to him and asked him to train them as laymen for missionary service. In 1837 the congregation sent out the first missionaries to Australia and one year later some men to Calcutta. Since the church was sending out missionaries, church officials asked Gossner to officially organize his mission ministry. In 1842 the *Evangelische Missionsverein zur Ausbreitung des Chirstentums unter den Eingeborenen der Heidenländer* was founded, out of which the Gossner Mission organisation developed. See Bautz, "Johannes Evangelista Gossner."

67. Christian Friedrich Spittler (1782–1867) was secretary to the *Basler Christentumsgesellschaft* and founder of various organizations like the *Pilgermission St. Chrischona*, the *Rettungshaus in Beuggen*, the *Diakonissenhaus in Riehen* and co-founder of the *Basler Mission*. See Wesseling, "Christian Friedrich Spittler."

68. Wesseling, "Christian Friedrich Spittler."

69. *MadB* 18:5–6; and P. Jellinghaus, *Bibelschule*, 5–6.

party was training "thousands of young men" with hardly any educational background in "agitator schools" for five months to become political orators. He felt that if "atheists" could do this then "faithful believers could be trained in Bible schools to be able to share the gospel and to lead Bible studies and prayer meetings."[70]

The idea of training lay people for evangelistic ministry and to lead small groups of believers occupied him to such a degree that he could not let it go. Around 1880 Jellinghaus met some of the leaders of the *Reichsbrüderbund*, among who were Johannes Seitz[71] and Martin Blaich.[72] They approached Jellinghaus to gather young men in his house to train them to lead Bible studies and prayer meetings, especially for the eastern part of Germany.[73] However, it would take another five years until these plans were realized. During his second pastorate in Gütergotz, Jellinghaus followed the advice of his friends from the *Reichsbrüderbund* and started a Bible school with one student, Wilhelm Fritz from Sammenthin/Pomerania on New Year's Day 1885.[74] The basic textbook for the curriculum was the first edition of his *Das völlige Heil*.[75] The student would take courses for three months. After that the Bible school courses were offered from beginning of November until end of March the following year.[76] In 1886 "three to four" men participated in the courses and in 1887 twelve.[77] Jellinghaus reported that they studied different chapters in the gospels, Paul's letters to the Romans and Galatians, John's epistles, the first letter of Peter and various

70. *MadB* 1:2–3.

71. Johannes Seitz (1839–1922), was a preacher in Stuttgart. As a youth he was strongly influenced by Christoph Blumhardt (1805–1880) and Dorothea Trudel (1813–1862) and their ministry to the sick. He founded Christian convalescent homes in Preußisch-Bahnau (East Prussia) and Teichwolframsdorf (Saxony) to help people physically and spiritually. In 1885 he participated at a healing conference in London with William E. Boardman (1810–1886). When the Pentecostal movement came to Germany he supported it at the beginning. Later he turned against them and was one of the initiators of the *Berliner Erklärung* in 1909. See Seidel, "Johannes Seitz"; and Jung, *Kampf der Väter*, 282.

72. Martin Blaich (1820–1903), friend of Johannes Seitz and co-founder of the *Reichsbrüderbund* in 1878.

73. *MadB* 1:3; ibid. 18:6–7; and P. Jellinghaus, *Bibelschule*, 5–6. See also Fleisch, *Gemeinschaftsbewegung*, 1:37.

74. *MadB* 1:3.

75. It would remain the basic textbook for the school until the end of the school in 1914, even after Theodor Jellinghaus did not lead the school anymore (1906) or even recanted his teachings (1912).

76. *MadB* 1:3.

77. For 1886 there is a discrepancy from reports of 1899 and 1905 (see *MadB* 1:3 and *MadB* 18:7). See also Fleisch, *Gemeinschaftsbewegung*, 1:37.

chapters in the Old Testament. In addition they reviewed the main epochs of church history and studied the most important doctrines of the church, especially "that Jesus was the complete Redeemer who can save from all guilt, fear, chains of sin and the powers of darkness."[78] In other words, he taught them his basic understanding of justification and sanctification. The school used the classroom of the candidates for confirmation who only met twice a week, which was located in a house adjacent to the manse. A former barn was converted into accommodation for the students. The enterprise was financed by the students (accommodation, meals, and tuition) and special gifts by friends and supporters.[79]

In the early years of the Bible school Paul Jellinghaus summarized his impressions as a ten-year old boy, recalling that some people made fun of the school. One newspaper wrote about "the pastor and his twelve apostles" and ridiculed the enterprise. However, the church authorities tolerated this special ministry.[80] In 1893 the last courses of the Bible school were taught in Gütergotz. Up to that time seventy-three men had been students of Theodor Jellinghaus.[81] In the years 1892 and 1893 he fell ill to a "nervous affection."[82] This illness constrained him in such a way that in 1893 he had to resign as pastor and was retired with a "fifty percent salary."[83] There is no mention of the trigger of the illness. However, Jellinghaus would have to deal with these symptoms until the end of his life. After his retirement he began to feel better and thought about "independent ministry for the Lord."[84] He wanted to continue the ministry of the Bible school.

This beginning stage of the Bible school was dominated by two developments: First of all, there was a need and the opportunity for starting the Bible school. It took five years (1880–1885) from the planning stages until the first course was taught. Three circumstances were important. One, there was a need in eastern Germany for young men to be trained for Bible studies and prayer meetings. The *Reichsbrüderbund* played an important role in this development. The second was that the parish Jellinghaus was responsible for was rather small. This gave him time and opportunity for this ministry.

---

78. *MadB* 18:7 and 8–9.

79. P. Jellinghaus, *Bibelschule*, 9.

80. Ibid., 13–4.

81. *MadB* 1:3 and P. Jellinghaus, *Bibelschule*, 18:7.

82. Ibid. 18:10. He described the symptoms of the disease as "states of anxiety" and "weight loss."

83. Ibid.

84. Ibid.

Third, Jellinghaus's vision was too big for the small parish. He wanted an impact on the kingdom of God.

The second development concerned Jellinghaus's book, *Das völlige Heil*. In the beginning stage of the Bible school the book went through three editions, with each edition being revised and enlarged.[85] This book influenced the *Heiligungsbewegung* in Germany and made Jellinghaus and his school well known in the Pietist circles. It was unique in the sense that it was an academic book which was reviewed in some theological magazines, and therefore had no equal in the entire *Gemeinschaftsbewegung*.[86] The groundwork was laid: *Das völlige Heil*, which became the primary textbook for the entire Bible school era, was published and the basic concept of the school was developed. The following years would bring various developments; however, the basic orientation remained.

Stage 2 (1893–1895): Interim period—No Bible school courses

Because of the illness and his retirement as pastor in 1893, no Bible school courses were held in the years 1893 until 1895. Not much is known about this interim period, except that the family moved to Potsdam.[87] In 1895 Jellinghaus felt better and was beginning to make plans for his school.

Stage 3 (1895–1898): Bible school courses in different cities

In Potsdam there were no facilities for the Bible school. Jellinghaus decided if the students could not come to him, he would go to them. He planned Bible school courses in meeting rooms of Pietist groups in cities where students lived, or at least close to them. An extensive travelling ministry began, which was quite astonishing considering the fact that he was too ill to continue pastoral ministry. One of the modifications with this new approach was that women were participating in the Bible school courses.[88] A cause for this change is not mentioned. It could have had various reasons. First, the close and simple facilities in Gütergotz made it impossible to have accom-

---

85. The first edition was published in 1880, the second in 1886 and the third in 1891.

86. Already in 1881 we find a review in *NKZ*, vol. 23, issue 19, 345–46. See also Hardeland, *NKZ* 10; and Clasen, *ZThK* 10.

87. Jellinghaus mentions that a couple of times in *MadB* 1–4.

88. *MadB* 1:3.

modation for both men and women. Second, the emphasis in the beginning of the Bible school was on training persons to lead Bible studies and prayer meetings. At that time this was possible only for men. Now the goal was to help the believers (men and women) grow in their faith, although the curriculum had not changed significantly. Third, at the holiness convention in Oxford they had male and female participants. Since that time women's meetings had become quite popular in Pietist groups in Germany.[89] Women had to be trained for that ministry. Fourth, Jellinghaus began to develop close ties to deaconesses' homes in Germany. The Bible school education laid a good foundation for this growing ministry in the *Gemeinschaftsbewegung*.[90] Last, it is important to bear in mind the changes in general society in Germany, especially the role of women.[91]

The first Bible school courses in a different city were held from January to March 1895 at the *Christlicher Verein Junger Männer (CVJM)*[92] in Hamburg.[93] The second such event in that year took place at the end of September after the tenth conference of the *Evangelische Allianz* in Blankenburg

---

89. See Voigt, *Heiligungsbewegung*, 40 and 90; Ohlemacher, *Evangelikalismus und Heiligungsbewegung*, 374; Sauberzweig, *Er der Meister*, 353–54, 359–60, 472–73; Fleisch, *Gemeinschaftsbewegung*, 1:261–62, 268–73, 383, 429–30; Albrecht, "Frauen" in *GdP* 4, 522–55.

90. *MadB* 11:15–16; 15:28; 17:3. Jellinghaus worked together with the following persons who emphasized compassionate and social ministries: Friedrich von Bodelschwingh (1831–1910), Karl Ferdinand Blazejewski (1862–1900), and Theophil Krawielitzki (1866–1942). Blazejewski founded in 1899 a deaconesses' home in Borken (East Prussia), which was continued after his death in 1900 by Theophil Krawieliktzki and moved to Vandsburg (West Prussia). About the particular relationship to this deaconesses' home, see *MadB* 4:3; 9:21–22; and 21:4.

91. Regarding the status and the prominence of women in the *Gemeinschaftsbewegung*, see Albrecht, "Am Anfang eines langes Weges—Frauen- und Geschlechterforschung in der Kirchengeschichte," in *Feministische Theologie und Gender-Forschung*, 67–96; and Albrecht, "Daß wir andere zu Jesus rufen. Frauen in der Erweckungsbewegung Norddeutschlands" in *PuN 30*, 116–39; and Albrecht, "Chancen und Grenzen der Idee des geistlichen Priestertums für Frauen" in *Interdisziplinäre Pietismusforschungen*, 257–62; and Albrecht, "Adeline Gräfin von Schimmelmann. Deutsche Evangelistin nach amerikanischem Vorbild?" in *Transatlantische Religionsgeschichte*, 72–108; and Albrecht, "Modelle weiblicher Frömmigkeit im Protestantismus des 19. Jahrhunderts" in *Zwischen Vernunft und Gefühl*, 173–98; and Albrecht, "Pietism and Women" in *The Cambridge Dictionary of Christianity*, 962.

92. This is the German branch of the Young Men's Christian Association (YMCA). The first branch in Germany was founded in Berlin in 1883. Jellinghaus was present at that occasion and knew the first leaders, Friedrich von Schlümbach and Eberhard von Rothkirch, personally. Kupisch, *Der Deutsche CVJM*. *MadB* 8:12–15.

93. Jellinghaus was invited by Emil Köhn from *CVJM* Hamburg. *MadB* 18:10. See also *Der Evangelische Botschafter. Sonntagsblatt der Evangelischen Gemeinschaft* 31 (1895) 134.

(Thuringia).[94] The following year, Jellinghaus went again to Hamburg.[95] In summer 1896 he travelled with his friend Rev. Theodor Ziemendorf[96] and the latter's wife and daughter to England, where they participated at the golden anniversary events of the Evangelical Alliance in London and the twenty-second Keswick convention. These meetings made a big impression on Jellinghaus and reinforced his optimism of the positive effects of the holiness movement on worldwide Christianity.[97] Following this journey, Jellinghaus held Bible school courses in Wiesbaden (with Rev. Ziemendorf) for a period of eleven weeks.[98]

The Bible school courses in different cities became a success in these two years. It was an important transitional period for the future ministry of the school. Three developments can be observed. First, Jellinghaus opened the Bible school to women. This move broadened his influence and it gave him a greater base for recruiting students as well as financial supporters. Second, by travelling to different cities in Germany Jellinghaus was able to reach a greater audience for his teaching and his Bible school concept within the *Gemeinschaftsbewegung*.[99] In addition he was able to build important contacts for his ministry.[100] Third, the circle of friends and supporters was built and kept growing.[101] The travelling ministry and holding Bible school courses in different cities would remain an important source of income for his ministry in the future.

---

94. *Der Evangelist. Sonntagsblatt der Bischöflich-Methodistischen Kirche* 46 (1895) 279.

95. *MadB* 18:10 and *Der Evangelist*, 279.

96. Theodor Ziemendorf (1837–1912), since 1869 pastor in Wiesbaden, founder and leader of the city mission in Wiesbaden. See Ohlemacher, *Reich Gottes*, 62.

97. Jellinghaus reported on the twenty-second Keswick convention in an article and wrote that while in Oxford the movement began enthusiastically, there still remained doubts if it would bear fruits. At the event in Keswick he heard reports from missionaries and other leaders that were encouraging. In fact, he mentioned that "970 English students indicated at this event that they were willing to go to the mission field." Jellinghaus, 22. *Keswick-Konferenz*, 178–79.

98. *MadB* 18:10 and P. Jellinghaus, *Bibelschule*, 15.

99. *MadB* 1:3.

100. This becomes clear by the lists of participants, which he published in different issues of the *MadB*.

101. See lists of donors in different issues of *MadB*.

Stage 4 (1898–1904): Bible school in Berlin

The next stage of the Bible school was signaled in the year 1897. During this year Jellinghaus felt that it was best for his ministry to have a residential Bible school in Berlin.[102] However, he did not want to give up his travelling ministry. He planned to have students come to the residential school in the first quarter of the year and travel the rest of the year to lead Bible school courses and speak at faith and holiness conventions in Germany and Switzerland.[103] This sequence was introduced in the year 1898. From January 3, until March 30, Bible school courses for men and women were conducted at facilities of *CVJM* in Berlin. This was made possible through an acquaintance, Eberhard von Rothkirch.[104] Jellinghaus used the facilities for his courses from Monday through Friday every morning (10:30–12:00 hours) and every afternoon (16:30–18:00 hours). On Tuesday evenings (20:30–22:00 hours) he held Bible studies for the young men of the local *CVJM*.[105]

Meanwhile a men's dormitory for these three months was rented in Wilhelmstrasse (Berlin-Kreuzberg).[106] One year later, starting on January 1, 1899 a women's dormitory was arranged under the leadership of Martha Ebers, who got into contact with Jellinghaus in Wiesbaden, when he had Bible school courses there.[107] In this year twenty-five men and ten women were students at the Bible school.[108] Three of the students came from Latvia and Jellinghaus was excited about the unity among the students although they came from different cultures, spoke different languages and were members of different churches. He felt that "true *evangelische Allianz* happened" in his Bible school.[109] This reminded him of his experiences both in Oxford (1874) and London (1896). From Easter 1899 the school obtained a permanent men's residence in Kochstrasse (Berlin-Mitte). Outside of the Bible

---

102. *MadB* 18:10.

103. Ibid. 1:3.

104. Eberhard Carl Siegismund von Rothkirch und Panthen (1852–1911). While serving at the royal court chamber office in Berlin he met Count Eduard Pückler (1853–1924) and Count Andreas Bernstorff (1844–1907), early leaders of the *Gemeinschaftsbewegung*. Together with them he founded the Berlin *CVJM* on January 22, 1883. He became the first president and served in this position for many years. Rothkirch, "Eberhard von Rothkirch und Panthen"; Hassell, *Eberhard von Rothkirch und Panthen*.

105. P. Jellinghaus, *Bibelschule*, 19.

106. *MadB* 18:12.

107. Ibid.

108. Ibid. 3:2.

109. P. Jellinghaus, *Bibelschule*, 21–22.

school season the facilities were used for alumni and lay ministers of the *Gemeinschaftsbewegung* who stayed in Berlin or travelled through Berlin. To finance the enterprise Theodor Jellinghaus started the *Bibelschulbund* (Bible school association), which people could join for an annual fee.[110]

Encouraged and supported by his son Paul, he began to publish the *Mitteilungen aus der Bibelschule und der Evangelisationsarbeit ihrer Mitglieder* (information from the Bible school and the evangelistic work of its members).[111] This publication helped the school to stay in contact with alumni and to inform supporters of the ministry. In the first issue Jellinghaus reported of the goal to work closely with persons and organizations of the *Gemeinschaftsbewegung* on the common foundation of the *Evangelische Allianz*.[112] Another sign of cooperation with other organizations of the *Gemeinschaftsbewegung* was his relationship with the president of the youth organization *Jugendbund für Entschiedenes Christentum (EC)*,[113] Count Eduard von Pückler,[114] who used many of the Bible school alumni for his association.[115] Through the regular publication of the *Mitteilungen* (four times a year was the goal) more detailed information became available about the ministry of Theodor Jellinghaus. In 1899 he spoke at various holiness and faith conventions,[116] at the fourteenth Alliance Conference in Blankenburg,[117] and held Bible school courses in different cities of Germany.[118]

110. *MadB* 1:5–6. The annual fee was "Eine Mark" (one mark), and included a subscription of the newsletter.

111. Ibid. 18:13. See also Fleisch, *Gemeinschaftsbewegung*, 1:265–66.

112. *MadB* 18:4–7. He mentions working closely with Rev. Jonathan Paul in Pomeria and with Rev. Friedrich Gustav Johannes Gotthold Hahn from the *Magdalenenstift* in Berlin-Teltow, who organized weekly meetings of the youth organization Endeavors for Christ at the men's residence. Rev. Hahn would later play an important role when Jellinghaus recanted his teachings in 1912. In addition Jellinghaus mentions the cooperation with "my dear friend and brother Dr. Lepsius."

113. The *EC* is the German branch of the Christian Endeavour (CE). Again, Jellinghaus had good connections to the early leaders in Germany and Berlin, Graf Eduard von Pückler, Curt von Knobelsdorff, Friedrich Blecher, and Adolf Stoecker. Pagel, *EC-weltweit—Entschieden für Christus*. *MadB* 2:23; 4:1–2; 5:18–19.

114. Count Eduard von Pückler (1853–1924) was one of the leaders of the *Gemeinschaftsbewegung*. Among other things he was one of the initiators of the *Gnadauer Konferenz* in 1888, co-founder of the *CVJM* in Berlin in 1883, and co-founder and chairperson of other organizations of the *Gemeinschaftsbewegung*. See Sauberzweig, *Meister*, 134–43; and Ohlemacher, *Reich Gottes*, 35–79.

115. *MadB* 2:23.

116. Ibid., 4–6.

117. Melle, *50 Jahre Blankenburger Konferenz*, 143.

118. *MadB* 2:5–6.

The following year (1900) looked similar. From January until March the residential programme of the Bible school was conducted in Berlin at which twenty-five men and ten women participated.[119] The number of supporters of his ministry was growing to 560 members of the *Bibelschulbund* in mid-1900.[120] In April Jellinghaus travelled to his family in Westphalia to visit his brother Karl who had succeeded their father as pastor in Wallenbrück.[121] He also participated at a faith convention while there and on his way back to Berlin he took part at various conferences again.[122] In addition Jellinghaus conducted different Bible school courses in that year.[123] These lists of events and speaking engagements point to a quite intensive ministry of Theodor Jellinghaus. Travelling all these distances was a strain. In addition to speaking and preaching (sometimes more than once a day), he had counselling sessions with participants. In light of his previous illness, it becomes clear that this ministry must have been exhausting. It is significant to note that Jellinghaus met with other important leaders of the *Gemeinschaftsbewegung* at many of the conferences and conventions. Although they spoke to different audiences in the different cities, many of the speakers were the same. Jellinghaus did not report much about these encounters during his travels, just that they met and who was there. Reasons for the lack of reports about deeper personal or theological conversations might include that they were busy with correspondence which they had to take care of during their travels, and that many of them published devotional material which had to be managed. It is also known that some of the men had different theological convictions which brought about tensions. This became clear towards the end of Jellinghaus's ministry when he recanted his teachings. Nevertheless, the constant meetings of these leaders contributed to the close relationships between the different organizations which they represented. Many of them were members of diverse associations, like Jellinghaus himself. This is an indication that the travelling ministry of Jellinghaus strengthened his position within the *Gemeinschaftsbewegung*. At the end of the year 1900 Jellinghaus indicated for the first time that it would be important for his ministry in all of Germany to have a "all year, independent, Christian seminary" for training men and women. To make this possible he asked his supporters to

---

119. Ibid. 3:2.

120. Ibid. 4:15.

121. Ibid., 1–2. During his stay in Wallenbrück, he became co-founder (with two of his students and his son Paul, who accompanied him on that trip) of an *EC* chapter in Wallenbrück.

122. *MadB* 1–3, 5:1–5, 6:4–5. See also Melle, *50 Jahre Blankenburger Konferenz*, 143.

123. *MadB* 4:2–3; 5:1–2; 6:1–3.

pray and give generously. Membership of the *Bibelschulbund* rose to 670 in that year.[124]

The year 1901 was not as busy as the previous two years, mostly because Theodor Jellinghaus's travelling plans were not as extensive. His son, Paul Jellinghaus, had joined him as assistant, helping ease his workload. Paul took care of most of the extensive correspondence with all the contacts the school had made. He also participated in some meetings to represent his father, and he held some Bible studies. Another area was the administration of the school, dealing with the buildings and working with teachers and students.[125] At the Bible school in Berlin from January 3 until March 30, 1901 fifty men and ten women registered. Since many of them came from outside Berlin, more rooms needed to be rented for accommodation. The school continued to grow.[126]

Three events influenced the ministry of Jellinghaus that year. The first was a court case with one of the landlords of the student accommodation regarding the termination modalities.[127] Jellinghaus lost the case and had to pay the court fees of "400 to 500 marks."[128] The school had to relocate the housing for the men to Berlin-Kreuzberg.[129] Another event was rather turbulent and was connected to his daughter and son-in-law, Rev. Richard Horst, who was pastoring a church in Mansbach/Hessen. A conflict in the local church developed which would occupy the family until 1904. Apparently the congregants were split over the theological position of the Pietist minded pastor, some of whom even went to court to ensure the dismissal or relocation of the minister. Theodore Jellinghaus reported regularly of the developments and asked for prayer support for what he called "persecution."[130] Later that year, Theodor Jellinghaus celebrated his sixtieth birthday. The funds he received as birthday gifts were planned for establishing a convalescence center in Soislieden (close to Mansbach, where his son-in-law pastored), where people "could come and find some rest for body and soul."[131]

---

124. Ibid. 4:16; 5:6–7.

125. Ibid. 8:8.

126. Ibid. 6:17–18.

127. The landlord wanted to end the lease of the facilities used by the Bible school in Berlin, which Jellinghaus rejected.

128. *MadB* 8:11.

129. Ibid. 18:14.

130. Ibid. 9:3.

131. Ibid., 3, 6.

The year 1902 would mark a decisive modification regarding the target group of students. Until then students would come from different parts of Germany. For some years Jellinghaus had been working closely with Dr. Johannes Lepsius and his mission organization, *Deutsche Orient-Mission*.[132] Through this connection, Andrej Stefanowitsch, a Bulgarian with Russian origins, participated in courses at the Bible school. He already had a theological education, but he wanted to learn German in a Christian community. Because of him other students from Bulgaria, Persia, Russia and Estonia were recruited in the years 1902 and 1903.[133] At the 1902 Bible school sessions from January through March, sixty-six men and forty-seven women participated.[134] Paul Jellinghaus had moved to Münster for his studies and other young men worked as his assistants.[135] In the July edition of the *Mitteilungen*, Jellinghaus wrote that because of recent developments he planned "to build a permanent home for the Bible school for Christians from Germany, Russia and Bulgaria in the Berlin area."[136] He bought, secured through a mortgage, a piece of land in Lichtenrade, south of Berlin.[137] This transaction was initiated and supported by Rev. Ernst August Ferdinand Klein,[138] Protestant minister in Lichtenrade. Jellinghaus participated again

---

132. The *Deutsche Orient-Mission* was founded in 1895 by Rev. Dr. Johannes Lepsius (1858–1926) and worked in eastern and southeastern Europe. Originally Lepsius wanted to work among Muslims. However, the hostilities between the Turks and Armenians with a wave of persecutions in 1895–1896 changed the direction of the organization. Lepsius wanted to inform about the fate of the Armenians and organized help for them in form of orphanages, clinics, dispensaries, schools, and workshops in the Ottoman Empire, especially in the areas of Bulgaria and Persia. See Baumann, *Der Orient für Christus*.

133. *MadB* 10:5. In this issue of his *Mitteilungen* Jellinghaus reported, "Since I am a member now of the board of trustees of the *Deutsche Orient–Mission*, I see an opportunity for an open door for mission work in the east of Europe." Ibid., 15–16.

134. Ibid., 9–11.

135. Two of them would later become missionaries, Adam Seipel and Karl Hannemann. *MadB* 10:3–4 and ibid. 11:4.

136. Ibid. 11:9.

137. Ibid.

138. Ernst August Ferdinand Klein, studied theology in Halle and Berlin and came as pastor to Lichtenrade in 1893. Klein was the brother-in-law to Carl Franklin Arnold, professor for church history at the university in Breslau. C. F. Arnold's son, Eberhard Arnold, visited Rev. Klein in summer of 1899 and reported later that the "vital and joyful faith" of his uncle, impressed him and helped him, together with the reading of the New Testament, to come to a "deliberate commitment to Christ," which would influence his future life. Later he became a writer, educator, and founder of the Bruderhof community. See Bautz, "Eberhard Arnold"; and Baum, "Eberhard Arnold" in *BBKL* XIX, 23–32. *Evangelisches Pfarrerbuch für die Mark Brandenburg seit der Reformation* 2, no. 1 (1941) 412.

at various faith and holiness conventions in Germany, the meeting of the *Evangelische Allianz* in Bad Blankenburg, and taught Bible school courses in various cities.[139] It is important to note that he also participated at the first *Eisenacher Konferenz* in that year.[140]

The year 1903 would prove to be a critical year; actually a turning point for Jellinghaus as well has his ministry. The Bible school continued to grow; seventy men and forty-nine women were enrolled from January to March.[141] He continued to plan the permanent all-year Bible school and tried to raise support.[142] He did that as he was travelling after the Bible school was finished in Berlin. He participated at various conferences and the second *Eisenacher Konferenz*.[143]

The first crisis of that year developed at the conference of the *Evangelische Allianz* in Bad Blankenburg. Lepsius had published an article with a rather idiosyncratic interpretation of Genesis 4. He speculated that the dispute between Cain and Abel was connected to which of the two brothers was favored by their sister.[144] The dispute at the conference was not connected to the rather weak quality of the article, but that it indicated that Lepsius apparently rejected the verbal inspiration of Scripture. Lepsius himself was not present to defend himself. Jellinghaus felt that it was unfair not to give the attacked person a chance to respond to the accusations and defended his friend. His position was interpreted by many as also rejecting the verbal inspiration of the Bible. Jellinghaus was upset about the whole affair, which would later be called the Lepsius case.[145]

In September 1903 Theodor Jellinghaus became very ill. After a rather harmless fall, where he dislocated his arm, he developed pneumonia and pleurisy. He was physically so weakened that the worst was expected. His recovery took some time and in November he had a physical relapse.[146] This crisis was increased by the fact that the school was in the midst of a building project for which they urgently needed additional money. However,

---

139. *MadB* 10:4–5; 11:4–8; 13:1.

140. Lepsius, *Erste Eisenacher Konferenz*, 18–19. *MadB* 11:5–7. See also Fleisch, *Gemeinschaftsbewegung*, 1:302–7. More information on the *Eisenacher Konferenz* will follow later.

141. *MadB* 13:3–5.

142. He mentioned that in a review in 1905. *MadB* 18:17.

143. Ibid., 14:2–4.

144. *RCJL* 1903, 208ff. The article was *Der Text der Schöpfungsgeschichte*. See also Fleisch, *Gemeinschaftsbewegung*, 1:297.

145. *MadB* 16:12–13.

146. Ibid., 13:6; 15:1–2, 8, 33. See also 49:2.

Jellinghaus was unable to travel and raise funds.[147] This was quite a burden to him. He became aware that he could not continue his ministry without additional help, which in fact would even increase the financial need.[148] Because of his physical condition it was not clear if Jellinghaus could teach the Bible school courses from January to March 1904. However, he recuperated to such an extent that he could teach the courses in the mornings. The other courses as well as the administration of the school were assumed by a new assistant, Walter Jack, who had just finished his theological studies and was a candidate for missionary service to Russia.[149] The school continued to thrive with seventy men and fifty-four women participating in the courses.[150]

It became clear that the Bible school would stand or fall with Jellinghaus, if there were no other key persons to continue the ministry. However, this was not thoroughly dealt with. The physical and psychological condition of Jellinghaus began to decline. It becomes evident that his ministry since his retirement as pastor with its intensive travelling took its toll on him. In addition to these developments the different theological tendencies within the *Gemeinschaftsbewegung* created tensions on another front.[151]

Stage 5 (1904–1906): Bible school in Berlin and Bible seminary in Lichtenrade until the end of the leadership of the school by Theodor Jellinghaus

Two tensions need to be mentioned at this point. The first one was with his friend Johannes Lepsius. A dispute arose between them. The latter wanted to establish a theological seminary himself to support his mission organization. Jellinghaus felt that this was a betrayal because his own school wanted to develop a Bible seminary (all-year residential school) in addition to the Bible school (short-term school). They had openly discussed these plans, but Lepsius did not disclose his own agenda until a public announcement was made. Many of Jellinghaus's students were supposed to work with Lepsius later on. The conflict progressed from June to September 1904 when Jellinghaus resigned from his post as vice-chairman of the board of Lepsius's mission organization, the *Deutsche Orient-Mission*.[152] All ties were broken.

---

147. Ibid. 15:5; 16:34–36.
148. Ibid. 13:6; 15:8.
149. Ibid. 16:3; and Renstich, "Walter Ludwigowitsch Jack" in *BBKL* II, 1398–99.
150. *MadB* 16:44–46.
151. This will be dealt with in more detail in chapter 7.
152. Jellinghaus described the whole process at length in *MadB* 18:18–20. See also Fleisch, *Gemeinschaftsbewegung*, 1:380–81.

This meant that no students could be expected from Lepsius's organization in either his Bible school or the planned Bible seminary. The second tension arose in connection to the *Evangelisches Allianzhaus* in Blankenburg. Because of its strong connections to speakers at the Keswick convention in England,[153] this organization had been open to the teachings of Jellinghaus, as it was open to other doctrines as well. Jellinghaus was one of its leaders and spoke there every year. At the turn of the century Darbyite[154] teaching gained wide influence. This manifested itself by tendencies to withdraw from the established churches and strong dispensational teaching. Jellinghaus felt that this development was against the spirit of the *Evangelische Allianz* which wanted to be non-denominational and against his conviction that the *Gemeinschaftsbewegung* should stay within the established church. Therefore, he spoke up and criticized leaders who established the new teachings. However, adherents of Darbyite teaching gained more and more influence which led to an isolation of Jellinghaus and his position. He finally resigned from all posts in Blankenburg.

In the midst of these conflicts and his declining health Jellinghaus did not want to give up his plans to create a Bible school and a Bible seminary. The Bible school should continue to work as it did so successfully in the last years. The Bible seminary was geared toward people planning to go into full time ministry both in Germany and on the mission field. However, he did not want to offer a full programme of theological education, but rather planned to prepare those students for theological studies at the university. The influence should aim at two areas: first, the importance of laypersons in the ministry of the church in all areas should be a priority for every pastor and missionary. Second, Jellinghaus's understanding of justification and sanctification would be transported to all layers of the established church. He felt that his ministry as well as the work of the entire *Gemeinschaftsbewegung* could only be really fruitful if it was done within the established

---

153. Among the speakers in Blankenburg were Hudson Taylor (missionary to China), George Müller (leader of an orphanage in Bristol) and F.B. Meyer (Baptist itinerary preacher).

154. The term is based on the teachings of John Nelson Darby (1800–1882) who greatly influenced the doctrines and practices of the "exclusive brethren." The term "Darbyites" is not used by themselves; they prefer the term "brethren." In this work the term is used to describe those who adhered to the following teachings (among others): holy or pure fellowship (no open communion), dispensationalism, pre-tribulationalism, pre-millenialism, eternal security, rejection of central hierarchy or connection to state churches by emphasizing fellowship rather than membership, and criticism of ordained ministry (clergy).

Protestant church. It was to be beneficial for the established Protestant church and the entire kingdom of God.[155]

After the Bible school courses ended in March, the first courses of the Bible seminary were held in April 1904. Students from different nations studied in the new facilities in Lichtenrade.[156] Because of his health situation and the conflicts, Jellinghaus did not travel much in 1904. Some of the travels where taken over by Rev. Stefanowitsch, who was quite successful in raising funds for the projects.[157] In addition, Jellinghaus contacted sponsors to support the new ministry with extra gifts. He had personally taken a loan to cover some of the costs of the school.[158] He taught for the last time at the Bible school in Berlin (Wilhelmstrasse) from January until March 1905. After that the Bible school moved to Lichtenrade where the Bible seminary was meeting already.[159] During this period his son, Paul Jellinghaus, joined the ministry of the Bible school. A preliminary part-time involvement developed into full-time work for the school in 1905 after he finished his doctorate.[160] It is doubtful that joining his father's ministry was the original plan, because Theodor Jellinghaus mentioned different times that he was looking for a successor, but did not mention his son. However, there was no other successor and because of his father's declining health and the desire to support the lifework of his father, the younger Jellinghaus took on more and more responsibilities. In the second half of 1905 Theodor was bedridden for extended periods of time.[161] This led to the complete change in leadership in 1906. Theodor Jellinghaus could only teach part of the time at the Bible school in January through March in Lichtenrade. He taught mainly in the morning and his son taught in the evenings. Rev. Klein lectured in church history. At the closing ceremony in March, 1906 Theodor Jellinghaus spoke briefly and his son addressed the difficult times and crises within the *Gemeinschaftsbewegung* and the effects on the ministry of the school.[162] The following courses of the Bible seminary starting in May were attended by twenty-six men and eight women. In addition, some persons took individual courses, but not the full programme.[163] Theodor Jellinghaus was not

155. His reasoning for this position will be demonstrated in chapter 6.
156. *MadB* 17:19; 18:18–20.
157. Ibid. 17:20.
158. Ibid.
159. Ibid. 18:38.
160. P. Jellinghaus, *Bibelschule*, 19–20.
161. Ibid.
162. *MadB* 21:4–7.
163. Ibid., 13; 22:6.

able to teach anymore, and what had been feared became true; he became so ill that his son took over as editor of the *Mitteilungen* in August 1906 as well as teaching all the courses of his father. In September Dr. Paul Jellinghaus became the successor of his father in leading the entire enterprise.[164]

Stage 6 (1906–1912): Bible seminary in Lichtenrade under the leadership of Paul Jellinghaus

This next stage in the history of the Bible school and Bible seminary was characterized first of all by the health situation of Theodor Jellinghaus. Many issues of the *Mitteilungen* reported on his illness and the developments of his health. The second characteristic was that the numbers began to decline. With the change in leadership, two small external changes took place. First, the newsletter (*Mitteilungen*) received the addition "in Germany and Russia," focusing on the students from these two countries. Second, the invitations to participate at courses were changed from "Bible courses or Bible school of Pastor Jellinghaus" to "at the Bible seminary of Pastor Jellinghaus."[165] Under the designation Bible seminary, all educational programs (individual Bible courses, the short-term Bible school and the all-year residential Bible seminary) were summarized now.[166]

In October 1906 Paul Jellinghaus reported that Johannes Seitz,[167] a friend of his father's for over thirty years, came to visit the patient and actually took him to his convalescent home in Teichwolframsdorf in Saxony.[168] However, the illness of Theodor Jellinghaus was so severe that the provisions at the facilities of Seitz did not suffice. Jellinghaus's condition deteriorated fast so that on December 10, 1906 he was admitted to a private psychiatric hospital in Lichtenrade.[169] About a year later, on November 2, 1907, he was

---

164. Ibid., 23:10; 24:8–9.

165. Ibid., 23:1.

166. The term "Bible seminary" is never defined by Jellinghaus. In fact, there is some confusion in its usage. It is clear that the seminary did not have a degree-granting status. It was designed to support students at theological faculties with theological concepts and practical courses to become ministers who would be influenced by the *Heiligungsbewegung*. The basic concept was that while the Bible school was geared toward laypersons, the Bible Seminary was geared toward ministers. However, later the term 'seminary' was used for courses for both laypersons and ministers.

167. Johannes Seitz was actually one of the men who had encouraged Jellinghaus to start a Bible school.

168. *MadB* 24:8.

169. Ibid. 25:1; and 27:3. The costs for the hospital stay were covered by friends. The psychiatric hospital has been the *Sanatorium für Gemüts- und Nervenkranke* of Dr.

transferred to the *Evangelische Heil- und Pflegeanstalt für Gemütsleidende Tannenhof* (Protestant Curative and Care Institution for Persons with Mental Disorders Tannenhof) in Lüttringhausen (close to Remscheid in western Germany).[170] Theodor Jellinghaus spent a total of five years (until 1911) in closed institutions.

The programme of the Bible seminary continued. Paul Jellinghaus taught the courses of his father and other teachers were responsible for other subjects.[171] In addition, the younger Jellinghaus travelled to some extent, especially to Russia in 1907 in order to foster the relationships to Christian organizations there for future co-workers who were trained in his school and to visit former students.[172]

In the year 1907 critique was raised in the circles of the *Gemeinschaftsbewegung* against Jellinghaus's teachings on reconciliation and sanctification and against the Bible seminary. The reason for this was that Theodor Jellinghaus wrote letters while he was in the psychiatric hospital. These letters were addressed to different leaders of the *Gemeinschaftsbewegung* in which he asked for their help to stop the circulation of the teachings expressed in his book, *Das völlige Heil*. Part of the psychological problems he had were deep depression paired with feelings of guilt for the theological tensions within the *Gemeinschaftsbewegung*.[173] Paul Jellinghaus had tried to keep details on the illness of his father secret since they were hoping he would get better. However, since his father's letters had become the subject of discussion at various conferences, this had negative consequences on his reputation as well as the Bible seminary because he put into question both his earlier beliefs and his school which helped to disseminate his teachings. Some even visited him at the psychiatric clinic in Lichtenrade with the intention to help him, and they reported about it. In a desperate effort to stop the public discussions, Paul Jellinghaus printed the medical certificate of Dr. Anker who had declared Theodor Jellinghaus legally insane in August 1907.[174] In

---

Anker in Lichtenrade.

170. The medical records of Theodor Jellinghaus of the *Evangelische Stiftung Tannenhof* have been made available to me with the kind assistance of Prof. Dr. Windgassen and Rev. Martin Wolff.

171. Pastor Klein continued to teach as well as some university students who had taken some courses at the Bible Seminary, like A. E. Damerow, Pastor Eduard Klautzsch—brother-in-law to Paul Jellinghaus and missionary in East and South Africa—and A. O. Müller. See *MadB* 23:14; 24:13; 25:1; 26:2, 29; 27:3, 19–20; 28:19–20; 36:9–13; 39:1. P. Jellinghaus, *Bibelschule*, 31–33.

172. *MadB* 26:2, 29; and P. Jellinghaus, *Bibelschule*, 31–33.

173. More details on his illness and the final recantation from his teachings will be reviewed and assessed in chapter seven.

174. *MadB* 27:3.

addition, he was transferred to the psychiatric hospital in Lüttringhausen, which was kept secret.[175] In the year 1908 the invitation to enroll at the Bible seminary was changed from "at the Bible seminary of Pastor Jellinghaus" to "at the Bible seminary in Lichtenrade."[176] Reasons for that change were not mentioned. However, since the change was made just after the discussions about the teachings and health situation of Theodor Jellinghaus were published, it seems like the leadership of the school wanted to demonstrate a certain distance to Jellinghaus in the mental hospital.

In the following years the numbers of students declined; and in the December 1911 issue of the *Mitteilungen* it was announced that for the first time in seven years no Russian student was enrolled in the programme.[177] These were final consequences of the break with Lepsius's mission organization in 1904, which was still flourishing at the time. In addition, another Bible school was founded in Berlin (*Allianz-Bibelschule*) in 1905 with Darbyite tendencies. The Bible seminary in Lichtenrade in this context could not compete with these schools. The year 1911 became the most critical year for the future of the school. Back in 1906 Theodor Jellinghaus had been placed in a voluntary wardenship,[178] however, he was not fully deprived of the right of decision. The family had objected to this step, because they wanted to defend the dignity of their husband and father. In 1911 Theodor Jellinghaus left the mental hospital on his own account and contacted a lawyer who helped him to repeal the voluntary wardenship, against the wishes of the family. Following that decision he immediately prompted the sale of the real estate of the Bible seminary in Berlin, which was privately owned by him.[179] Theodor Jellinghaus was on a mission: the mission was the battle against his so-called heresies, which meant for him to recant from his teachings, stop the dissemination of his book and close the Bible seminary.

This stage of the Bible seminary ended dramatically. However, the situation in 1906 already pointed to a difficult future. With the change of leadership the school not only lost its founder, but most of all its theological thinker and original leader, who through many relationships and networking within the *Gemeinschaftsbewegung* had created a place for his school and secured financial support. This became especially critical in the crises of the school and the entire *Gemeinschaftsbewegung* in the years 1904 through 1909. The questions that came up with the sinlessness-debate, the

---

175. Ibid., 28:4.
176. Ibid., 19; 26:29.
177. Ibid., 43:2.
178. This will be dealt with in more detail in chapter 7.
179. *MadB* 43:2; P. Jellinghaus, *Bibelschule*, 26; Jellinghaus, *Erklärung*, 4.

Pfingstbewegung and the challenges of the Darbyite tendencies within the *Gemeinschaftsbewegung* were not met with clear theological arguments; the new leadership of the school just repeated the teachings of the early Jellinghaus. *Das völlige Heil* remained the main textbook of the school. There were no significant developments after 1906. Because of the various crises the Bible seminary became more and more isolated and became secluded from the development of the *Gemeinschaftsbewegung*. What seems like an irony of history is the fact that it was Theodor Jellinghaus himself who brought about the mortal blow to his school and his theological legacy. The final eight years of the school can be described as administering the legacy of Theodor Jellinghaus with a final verdict.

Stage 7 (1912–1914): Bible school and convalescence home in Wilhelmsdorf/Havel and end of the Bible school

Because of the sale of the real estate, Paul Jellinghaus was forced to look for new facilities for the Bible school. He first planned to move the school to the former monastery Zinna/Brandenburg with the goal to move into the facilities by July 1912.[180] However, in the next issue of the *Mitteilungen* the move was questioned again without any further explanations.[181]

By that time the recantation of his father was published and became a topic for discussion in different publications of the *Gemeinschaftsbewegung*.[182] Paul Jellinghaus was upset that it seemed that many writers were not aware of the illness of his father and therefore did take heed of the motivation for his writings.[183] In a review in 1913 Paul Jellinghaus wrote that he and the school experienced "suspicion and persecutions" during this time.[184] The new location of the Bible school was not Zinna but rather Wilhelmsdorf/Havel, close to the city of Brandenburg.[185] No reasons were mentioned for the change of location. The goals of the school had not changed, except that the facilities were also used by friends and alumni for recreation.[186] With the move to Wilhelmsdorf/Havel it became clear that this was a significant change in the direction of the school. Although there

180. *MadB* 43:2.
181. Ibid., 44:18.
182. Especially in the periodicals *Licht und Leben* and *Glaubensgrüße*.
183. *MadB* 44:1–2.
184. Ibid., 49:4.
185. Ibid., 44:18; 48:2–4.
186. Ibid., 48:1–4.

were still Bible courses, there were no students from Russia or other eastern European countries. The participants came almost exclusively from Germany. Other visitors came from the area to use the facilities for recreational purposes—individuals and groups.[187]

Issue forty-nine of the *Mitteilungen* (December 1913) recorded the death of Theodor Jellinghaus on October 4, 1913. Paul Jellinghaus summarized the life and ministry of his father, including their dispute during the time of his father's illness. Although his father had tried to destroy the work of his life, Paul believed that the fruit of his ministry would remain in the future.[188] With the beginning of the Great War in 1914 no courses were offered and the school was closed forever. The war became the occasion to finally close the school; nevertheless its end seemed to be inevitable for different reasons. Primarily the crises and conflicts within the *Gemeinschaftsbewegung* and in the personal life of Theodor Jellinghaus led to this conclusion. Especially since the change of leadership there were no new developments either in the school's organization or in the theology it promoted. This became especially clear in the theological disputes within the *Gemeinschaftsbewegung* between 1904 and 1909. As Jellinghaus became ready to address the issues, he became ill. His successors at the school repeated his former teachings, but were not ready to meet the new challenges.

With the beginning of the Great War, all young men were recruited as soldiers or, at least in the beginning of the war, volunteered to the armed forces. Even Paul Jellinghaus wanted to serve his *Vaterland*. However, because of cardiac insufficiency and myopia, he was unfit for military service. He served in the area of pastoral care in connection to the German Christian Student Union to German soldiers in Libau/Latvia, Vilnius/Lithuania, Riga/Latvia and Dünamünde/Latvia.[189] After the war the Bible school was not opened again. Not only was the era of the school over but also the time of the *Heiligungsbewegung* in Germany. It becomes clear that both the school and the *Heiligungsbewegung* in Germany, which were focused on and expressed by the life and work of Theodor Jellinghaus, were intrinsically connected. Both kept each other alive and continued as long as there were students who continued to teach what they had learned in different organizations of the *Gemeinschaftsbewegung*. In addition, his teachings were spread and the school was financed by Jellinghaus's extensive trips all over Germany. This had also come to an end. And third, his publications, especially *Das*

---

187. Ibid., 3.

188. Ibid., 49:2–5.

189. *Evangelisches Pfarrerbuch für die Mark Brandenburg seit der Reformation*, 379, and *PSJ*.

völlige Heil as well as the commentaries and other small pamphlets served both the school and his teachings. Since Jellinghaus failed to find adequate successors in theological scholarship and school leadership, both came to an end together with the end of his life and work.

Relationship to the Gemeinschaftsbewegung

Theodor Jellinghaus was not only raised in the Pietist tradition, he himself embraced and practiced Pietist teachings. As the Pietist tradition developed organizationally in the last quarter of the nineteenth century in Germany into the *Gemeinschaftsbewegung*, he was an integral part of the movement.

After returning from the mission field in India to Germany, Theodor Jellinghaus moved to Berlin, close to his father-in-law, Johannes Prochnow. Through him he came to know the Pietist circles in Berlin and Germany. A few years after his arrival in Berlin he was invited to participate at the holiness convention in Oxford. It was there that he met many of the leaders of the Pietist tradition in Germany and Switzerland as well as England, France and other countries.[190] It was in Oxford that he experienced the spirit of *Unum Corpus Sumus in Christo* (used in English by the Evangelical Alliance as: One Body in Christ), the original motto when the Evangelical Alliance was founded in 1846.[191] People from different countries and denominations had participated and enjoyed spiritual unity. That experience would influence and shape his ecclesiological understanding tremendously.

In the first issue of the newsletter of his Bible school, the *Mitteilungen*, Jellinghaus wrote that his ministry must focus on the "essentially important cooperation with the *Gemeinschaftsbewegung* on the basis of the *Evangelische Allianz*."[192] This statement expressed an important aspect in his ecclesiological concept; namely that participation in the kingdom of God through the church depended on a person's relationship to Jesus Christ. Membership in an organized church is important, but secondary. Jellinghaus felt this was the best way to make possible fruitful cooperation of Christians from different traditions for the good of the kingdom of God.[193]

His relationship to the different groups and persons within the Pietist tradition in Germany developed in the next decade in such a way that

---

190. After his return from Oxford he immediately began to work closely with Carl Heinrich Rappard and Paul Kober-Gobat, Otto Stockmayer, Baron Julius von Gemmingen, and Theodor Ziemendorf.

191. Randall and Hilborn, *One Body in Christ*. Voigt, *Evangelische Allianz*, 11.

192. *MadB* 1:4–7.

193. This will be dealt with in more detail in chapter 6.

Jellinghaus participated in the important meeting of the *Deutscher Evangelisationsverein* (April 13–14, 1887)[194] which prepared and invited people to the first *Gnadauer Pfingstkonferenz*, which met May 22–24, 1888.[195] This meeting was later referred to as the beginning of the *Gemeinschaftsbewegung* in Germany. He would participate not only at the first meeting, but many more that were to follow.[196] In Berlin the connection to and cooperation with two important movements of the *Gemeinschaftsbewegung* became an important part of his ministry and his Bible school—the *Christlicher Verein Junger Männer* (*CVJM*) and the *Jugendbund für Entschiedenes Christentum* (*EC*). This connection and cooperation not only took place in Berlin but in many cities in Germany. When he was touring and speaking in Germany, many of the meeting places were connected to either the *CVJM* or the *EC*.[197] He also worked closely with the *Gemeinschafts- und Schwesternhaus Vandsburg* (House of Fellowship and Deaconesses' Home Vandsburg) under the leadership of Theophil Krawielitzki. Not only did women from this organization participate in the Bible school, but quite a few of the alumni of Jellinghaus's school would later join Krawielitzki's association.[198]

The organization where Jellinghaus invested most time and interest, was the *Evangelisches Allianzhaus* in Blankenburg and their annual *Allianzkonferenz* (Alliance Conference). He worked closely with the leader Anna von Weling[199] from 1892 to her death in 1900. One of the characteristics of the conferences in Blankenburg was that they had more speakers from the United Kingdom than any other conference in Germany.[200] This gave Theodor Jellinghaus an open door for his theological teachings, which he was able to share at many conferences and through the periodical of the

---

194. Ohlemacher, *Quellen*, 33.

195. Pfleiderer, *Gnadauer Pfingstkonferenz 1888*, 17. See also Fleisch, *Gemeinschaftsbewegung*, 1:92–94. Ohlemacher, *Gemeinschaftsbewegung*, 34.

196. For an overview of the *Gnadauer Pfingstkonferenz* from 1888–1940, see Lange, *Eine Bewegung*, 267–79.

197. *MadB* 13:28–29; 14:42–43; 17:3; 18:1.

198. Ibid., 4:3; 5:19; 9:22–23.

199. Anna von Weling (March 20, 1837—May 21, 1900) started faith conferences in 1886 at her own facilities in Blankenburg for ministers, evangelists and laypersons from different denominations. What was peculiar with the meetings in Blankenburg was the fact that there were strong ties to the Evangelical Alliance in London as well as the Keswick Conference. Karl Heinz Voigt asked the question if the meetings in Blankenburg were "Alliance meetings with holiness character or were they holiness meetings with an Alliance character?" Voigt, "Weling, Anna Thekla von" in *BBKL* XXIII, 710–15.

200. Voigt, "Weling," 710–15. Among the speakers were Hudson Taylor (missionary to China), Georg Müller (leader of an orphanage in Bristol) and F.B. Meyer (Baptist itinerary preacher).

association. From 1894 until 1904 he was co-editor of the periodical, *Evangelisches Allianzblatt* and since 1902 until 1905 a member of the board of the *Evangelisches Allianzhaus* in Blankenburg.[201] Another important involvement was in connection with his friend Johannes Lepsius. They shared mission objectives in reaching out to eastern and south-eastern Europe and Asia. Johannes Lepsius was leading the *Deutsche Orient-Mission*, which Jellinghaus joined as a member of the board in 1900. Many of the students from eastern and south-eastern Europe and Asia at the Bible school came in connection to that mission organization.

The last important engagement with a non-denominational organization was the *Eisenacher Konferenz*. Together with Johannes Lepsius, Samuel Keller[202] and Friedrich Zeller[203] they founded this organization in 1902. It is not to be confused with the *Eisenacher Konferenz* (same name) which was founded by the various governing bodies of the Protestant churches in Germany in 1852 to form a platform in order to coordinate their work. One of the main reasons for founding the organization in 1902 was to counter tendencies in the *Gemeinschaftsbewegung* which fostered distance to the established Protestant churches in Germany as well as a hostile relationship to academic theology. The *Eisenacher Konferenz* aimed at a dialogue between the *Gemeinschaftsbewegung* and the established churches. At the first conference quite a few well-known professors of theology from different universities were willing to participate. Some came from Greifswald (Karl Bornhäuser, Hermann Cremer, Friedrich Kropatschek and Martin von Nathusius) and Halle (Hermann Hering, Martin Kähler, Wilhelm Lütgert and Gustav Warneck). Other renowned participants were Gustav Ecke (Königsberg), Ernst Friedrich Karl Müller (Erlangen), Eduard Riggenbach (Basel) and Adolf Schlatter (Tübingen).[204] Some of the participants from

---

201. Melle, *50 Jahre Blankenburger Konferenz*, 143; Fleisch, *Gemeinschaftsbewegung*, 1:283; *MadB* 5:3.

202. Samuel D. Keller (1856–1924), Protestant minister and evangelist, born in St Petersburg as son of a Swiss teacher. He served as minister and evangelist in Germany. Together with Elias Schrenk Keller was probably the most popular evangelist in Germany and Switzerland. Krug, "Samuel D. Keller."

203. Friedrich Samuel Zeller (1860–1909) was born as missionary child in Nazareth (Holy Land). After his theological studies he served as pastor in different parishes and as lecturer at the Theological Seminary in Blaubeuren. He then let the city mission in Magedburg and from 1906 until his death he was the director of the *Evangelischer Diakonieverein* in Berlin-Zehlendorf. Archives of the Evangelischer Diakonieverein Berlin-Zehlendorf, files H 753 and 754.

204. Lepsius, *Erste Eisenacher Konferenz*. See also Fleisch, *Gemeinschaftsbewegung*, 1:302–7. Beyreuther, "Eisenacher Bund"; Ruhbach, "Eisenacher Bund"; and Lange, *Eine Bewegung*, 142.

the *Gemeinschaftsbewegung* included Friedrich Blecher, Julius Dammann and Johannes Ziegler.[205] The conference was held from May 26–27, 1902 in the ballroom of the conference center Fürstenhof in Eisenach. About four-hundred persons participated. As Jellinghaus reflected on this meeting, he stated that it would be important for the future of the church to educate theologians and ministers who believed in the revelation of God in Jesus Christ. Therefore, theological education must happen on two levels. First, a solid academic theological education was indispensable. Second, a good education of laypersons for engaging in Bible studies and prayer meetings as well as evangelistic work must be introduced widely. Both levels should not exclude but rather complement each other.[206] The second *Eisenacher Konferenz* in 1903 was the last one where Jellinghaus could participate because of his illness in 1904 and the following years. The second conference was held at the same place from June 8–10, 1903.[207] Jellinghaus remarked that not as many persons from the *Gemeinschaftsbewegung* participated as in the year before. Nevertheless approximately four-hundred persons were counted.[208] However, there was from the beginning a distance to the *Allianzkonferenz* in Blankenburg and many leaders of the *Gemeinschaftsbewegung*, because of the goals of the new organization and impending theological disputes on the inspiration of Scripture and the doctrine of the church. After 1905 the organization changed its name to *Eisenacher Bund* in order to not be confused with the other organization; however, the distance to the *Gemeinschaftsbewegung* grew and the goals were not reached. The start was rather spectacular, but the interest on all sides faded quickly and the organization remained insignificant.

At the end of this section on Theodor Jellinghaus's relationship to the *Gemeinschaftsbewegung*, it must be noted that various conflicts arose within the movement in which he participated in different degrees. The first conflict occurred in 1900 and 1901 about the understanding of the new birth.[209] Some leaders of the *Gemeinschaftsbewegung*[210] taught a substantial change in human nature in regeneration, which Jellinghaus and others rejected. He believed that there is a change in relationship but not in human nature.[211]

205. Lepsius, *Erste Eisenacher Konferenz*.

206. *MadB* 11:5–7.

207. Lepsius, *Zweite Eisenacher Konferenz*. See Fleisch, *Gemeinschaftsbewegung*, 1:302–7.

208. *MadB* 14:3.

209. Fleisch, *Gemeinschaftsbewegung*, 1:295–96.

210. Ibid. Especially Eduard Graf von Pückler and Ferdinand Brockes were the spokespersons for this group.

211. *MadB* 6:14–17. Jellinghaus's understanding of regeneration will be addressed

The conflict was not fully resolved and lingered on over some years. The second and more significant conflict centered on the understanding of inspiration of Scripture. The occasion for this debate was an article written by Johannes Lepsius on the interpretation of the story of Cain and Abel in Genesis 4.[212] Lepsius tried to restore the original text in a rather speculative way. Because of the fear of liberal theologians and their criticism of Scripture, Lepsius was attacked by various leaders of the *Gemeinschaftsbewegung* especially at the *Allianzkonferenz* in Blankenburg in 1903.[213] The discussion was not so much on his article as more a fundamental suspicion against anyone who would not believe in the verbal inspiration of Scripture. Jellinghaus got involved in the debate and tried to defend his friend. By doing so he also stated his understanding of the inspiration of Scripture, which was not verbal inspiration.[214] This lead to some suspicion against him as well.

Connected to this debate, Jellinghaus continued to criticize the influence of Darbyite thoughts on the *Gemeinschaftsbewegung* in general and the *Allianzkonferenz* in Blankenburg in particular. He was critical of any ideas of trying to create the "perfect bride" of Christ on earth and withdrawing from the established church or any other denomination. He also criticized their dispensational teachings, understanding of the inspiration of Scripture and teaching of salvation, which he felt was too predestinarian.[215] In the course of this conflict Jellinghaus resigned as a board member of the *Allianzkonferenz* in April 1904 and as co-editor of the *Evangelisches Allianzblatt* in April 1904. In 1905 he was released as trustee of the *Allianzhaus* in Blankenburg. The relationship to Blankenburg came to an end. The situation did not change during Jellinghaus's illness.[216]

The last conflict to mention is in relation to the sinlessness-debate within the *Gemeinschaftsbewegung* and the emergence of the *Pfingstbewegung*. Both phenomena were connected in the person of Jonathan Paul,[217]

---

in detail in chapter 5.

212. *RCJL* 1903. In this issue of the periodical the following articles by Lepsius addressed the issue: "Laboreumus," "Die alttestamentliche Wissenschaft und die Ergebnisse ihrer Forschung" and "Der Text der Schöpfungsgeschichte." See also Fleisch, *Gemeinschaftsbewegung*, 1:297–301.

213. Fleisch, *Gemeinschaftsbewegung*, 1:297–301; Lepsius, "Ein menschlicher Tag" in *RCJL*, 5.

214. *MadB* 16:6–16. Jellinghaus's understanding of the inspiration of Scripture will be reviewed in chapter 6.

215. Ibid. 14:33–34; 15:19; 16:23–33.

216. Fleisch, *Gemeinschaftsbewegung*, 1:308–316. *MadB* 16:14–16, 30–33.

217. Jonathan Alexander Benjamin Paul (1853–1931), studied theology in Greifswald and Leipzig and served as minister, evangelist, writer, and later became the founder and leader of the *Christliche Gemeinschaftsverband Mühlheim/Ruhr*, which

who was a close friend of Jellinghaus and ministered in eastern Germany. As early as 1898 Jellinghaus warned against any perfectionistic tendencies in the understanding of sanctification.[218] He was outspoken when Jonathan Paul apparently taught that Christians could be sinless.[219] Those who were critical of Jellinghaus and his teaching felt that this was the natural consequence of any teaching of victory over sin. When the Pentecostal movement came to Europe and especially to Germany, it developed well in the circles of the *Heiligungsbewegung*, especially in eastern Germany. Jonathan Paul and his followers joined forces with the Pentecostals. These developments took place as Jellinghaus was already ill, and especially when he was in the psychiatric hospitals. He was aware of the tensions within the *Gemeinschaftsbewegung* which culminated in the *Berliner Erklärung* of 1909 where leading members of the *Gemeinschaftsbewegung* drafted a declaration against the *Pfingstbewegung* and any teachings of a subsequent work of grace. This development actually split the *Gemeinschaftsbewegung* and caused much confusion and hurt feelings for many years. Jellinghaus in his illness felt that he was responsible for this development and consequently recanted from all his teachings.

Theodor Jellinghaus and his relationship to the *Gemeinschaftsbewegung* was ambivalent. He supported its beginnings as it helped to unify the Pietist groups in Germany to join forces in the ministry for the kingdom of God. However, although he played an important role, he was not a core member. There are several reasons for that: First, Jellinghaus's teaching remained peripheral in the overall *Gemeinschaftsbewegung*. Some Pietist circles with strong Lutheran ties were always critical. For others it did not seem to be an influential teaching. His voice was one among many. Second, the conflicts promoted the differences and clouded the relationship of Jellinghaus to leaders and organizations within the *Gemeinschaftsbewegung*. Third, and strongly connected to the second point, was the illness of Jellinghaus which incapacitated him at the height of the personal conflicts and the beginning of the crises within the *Gemeinschaftsbewegung*. It was in the aftermath of the illness that he recanted from all his teachings and thereby brought an end to his school and his teachings.

---

was a secession organization of the *Gnadauer Verband* on the occasion of Paul's teaching on sinlessness and the emergence of the *Pfingstbewegung* (Pentecostal movement) in Germany.

218. Jellinghaus, *Johannesbrief*, 6.
219. *MadB* 16:32–33, 42; 17:25.

4

Doctrine of Salvation I
Doctrine of Reconciliation

THEODOR JELLINGHAUS STANDS OUT for two accomplishments in his ministry in the *Heiligungsbewegung* and *Gemeinschaftsbewegung*. First, he founded a Bible school to train laymen and laywomen to support the ordained clergy of the church and leaders of the *Gemeinschaftsbewegung* to fulfill the mission of the church. His school focused especially on preparing laypersons to lead small groups in Bible study, prayer and evangelism. Second, Jellinghaus composed the only major work on the theology of the *Heiligungsbewegung*. With both his academic education and his upbringing in the Pietist tradition he felt it necessary to have a sound biblical-theological treatment of the beliefs of the movement, especially after his exposure to the teaching and practice of the Anglo-American holiness movement in Oxford in 1874. He accomplished that in his work, *Das völlige, gegenwärtige Heil durch Christum*, which went through five editions between 1880 and 1903.

The major contributions of the book are Jellinghaus's views on *Versöhnung* (reconciliation) and *Erlösung* (redemption). He was clear that he preferred the term *Versöhnung* (reconciliation) over *Sühne* or *Sühnung* (atonement) because of his criticism of the so-called "old Anselmic ecclesiastical doctrine"[1], by which he meant the penal satisfaction teaching. He felt that a sound doctrine of reconciliation would be the necessary foundation for the doctrine of redemption. In fact, Jellinghaus believed that his doctrine of reconciliation would create the framework for a basic unity as

---

1. He called it in German the *alte anselmisch-kirchliche Lehre*. See for example: Lepsius, *Erste Eisenacher Konferenz*, 21; and Jellinghaus, *Das völlige Heil*, 19.

well as foundational distinction between the doctrines of justification and sanctification. His goal was to prove that in his work.

At this point it is important to observe that Jellinghaus separated reconciliation and redemption. Certainly he was influenced by Schleiermacher's differentiation between the two terms. This impact cannot be seen in the content of their doctrines because Schleiermacher interpreted redemption or salvation as liberation from the power of sin and reconciliation as liberation from guilt.[2] For Jellinghaus, liberation from the power of sin and from guilt can be found both in reconciliation and redemption. He distinguished between the terms not because of their content, but rather for practical purposes. Jellinghaus used the term 'reconciliation' primarily when he talked about the organic representation of Christ, and as such for the objective exposition of the work of Christ. The term 'redemption' on the other hand was used by him primarily in terms of the work of God in the believer, the order of salvation, and therefore in the subjective effects of the work of Christ. Two other parallels between Schleiermacher and Jellinghaus are the influence of Pietism on both of them and that both rejected the traditional Anselmic doctrine of the atonement (or at least how they perceived it). Despite these parallels, Jellinghaus did not follow Schleiermacher's theology. Any influence of Schleiermacher came through his university teachers, especially Johann Christian Konrad von Hofmann in Erlangen.[3]

DOCTRINE OF RECONCILIATION: CHRIST AS ORGANIC REPRESENTATIVE

In the history of dogma, the doctrine of reconciliation has always had a fundamental influence on the doctrine of redemption. Jellinghaus felt that his book, *Das völlige Heil*, needed to be grounded well in a doctrine of reconciliation that would give the biblical foundation and direction for its subsequent teachings on redemption.[4] He not only presented his doctrine of reconciliation especially in the first part of the book, but he also mentioned and explained it in all of his other publications.[5] Jellinghaus was aware of

---

2. Schleiermacher, *Der christliche Glaube*, 1:369–410 and 2:90–147. In this connection the discussion regarding the term reconciliation in Gunther Wenz is helpful. Wenz, *Geschichte der Versöhnungslehre*, 1:23–29.

3. Johann Christian Konrad von Hofmann (1810–1877) was a German Lutheran theologian and an important representative of the so-called "Erlanger Theologie" who had studied under Schleiermacher in Berlin. His influence on Jellinghaus will be reviewed later in this chapter.

4. Jellinghaus, *Das völlige Heil*, 15.

5. Jellinghaus, *Heiligungskraft*, 7. Jellinghaus, *Glaube und Erfahrung*, 5–6.

the different traditions and theologians who influenced his doctrine and at various points even referred to them. In the opening devotion at the first Eisenach Conference in 1902[6] Jellinghaus mentioned that in 1877 he realized that what he called the "old Anselmic ecclesiastical doctrine" on the atonement could not be maintained anymore.[7] He wanted to develop his own doctrine of reconciliation in which forgiveness of sins, justification, regeneration, sanctification and entering the kingdom of God fall together.[8] However, when the first edition of *Das völlige Heil* was published in 1880, his own doctrine of reconciliation had not been finalized yet. Only in the second edition in 1886 did he explain his own teaching, which he developed further until the fourth edition in 1898.[9]

Already as a student of Hofmann in Erlangen[10] Jellinghaus was persuaded that

> the Anselmic ecclesiastical doctrine of the propitiation of the wrath of God against humanity through penal substitution by Christ with its understanding of merit cannot be proven by Scripture and even goes against human reason which has been enlightened by God's Word and Spirit.[11]

At the same time he believed that Hofmann's "complicated doctrine of the sacrificial death of Christ" does not do justice to the "depth of the biblical

---

Jellinghaus, *Sieg und Leben*, 5. Jellinghaus, *Römerbrief*, v–vi. Jellinghaus, *Johannesbrief*, 4–6. His doctrine of reconciliation is also mentioned in many of the articles he wrote and in the publications of his Bible school (*Mitteilungen aus der Bibelschule*).

6. Monday, May 26, 1902, evening devotion. Lepsius, *Erste Eisenacher Konferenz*, 21.

7. Ibid.

8. Ibid.

9. Comparing the pages he gives to this doctrine in the second and fourth edition: Jellinghaus, *Das völlige Heil*, second edition, 1–37; and Jellinghaus, *Das völlige Heil*, fourth edition, 1–72. There is no further development in the fifth edition in this part of his work.

10. Hofmann began to outline his understanding of reconciliation in the two volumes of his work, *Weissagung und Erfüllung im Alten und Neuen Testamente: Ein theologischer Versuch*, and defended his understanding in his *Schutzschriften für eine neue Weise alte Wahrheiten zu lehren*. Quotations follow according to Haußleitner, *Grundlinien der Theologie Joh. Christ. K. v. Hofmanns in seiner eigenen Darstellung*, 1–29.

11. Jellinghaus, *Das völlige Heil*, 19. It is important to note here that, although Jellinghaus uses the term *anselmisch kirchliche Versöhnungslehre*, Anselm did not teach penal substitution; that was later developed by the Reformers. His doctrine stated that because Christ has offered the perfect satisfaction for us, we need not be punished. Jellinghaus did not distinguish between Anselm and the Reformers, he called it *anselmisch kirchlich*.

truth of the grace and forgiveness through the blood of Christ."[12] Hofmann portrayed Jesus as new humanity in whom there is salvation for the whole world. "Jesus Christ is the new being, the new consummation of the world, not in the way of an end in itself, but in the manner of a new beginning which is designed to encompass universality."[13] Hofmann summarized his doctrine of reconciliation in the following way:

> Man has been conditioned by Satan to sin, which made him subject to the wrath of God. But God wanted to bring to perfection in love that created relationship between himself and man. In order to accomplish that the triune God has allowed an opposition between the Father and the Son, which did not lead to self-denial of the trinity, but which was necessary because of the sin of man. The Son remained sinless when he became part of the human race. He endured the consequences of the sin of mankind and the death of a criminal which was brought upon him through Satan. Satan had done to the sinless one what he could bring upon him because of sin. But the Son stood the test and the relationship of the Son to the Father became the relationship for all humanity to the Father through the Son. In the Son humanity was not defined by the sin of Adam anymore, but by the righteousness of the Son.[14]

Here we find obvious parallels to Theodor Jellinghaus. First of all, Jellinghaus also stated that through sin humanity had been made subject to the wrath of God. Second, God wanted to re-establish the created relationship between himself and humanity again. Third, in order to save humanity, the Son of God became human without causing a contradiction within the Trinity. Fourth, the Son of God took upon himself death for all humanity. Fifth, the foundation for the perfection of humanity in a perfect relationship with God had been laid in Jesus Christ, the second Adam.[15] Sixth, both men taught that Jesus Christ as the second Adam had established a new beginning for humanity which was not determined any more by sin but rather by the righteousness of the Son of God. Seventh, both agreed that the doctrine of reconciliation needed to be different from the Anselmic ecclesiastical

---

12. Ibid.

13. Wenz, *Versöhnung*, 2:34

14. Hofmann, "Begründete Abweisung eines nicht begründeten Vorwurfs" in *Zeitschrift für Protestantismus und Kirche*, issue 31, 179–80, cited in Wenz, *Versöhnung*, 2:41.

15. Hofmann, *Schriftbeweis*, vol. 1, 40, cited in Wenz, *Versöhnung*, 2:42.

doctrine on the atonement, especially the "erroneous teaching" of Christ bearing the penalty of sin instead of humanity.[16]

That Jellinghaus was influenced by Hofmann's teaching is unquestioned. He stated it himself, and it has been noted by many of his critics. The first to mention the influence of Hofmann on Jellinghaus was Paul Gennrich.[17] Gennrich appreciated Hoffmann's teaching and liked Jellinghaus's doctrine on reconciliation. However, Gennrich rejected Jellinghaus's doctrine of redemption which he built upon it.[18] Despite the parallels between Jellinghaus and the influence von Hofmann had on him, there are some definite differences in their teaching. First, Jellinghaus did not ascribe the same active role to Satan in the fall of humanity as did von Hofmann. Jellinghaus did not argue that way, but he rather placed the misuse of the will by humanity in the center of his teaching of depravity. Second, while von Hofmann emphasized the importance of the example of the life and death of Christ, Jellinghaus did not follow that thought at all. He accentuated that redemption of humanity was only possible through death, because death was the consequence of humanity's detachment from God, the source of all life. Therefore, humanity had to face death. The Son of God took upon himself and suffered this death. Jellinghaus did not teach Christ's example as the key to the doctrine of reconciliation (i.e., that Christ stood the test), but rather the reality of his experiencing of death as the Son of God. Third, Jellinghaus coined the term 'organic representation of Jesus as the second Adam'. This expression is not found in von Hofmann. Fourth, Jellinghaus stressed the power of death and the power of life in Christ's death and resurrection. The powers of death had to do with the overcoming of guilt and the power of sin. The powers of life were connected to the presence of Christ in the believer for a victorious and godly life.

The question must be asked why von Hofmann had an influence on Jellinghaus and his doctrine of reconciliation. Gunther Wenz states correctly that von Hofmann's concept was nothing new. The traditional doctrine of reconciliation had been criticized for quite some time within Protestant dogmatics in the late eighteenth and nineteenth century, especially since

---

16. Hofmann, "Begründete Abweisung," 180–84, cited in Wenz, *Versöhnung*, 2:41.

17. Paul Gennrich (1865–1946) studied theology in Berlin, was founding rector of the Dembowalonka Seminary near Briesen (Western Prussia), councilor of the consistory, and professor in practical theology and university chaplain at Breslau University. Later he became general superintendent of the southeast parish of the church province of Saxony (Lutheran) and served in the same position at the church province of East Prussia. Wolfes, "Paul Gennrich."

18. Gennrich, *Wiedergeburt und Heiligung*, 24–25. Gennrich's rejection of Jellinghaus's doctrine of redemption will be dealt with in the next chapter.

Schleiermacher.[19] In addition to that von Hofmann himself was influenced by the Pietist tradition, especially by Samuel Collenbusch[20] and Gottfried Menken,[21] as has been stated by church historians.[22] Collenbusch had criticized the penal satisfaction doctrine.[23] In other words, the openness of Jellinghaus to von Hofmann's thoughts was promoted by his own immersion in Pietist tradition with its emphasis on personal relationship to Jesus Christ, which also influenced the doctrine of reconciliation. It can be concluded that Jellinghaus was influenced heavily by von Hofmann in his doctrine of reconciliation. However, Jellinghaus conceived and processed von Hofmann's thinking differently from his teacher. He reinterpreted the Pauline principles in Romans and created a different doctrine of reconciliation which would become the foundation for his doctrine of redemption.

A second source for his own doctrine was his own father, who shared his son's concerns about the doctrines of both Anselm and Hofmann. After a conversation with his father, Theodor Jellinghaus became aware that the reconciliation Christ has brought about can best be comprehended by the Pauline teaching of Christ as the second Adam, the new head of humanity.[24] Because the Son of God has become a member of "guilt-ridden and sin-infected humanity," he has taken upon himself the sins of humanity.[25] Humanity is "organically" connected to Christ; based on that believers can receive by faith "forgiveness through his death and life through his resurrection."[26] Here the influence of Johann August Wilhelm Neander (1789–1850), professor of theology at the University of Halle, upon his father can be detected, who emphasized the importance of the Pauline doctrine of Christ as second Adam in the doctrine of reconciliation.[27]

An important time of his theological reflection after his studies was Jellinghaus's ministry as missionary in India. He noted that through "inner experiences" and "study of Scripture" as a teacher he came to the conclusion

19. Wenz, *Versöhnung*, 2:61

20. Samuel Collenbusch (1724–1803), lay-theologian, medical doctor, and important representative of eighteenth-century Pietism in northwest Germany.

21. Gottfried Menken (1768–1831), Protestant minister and one of the most important figures of the *Erweckungsbewegung* (awakening movement) in northwest Germany in the early nineteenth century.

22. Wenz, *Versöhnung*, 2:61. See also Stephan, *Geschichte der deutschen evangelischen Theologie*, 110.

23. Wenz, *Versöhnung*, 2:61.

24. Jellinghaus, *Das völlige Heil*, 19.

25. Ibid., 20.

26. Ibid.

27. Neander, *Geschichte der Pflanzung und Leitung der christlichen Kirche*, 579–84.

that "true Christianity cannot be belief in the merit of Christ, but must be an inner communion of suffering, dying and resurrection through faith and love with Christ himself (Phil. 3:10; 2 Cor. 4:10–11)."[28]

Last, it is important to mention his experience at the holiness convention at Oxford in September 1874. Jellinghaus himself stated, that he was "confronted with clarity by the truth of Scripture that in the blood and death of Christ, there is not only forgiveness, but also direct and immediate breaking of the power of sin, cleansing from sin and continuous victory over sin through surrender by faith."[29] This new insight would become the heart of his doctrine of redemption. However, he still needed to work on the foundational doctrine of reconciliation. One of the persons Jellinghaus encountered through the relationships in Oxford was Frédéric Louis Godet.[30] Already in the first edition of his *Das völlige Heil* Jellinghaus mentioned Godet and his book, *Etudes Bibliques*, published in 1873 translated into German in 1875 and into English in 1876.[31] In the book Godet rejected both theories of the atonement which either only view Christ's death as "the perfect obedience offered to God by Christ in the active consecration of Himself," or the "old orthodox formula, according to which Jesus on the Cross became, as the representative of the sinful world, the object of the displeasure and reprobation of God."[32] Godet's thoughts were not exactly the same, but they were similar to Jellinghaus's. There is no indication that Jellinghaus read French; however, the 1875 translation was most probably available to him. Since Jellinghaus's basic convictions grew out of his university studies, Godet's thoughts did not give him new insights, but rather a confirmation for his teaching.

The overall influence of Jellinghaus's encounter with the protagonists of the holiness convention at Oxford, however, must be considered key to the development of Jellinghaus's doctrine. The written documents of both Smith and Boardman do not say much about their understanding of the doctrine of reconciliation. However, as will be shown later, their understanding of salvation by faith in both justification and sanctification had been adopted fully by Jellinghaus. Jellinghaus developed his doctrine of reconciliation after having formulated his doctrine of justification and sanctification in the first edition of his book in 1880. That means that the

28. Jellinghaus, *Das völlige Heil*, 20.

29. Ibid.

30. Frédéric Louis Godet (1812–1900), Swiss Reformed theologian, served for many years as professor for biblical exegesis in Neuchâtel, Switzerland.

31. I am referring to the first edition of the English translation in this work. Godet, *Studies on the New Testament*.

32. Godet, *Studies on the New Testament*, 174.

formulation of his doctrine of reconciliation was influenced and driven by his understanding of justification and sanctification. This interpretation is confirmed by comments made on the message of the Keswick conventions, which had developed out of the meetings in Oxford and Brighton. Steven Barabas made some important comments on Keswick's understanding of reconciliation. He summarized Keswick's teaching on Adam in the following way:

> The Scriptures are clear in teaching that Adam was constituted by God the representative of the entire human race. When he sinned, the entire race is considered to have sinned, and in him receives the results of sin. The results of his disobedience—death, sin and subjection—have been passed on to all of Adam's posterity.[33]

He also referred to Jesus' role as second Adam:

> In the same way, Christ was constituted by God the representative of the entire human race. He represented the entire race in His death at Calvary, and through its relationship to Him the race is considered to have rendered satisfaction and obedience. By virtue of Christ's capacity as man's representative, he therefore became the focal point of the entire problem of sin. Somehow the problem of mankind's sin became His personal problem at Calvary. Through the death of His Son, God undertook to deal with sin in such a way as to free sinners from the dominion of sin. The foundation of God's dealing with sin in man is the death of Christ on the cross. The cross is therefore the central event in history. There is no solution of the problem of sin apart from it.[34]

The parallels to Jellinghaus are striking. However, it is difficult to trace any direct literary links. Barabas wrote this summary of the understanding of the doctrine of reconciliation by the Keswick convention in 1952 and did not mention any references to who exactly it was who taught it this way. Nevertheless, it was taught from early on.[35] All the sources emphasize the centrality of Romans, chapter six for Keswick's teaching of reconciliation.

---

33. Barabas, *So Great Salvation*, 102.

34. Ibid.

35. Price and Randall, *Transforming Keswick*, 228–244, where they deal with Romans 6 in a chapter they call "Union with Christ and Death to Sin." They mention as the main source in the early Keswick teaching on this Evan Hopkins and his address at the Keswick Convention in 1906 in *The Keswick Week*, 94. See also Aldis, *The Message of Keswick and Its Meaning*, 53–57 on "Identification with Christ."

Barabas, for example, argued that Keswick strongly believed this to be a key passage to all of its teachings and then made an important reference in a footnote:

> In 1875 R.W. Dale, in his book, *The Atonement*, called attention in a memorable passage to the importance of Romans vi for the doctrine of sanctification; and in 1879 John Laidlaw, professor of Systematic Theology at New College, Edinburgh, and later to become one of Keswick's enthusiastic supporters, in his well-known book, *The Bible Doctrine of Man*, pointed out that the teaching of Romans vi is that the death of Christ, besides being an expiatory death for cancelling guilt and bringing in everlasting righteousness, is the ground of our sanctification. Our union with Christ in His death and resurrection, he says, secures moral renovation as well as justifying grace (pp.483–8).[36]

This is an important note, since it indicates parallel thoughts between the second edition of Jellinghaus's book (1886) and Laidlaw who published his work in 1879. Now, it is not clear if Jellinghaus was aware of this (probably not), nevertheless it is an interesting parallel development. And there is a connection (even if not direct or intentional) between Jellinghaus and Laidlaw, namely the development of an understanding of sanctification that was connected to the teaching of the Keswick convention.

Critiquing the Anselmic Ecclesiastical Doctrine of the Atonement[37]

From Jellinghaus's point of view, the Anselmic ecclesiastical doctrine of the atonement (at least as he understood and interpreted it), was a typical Roman Catholic doctrine which assisted Roman Catholic practice; but it did not promote a Protestant understanding of salvation. The doctrine's emphasis on expiation and merit supported any emphasis on the church mediating the merit of Christ through the sacraments and encouraged works-righteousness or self-improvement for becoming worthy to receive Christ's merit.[38]

He argued that even Luther and the other Reformers were too attached to this understanding of the doctrine of reconciliation. In the

---

36. Barabas, *So Great Salvation*, 104.

37. Jellinghaus preferred the term "reconciliation," which will be used primarily in this work. It is important to note that both terms refer to the same doctrine.

38. Jellinghaus, *Das völlige Heil*, 16.

post-reformation period and especially in the time of Lutheran orthodoxy the Anselmic ecclesiastical doctrine was even more emphasized, particularly in their doctrine of the sacraments.[39] Jellinghaus referred here specifically to the doctrine of baptismal regeneration which he rejected, because it suggested the idea of a seed of spiritual life being implanted into the infant. Even though it was not stated this way, Jellinghaus claimed that the doctrine of baptismal regeneration would lead to this logical conclusion. This would mean that salvation would be possible without faith.[40] He concluded that the act of baptism functioned as *opus operatum*, which must be rejected.[41] After this short review of the history of the doctrine, Jellinghaus continued to justify his rejection of the Anselmic ecclesiastical doctrine of the atonement by spelling out its theological difficulties, biblical inconsistencies and pointing to weaknesses and possible misunderstandings which have arisen from it.

Theological critique

Jellinghaus presented his theological critique in three arguments. First, the Anselmic ecclesiastical doctrine on the atonement considered redemption through the blood of Christ as remedy in the struggle between God's holiness and righteousness on the one side and his love and mercy on the other side. His holiness and righteousness required the eternal death of the sinner. At the same time his love and mercy would appease God's holiness and righteousness through the self-sacrificial death of Christ.[42] This concept assumed a contradiction in the attributes of God. According to Jellinghaus, this would be an intolerable thought, because God was a consistent being of integrity.[43]

Second, many of those who taught the Anselmic ecclesiastical doctrine, held that "Christ by paying the penalty and fulfilling the law has reconciled man and made it possible that God can send the Holy Spirit who can cleanse from sin and sanctify."[44] In this understanding Jellinghaus saw the danger that sanctification and cleansing from sin were separated from the person and work of Jesus Christ, which he felt had happened. He mentioned two extreme views: one he called sacramentalism and the other works-righ-

39. Ibid., 17–18.
40. Ibid., 306–18.
41. Ibid., 309.
42. Ibid., 31.
43. Ibid., 31–32.
44. Ibid., 50.

teousness. In the first, grace was received without a personal relationship to Christ himself; in the latter, people were taught that they had received grace with which they needed to improve their lives to be acceptable before God or even become like God.[45] Both teachings were theologically unacceptable for Protestants.

Third, Jellinghaus criticized the introduction and use of the non-biblical terms 'satisfaction' and 'merit of Christ'. 'Satisfaction', he argued, was a term which had an extra-biblical background (Roman law and legal system of Germanic tribes).[46] It was contradictory to the fundamental biblical teaching of love. Therefore Jellinghaus rejected the use of the term altogether.[47] The second term, 'merit of Christ', had been introduced by Tertullian (c. 160–220) and implied the misunderstanding that one could have the merit of Christ without a faith relationship to Christ himself, to receive the gift without the giver. This had led to the abusive teaching and practice that the church was in charge of the merit of Christ and passed them on through the sacraments.[48]

Biblical critique

Jellinghaus's biblical critique of the Anselmic ecclesiastical doctrine on the atonement focused on the use of the biblical terms 'righteousness', 'reconciliation' and 'ransom'. He tried to point out how the terms were misunderstood and how they should be comprehended biblically.

Regarding the term 'righteousness' Jellinghaus criticized an understanding which could be detached from the biblical context and viewed it primarily in a judicial and legal way. According to Scripture, he argued, humans were not righteous because they always kept the law.[49] Neither in the Old Testament nor in the New Testament was righteousness applied to persons by judicial imputation. Righteousness in the Bible was rather something vital and dynamic, which for Christians was portrayed as coming "through the relationship with the Risen Savior (John 16:10; Rom. 4:25; 16:10; 1 Cor. 15:17; 1 Peter 2:24)."[50] In the salvation of humanity the Bible did not portray God "as judging in a courtroom, but rather in the temple."[51]

45. Ibid., 16.
46. Ibid., 22.
47. Ibid., 22–23.
48. Ibid., 23.
49. Ibid., 25.
50. Ibid., 26–27.
51. Ibid., 28.

The righteousness of God was for the people of God always aiding and redeeming righteousness.[52]

Jellinghaus continued his biblical critique by examining the word 'reconciliation'. The New Testament word *katallassein* meant basically "to put in right relation" and therefore carried the basic meaning of reuniting.[53] Therefore we should not even consider an understanding of propitiation or atonement or appeasing the wrath of God against humanity. God was not reconciled to humans but rather humans were reconciled to God through the second Adam, when they participated in the death and resurrection of Christ through faith.[54] Jellinghaus went on and explored the Greek word *hilasmos* and gave it the meaning of redemption and reconciliation. That would mean that the term signified wiping, cleansing, redeeming, forgiving, and pardoning of sin. This was not to be misunderstood as propitiating the wrath of God, but rather a redeeming and cleansing of sin. Because of the love of God, Jesus' blood redeems, wipes away, and does away with sin and offers instead holiness and eternal life.[55]

The last biblical term Jellinghaus studied, was 'ransom'. The most common misunderstanding regarding ransom was to use it in the sense of a purchase, where a buyer paid a price (the blood of Christ) to a seller or owner. In that case the first question would need to be, to whom the price was being paid? It could not be the devil, because God did not owe him anything. The better translation or understanding of the term would be redeeming in the sense of liberation or deliverance. The goal was salvation from sin. Therefore, "Christ, the priestly king who has died and has been raised, redeems and liberates the soul from the dominion of sin, the world, death and the devil to become God's loved and liberated ownership."[56]

Besides criticizing the use of the three biblical terms, Jellinghaus also turned to the biblical teaching of the sacrifice or blood sacrifice of Christ. He first examined the use of blood sacrifice in relation to animals in the Old Testament. He argued that in the Old Testament it was connected with the awareness of sinful humanity of being unholy and guilty before a pure and holy God.[57] When we read of animal sacrifices and their blood, then it was always viewed in terms of restoring the relationship with God, a reinstallation of right relation with God, so that humans can approach God and come

---

52. Ibid., 24.
53. Ibid., 32–33.
54. Ibid., 33.
55. Ibid., 33–34.
56. Ibid., 34.
57. Ibid., 11.

near him.[58] Jellinghaus claimed that he followed the teaching of Seligman Baer[59] by opposing the notion of the Old Testament sacrifice in terms of a judicial substitutionary death. The principal thing in the sacrificial system of the Old Testament was the altar and the sprinkling with blood of the altar and the person who brought sacrifice. The altar always signified God's presence.[60] The blood and life of an impeccable animal represented the person on the altar in order to cleanse the person and make possible a sanctifying relationship with God.[61]

> By laying on of hands before slaughtering the animal the person who brought sacrifice did not transfer his guilt on the animal. He rather substituted (put in his place) the blood or the life of the animal for the cleansing and sanctifying surrender of himself, so that his sin, which would fall like a polluting shadow on the altar of God, would be cleansed (Lev. 16:18–19).[62]

Jellinghaus claimed that the basic meaning of the Hebrew term *kaphar* was not "to cover," but rather "to cleanse" or "to redeem."[63] That was how he believed the sacrifice of Christ needed to be understood in the New Testament.

> Jesus' sacrifice does not only mean Jesus' sacrificial death, but rather his slaughtering on Calvary and his approach to the altar as high priest so that from there he can forgive sins, cleanse hearts and present comfort, peace, life, righteousness, holiness, love and hope. The blood of Jesus does not only signify the death of Jesus, but also the risen life of Jesus. In the blood of Jesus there is not only the power of death of Jesus, but also the power of life which gives eternal life, love, truth, righteousness and sanctification.[64]

Only in and through Christ could all the provisions and orders of the old covenant be truly interpreted, because they pointed to him and he fulfilled them. It was faith which gave the covenant people Israel the strength to keep

---

58. Ibid.

59. Seligman Baer (1825–1897) Professor for the Hebrew language and the Masoretic text of the Bible, taught at the Jewish school in Wiesbaden-Biebrich, Germany. From 1869–1890 Baer and Franz Delitzsch (1813–1890), edited the critical text of the Old Testament, except the books of Exodus, Leviticus, Numbers, and Deuteronomy. Bautz, "Seligman Baer," 341.

60. Jellinghaus, *Das völlige Heil*, 11.

61. Ibid.

62. Ibid., 12.

63. Ibid.

64. Ibid., 13.

the laws. The laws must also be understood as taskmaster to make clear that God's people needed a new heart and a cleansing of sin through a redeemer which God would provide. This redeemer was Jesus Christ, the second Adam, who had redeemed the human race and sanctified them so that they could become members of the kingdom of God.[65] Jellinghaus insisted that already the old covenant with Abraham had been a covenant of grace. It was not based on merit, but Abraham did trust in God's promises. Therefore, he was declared righteous in respect of the coming redeemer. That had been true for all believers in the Old Testament. They might not have been aware of the fact that they were declared righteous through the future sacrificial death and resurrection of Christ; but their trust in God's grace and promises had been "in nucleus and nature" faith in Christ.[66]

One of the greatest critics of this biblical interpretation was Benjamin Breckinridge Warfield.[67] He argued that Jellinghaus had a Lutheran foundation in the original doctrine of redemption. However, this foundation was withdrawn through different influences. This began already during Jellinghaus's studies under von Hofmann, who "had taken from him the central doctrine of the penal satisfaction of Christ, without, however, conveying to him anything positive in its stead."[68] Warfield continued by stating that other early influences were J.A.W. Neander and the so-called

---

65. Ibid., 15.

66. Ibid., 13–14.

67. Benjamin Breckinridge (B. B.) Warfield (1851–1921) studied theology at Princeton Theological Seminary, Princeton, New Jersey and spent some time in Germany in Heidelberg and Leipzig. He served as professor for New Testament language and literature at Western Theological Seminary in Pittsburgh (1878–1887) and as professor for systematic theology at Princeton Theological Seminary (1887–1921). See Barry Waugh, "Benjamin Breckinridge Warfield" in *The Southern Presbyterian Review*. Digitization Project: Author Biography. St. Louis, MO: PCA Historical Center, 2003. Warfield wrote the most important and comprehensive work on Jellinghaus and the *Heiligungsbewegung* in Germany in the English language. In 1931, ten years after his death, a two-volume work with the title *Studies in Perfectionism* was released. In it we find a collection of articles by Warfield on the holiness movement in the United States, the United Kingdom, and continental Europe, which were originally published in various theological magazines. Warfield had much better access and a more developed overview of the history and theology in the United States and the United Kingdom than his colleagues in Germany. However, he was also well informed about the movement in continental Europe, especially in Germany, owing to his studies in Heidelberg and Leipzig. He wrote two articles on the situation in Germany: "The Fellowship Movement (*Gemeinschaftsbewegung*)," originally published in *Bibliotheca Sacra* 76 (1919) 1–40; and "The German Higher Life Movement and Its Chief Exponent," originally published in *The Biblical Review* 4 (1919) 376–406 and 561–90; published by The Biblical Seminary in New York. The second article assessed the theology of Theodor Jellinghaus.

68. Warfield, *Studies in Perfectionism*, 1:348–49

"mediating theology," which was conveyed to him also by Frédéric Godet, whose book, *Studies on the New Testament*, was known to Jellinghaus and already published before the convention in Oxford.[69] Warfield believed that Jellinghaus's doctrine of sacrifice belonged to the class of symbolic theories based on the hypothesis of Seligman Baer. Warfield summarized it thus:

> There is no "juristically substitutive, bloody penal death"; the significance of the rite lies not in the idea of "expiation," but in that of "drawing near." The chief matters are the "altar" and the "blood," the symbols respectively of the presence of God and the life of the offerer. The offerer approaches God, but being himself impure, comes into His presence through a substitute pure life. This is somehow supposed, by an organic union with the victim, to purify him.[70]

Warfield concluded that according to this doctrine it was possible through the mediation of the religious life of Christ to also live religiously, through which the believer can have communion with Christ in his death and resurrection. At that point he would have arrived at Ritschlianism. However, it would be doing injustice to Jellinghaus to think that he taught that the sacrifice of Christ was merely to be imitated by believers. He rather believed that through the faith relationship with Christ supernatural powers were released and at work in believers.[71] Warfield deduced that such a doctrine of redemption opened a wide door for Robert Pearsall Smith's teaching of sanctification by faith alone. It could even be stated that this teaching was implicitly present in Jellinghaus; it only needed to be explicitly formulated, which happened at Oxford.[72] This assessment by Warfield will be reviewed later in this chapter.

Weaknesses and possible misunderstandings of the Anselmic doctrine

Jellinghaus felt that it was important to point out weaknesses and possible misunderstandings of the Anselmic ecclesiastical doctrine on the atonement. In his understanding these were primarily connected to the order of salvation and the appropriation of salvation, especially in regard to

---

69. Ibid., 349. Frédéric Godet's book was originally published in 1873, one year before the convention in Oxford.
70. Ibid..
71. Ibid., 349–50.
72. Ibid., 350.

sanctification.[73] This part of the critique received the greatest space in his book, *Das völlige Heil*, mainly because of the purpose of the book, helping lay leaders to teach the biblical order of salvation in Bible studies, devotions, sermons, and other addresses in church settings.

Jellinghaus claimed that because of the strong influence of the Anselmic ecclesiastical doctrine on the atonement the Protestant churches in Germany did not teach a clear and common order of salvation and appropriation of salvation. He felt that there was a lot of confusion.[74] Following the discussion of Carl Heinrich von Weizsäcker,[75] he differentiated three groups within Lutheranism. First he mentioned the Lutheran confessions and old dogmatics. They placed the doctrine of the sacraments parallel to the order of salvation and appropriation of salvation without specifying their relationship. Second, there were those who had been influenced by Pietist and Methodist concepts. They gave the sacraments a secondary place, especially baptism. Priority was given to the personal and subjective appropriation of salvation in repentance, faith, justification, regeneration and sanctification. And third, there was what he called the Lutheran high church group. They tended to accept the old Roman Catholic view of sacramentalism and give up the primacy of faith.[76]

Ernst Cremer[77] criticized this interpretation, because with it Jellinghaus abolished the Lutheran center of justification by faith, which was already a danger in Hofmann.[78] Regarding the doctrine of reconciliation, he argued that Jellinghaus tried to position the doctrine of sanctification parallel to the doctrine of justification, and the former should even supersede the latter. In this endeavor Cremer commends Jellinghaus's "German thoroughness"; however, Jellinghaus ended up with an alteration of the traditional doctrine of atonement, because the teachings of the reformers seemed to be "not good enough."[79] This new teaching was not Jellinghaus's invention,

73. Jellinghaus, *Das völlige Heil*, 15.

74. Ibid., 74.

75. Ibid. Carl Heinrich von Weizsäcker (1822–1899) was professor for church history and history of dogma at the University of Tübingen. Jellinghaus does not make a direct quotation, but mentions Weizsäcker's classification.

76. Ibid., 75.

77. Ernst Friedrich Martin Cremer (1864–1922), son of the Protestant theologian and head of the so-called *Greifswalder Schule*, Hermann Cremer. Ernst Cremer taught for some time at the University of Marburg. He wrote the book, *Das vollkommene gegenwärtige Heil in Christo: Eine Untersuchung zum Dogma der Gemeinschaftsbewegung*, in which he noted that Jellinghaus had contacted him "to support his recantation." Cremer, 7. That was part of the motivation to write the book.

78. Cremer, *Das vollkommene gegenwärtige Heil in Christo*, 13–14.

79. Ibid., 13.

according to Cremer; he just processed, established and presented what he had received. The doctrine itself, according to Cremer, originated in the "English-American dissenters, especially in its Methodist form."[80]

This assessment by Cremer does not address Jellinghaus's question regarding the origin and formation of faith.[81] In order for faith to be reality, was it necessary that there was an awakening and conversion of the believer? Or could the Christian life be seen as a continuation of sacramental grace, which either happened through remaining in that grace or through ongoing return to baptismal grace?[82] Jellinghaus felt that the issue was very similar in Reformed doctrine. The doctrine of unconditional election and the irresistibility of grace in the elect would obscure the order of salvation. The Reformed tradition viewed regeneration and justification as the commencement of eternal salvation, which the believer more or less realized in their regeneration and justification.[83]

Since both Lutheran and Reformed doctrines still built upon the Anselmic ecclesiastical doctrine of the atonement, it was no wonder (according to Jellinghaus) that confusion and possible misunderstandings were present. While the orthodox Lutherans attempted to build on that foundation their doctrine of "justification by faith in the merit of Christ," they did well on the biblical truth that conversion, regeneration, sanctification fall together with justification.[84] However, Jellinghaus claimed that they were not able to develop a clear biblical doctrine of practical sanctification. They stopped half-way by stating that the Christian life was a "daily apprehension of the merit of Christ" and a "daily drowning of the old man" in repentance and faith.[85] Jellinghaus believed that the Reformed theologians[86], on the other hand, placed the regenerated person again under the law, because, in contrast to the Lutherans, they attributed sanctifying power to the law for the life of the believers.[87] Jellinghaus concluded that both Lutheran and Reformed views would necessarily lead to the realization that the "dead faith in the merit of Christ" did not lead to a victorious life over sin and did not give

---

80. Ibid., 13–14.
81. Jellinghaus, *Das völlige Heil*, 75.
82. Ibid.
83. Ibid.
84. Ibid., 76.
85. Ibid.
86. Jellinghaus did not name any of the "Reformed theologians," but made a general statement.
87. Jellinghaus, *Das völlige Heil*, 76.

any assurance of salvation.[88] They were rather looking for "other crutches" to sustain the Christian life.[89] Jellinghaus mentioned three: some were using the "crutches" of orthodox doctrine, the right practice of the sacraments and obedience to the Word and the regulations of the church. This led, in spite of Luther, to a "high church half-Roman" character of church and faith.[90] Others, especially the Mystics and the Pietists, emphasized the inner life and experiences. By stressing inner warmth and perceptible vitality, a clear and true doctrine had been neglected or viewed as inferior. That had been one of the weaknesses of Pietism.[91] Because Jellinghaus recognized that he was part of the Pietist tradition, he made the following remark:

> I realize that the present *Gemeinschaftsbewegung*, if it is not penetrated with clarity and assertiveness in regards to biblical doctrine, it will not be resistant neither to the right nor to the left. Therefore, I have tried to spell out in this book not only to voice, "That is the way it is," but also to say clearly, "That is not right!"[92]

Jellinghaus continued to argue that another group, especially in the Reformed tradition, seemed to accentuate their experience of justification and regeneration by faith as "revelation of their eternal election." Assurance of salvation meant in their belief that an elected Christian could not be lost.[93] Jellinghaus critiqued the above mentioned Lutheran and Reformed teachings because he felt that they focused in the best case on the salvation of individual souls. But they did not keep in mind the biblical teachings of Jesus as the "firstborn of the new humanity" and the "wonderful future of the kingdom of Christ."[94] Therefore he came to the conclusion:

> The total concept of the order of salvation and appropriation of salvation depends on the conviction that Christ . . . since Pentecost is near as full, present redeemer through the Holy Spirit so that each sinner looking for salvation through faith can receive in his arms forgiveness, righteousness and life as one who dies with Christ and is raised with him.[95]

88. Ibid.
89. Ibid.
90. Ibid.
91. Ibid., 77.
92. Ibid., 78.
93. Ibid., 77.
94. Ibid.
95. Ibid., 81–82.

In the general view of the order of salvation, this understanding had important consequences for the doctrine of sanctification. The common teaching of sanctification in the German Protestant churches understood the sacrificial death of Christ only as a binding holy commitment and strong motive "to put to death sin."[96]

However, Jellinghaus claimed that this was not biblical teaching. He maintained that Scripture taught that Christ through his sacrificial death had accomplished victory over the power of the flesh and sin and had acquired powers of life. Believers must accept and remain in Christ as victor through trust and surrender which was their holy obligation.[97] He came to the conclusion that the Bible clearly and unmistakably stated that through Christ's death and resurrection, through his blood and sacrifice, not only the guilt of sin had been cleansed, but every Christian could live in victory over sin, the world and the devil. That was possible when the believers through faith had died and had been raised in Christ and remained in constant relationship with him.[98]

In addition, the Anselmic ecclesiastical dogma, because of its teaching of the imputed perfect fulfillment of the law by Christ, led for Jellinghaus to an erroneous understanding of sanctification and perfection. Some, he mentioned specifically the Darbyites, had drawn the conclusion in the old atonement doctrine that not only forgiveness of sin and guilt but also perfection and sanctification had been judicially imputed to elected believers.[99] Followers of this understanding claimed that the flesh could never become holy and the righteousness and sanctification could not come from the law. He agreed that their conclusion was correct. However, he emphasized that was the reason why the Scriptures insisted that the flesh must be crucified with Christ if believers wanted to live a God-pleasing life.[100] At the same time, the idea that Christ's perfect fulfillment of the law was imputed to the believers, Jellinghaus argued, was nothing but law- or legal-righteousness. The Bible taught rather that the believer because of the law needed to die with Christ to the law. Therefore, eternal life, righteousness, holiness and all other Christian virtues did not come from the law but only through the new Adam with whom the believer must have a faith relationship through the

---

96. Ibid., 440.
97. Ibid., 442.
98. Ibid., 439.
99. Ibid., 554.
100. Ibid., 555.

Holy Spirit; then the believer actually participated in everything that Christ had accomplished.[101]

Jellinghaus continued to point out what he termed weaknesses and possible misunderstandings by addressing what he called the erroneous teaching of sanctification as a daily repeated justification through repentance and faith.[102] For him this credo also rested on the old Anselmic ecclesiastical doctrine on the atonement. He claimed that the often used dictum, justifying faith sanctifies, was not clear. It either meant that justifying faith did something to the believer by which he was also sanctified, a commonly held view that Jellinghaus believed was wrong and misleading. He claimed that not even the Fathers taught such a doctrine. It did not help the Christians in their daily life, but rather made them uncertain in their relationship to God.[103] Alternatively it meant that the same faith which receives Christ for justification must receive him also for sanctification, which Jellinghaus believed was absolutely correct. However, it would not necessarily mean that when the believer received Christ by faith as his or her justification that he received him for his or her full sanctification at the same moment.[104]

The last weakness Jellinghaus mentioned was related to the doctrine of sanctification. He felt that the Anselmic ecclesiastical doctrine was related to the erroneous teaching of an autonomous 'old man' versus the 'new man' in the life of the believer. This understanding would lead to two possible conclusions: first, justification was only a judicial act in heaven. Second, in justification at the time of regeneration a new nature or new human was created through the Holy Spirit. Jellinghaus rejected both beliefs. Both of them raised more questions than they answered. The term 'old man' in the New Testament described the inner being which was being dominated by the flesh, the sinful world and the devil. Even more, because this condition worsened because of sinful practice and habits, it became more and more destructive.[105] The term 'new man' was used by Paul to describe the image of Christ in the believer.[106] When Paul compared and contrasted the 'old man' and the 'new man' he did not speak of two autonomous humans or beings. He rather highlighted the either-or in the life of the believer. The

---

101. Ibid., 555–56.

102. He quotes a phrase used in the Protestant churches in Germany: "*Justificatio qotidie iterate est sanctificatio. Die täglich wiederholte Rechtfertigung ist die Heiligung.*" (The daily repeated justification is sanctification.) Ibid., 544.

103. Jellinghaus names specifically Ignatius, Polycarp, Justin, Irenaeus, and Tertullian. Ibid., 546.

104. Ibid., 544.

105. Ibid., 154.

106. Ibid.

Christian was dominated either by the law of Christ through the Holy Spirit as the motivating power in his life (new man), or by the law of sinful flesh (old man).[107]

Jellinghaus's Doctrine of Organic Reconciliation

Jellinghaus not only wanted to reject the Anselmic ecclesiastical doctrine of the atonement, he offered an alternative doctrine which he believed was biblically based, theologically sound and avoided the weaknesses and possible misunderstandings he had addressed. His presentation of the doctrine of reconciliation started with the biblical teaching of human depravity, which was based on the original sin of Adam and Eve. He defined original sin as turning away from God in unbelief, pride and evil lust. By sinning Adam and Eve had broken away from God, the source of all life, and had brought upon themselves guilt and death and had come under God's righteous and inevitable judgment.[108] Because of them, all of humanity lost the fellowship and relationship with the God of love, holiness, righteousness, peace, joy and eternal life. From that moment on humanity was separated from God. This situation is inherited by all humans, because all humans are born of Adam and Eve under the curse of sin and death and have the same corrupted, depraved, sin-loving, selfish, and God hating nature.[109]

The reason why God did not destroy corrupted humanity right away will never be fully known by finite humanity. All that is told is that from the very beginning God tried to save humanity from this lost state. God's plan of salvation, according to Jellinghaus, was not arbitrary but rather expressed his nature and was in line with the original creation of humanity. Jellinghaus developed three arguments: first, God created humanity in his own image with the ability to make free moral choices. God would not force salvation on humanity without their consent.[110] Second, complete contrition and repentance on the part of humanity is the necessary reaction to their sin and being ready to take upon themselves the consequences of their sin: death and damnation. However, this full contrition and repentance cannot come from a sinful heart. The sinfulness of sin is that humans are blind to it and even deny it.[111] Third, Jellinghaus wanted to retain the belief that God was a righteous God, who desired everything to be in the heavenly order of love,

---

107. Ibid., 155.
108. Ibid., 6.
109. Ibid.
110. Ibid., 7.
111. Ibid., 7.

purity and holiness. His fundamental declaration to Adam and Eve that disobedience would result in separation from God, the source of all life and would lead to death, could not be just suspended by an act of mercy. Sin had come into the life of humanity and sin would inevitably lead to death.[112]

How could humanity be saved from this terrible destiny? Jellinghaus believed that humanity must die and called the plan of salvation by God "through death to life."[113] This solution was not possible for humanity on their own; because of their sinfulness they would have never seen a way through death to life and because of the inevitable suffering and pain this involves they would have even more rebelled against God.[114] The only solution was a second Adam, a second new head of humanity, a new beginning. God himself provided for this solution. His Son, the eternal Word became a human being: Jesus Christ. In the incarnation he became the new head of humanity, the last Adam as Paul phrased it.[115] As the new head he had willingly borne the necessary and just judgment and the curse of death which the first Adam had incurred on all of humanity. Because of that Jesus Christ cancelled all guilt and broke the power of sin. But God did not leave him in death, but raised him from the dead. Through his resurrection he became the eternal high priest, mediator of life, righteousness and holiness for all humanity. In this way Jesus Christ restored the life and love relationship between God and humanity.[116]

Jellinghaus adopted what he called the concept of organic representation (*organische Vertretung*). Already the first Adam had represented all of humanity organically. When Adam sinned and was expelled from paradise, signifying the separation from the presence of God, all of humanity was expelled from paradise because all humans after him were born outside of paradise. In that sense all humans inherited depravity, because all were organically (through blood and life) related to Adam.[117] This concept of organic representation must also be applied to the second Adam, Jesus Christ, according to Jellinghaus. Christ, the new head, had died and had been raised from the dead as organic and not judicial representative of humanity. Through his incarnation, Jesus Christ had taken upon himself the burden and penalty of sin. This was not a judicial act, but rather lay in the nature of being human (organically through his human blood and life). Christ did

---

112. Jellinghaus, *Römerbrief*, 66.
113. Ibid.; and Jellinghaus, *Das völlige Heil*, 36.
114. Jellinghaus, *Römerbrief*, 66.
115. Ibid.; and Jellinghaus, *Das völlige Heil*, 36.
116. Jellinghaus, *Das völlige Heil*, 36.
117. Ibid., 46–47.

not do this because he was obligated. He was without sin; therefore he did not deserve death and damnation. It was an act of his free will out of love to the Father and to humanity.[118] When Christ died for humanity, he did not die instead of humanity, like someone who takes the penalty of another on himself without being necessarily related to that person. Christ died for humanity in that he represented all of humanity in his death. His death needed to be understood inclusively (he died for all humanity) and not exclusively (as if he died only for the elect).[119] Jellinghaus called this the doctrine of organic reconciliation. Because of that he spoke of Jesus Christ as the present and full redeemer, who through his death and resurrection had liberated humanity from guilt, the power of sin, the law, the world, death and the devil and has brought eternal life, the kingdom of God, love, righteousness and holiness.[120] Through this understanding of the doctrine of reconciliation, Jellinghaus claimed that according to biblical teaching the forgiveness of sins, justification, cleansing, regeneration, entering the kingdom of God, conversion, sanctification and the baptism with the Holy Spirit all fall together. That meant for him that the unity of the doctrine is found only in the person of Jesus Christ. Therefore, according to Jellinghaus, the gospel of the Redeemer can and must be presented clearly and easily understandable, which he felt was not the case with the old Anselmic ecclesiastical doctrine.[121]

Ernst Cremer could not see a logical difference between the terms judicial reconciliation and organic reconciliation. He felt that what Jellinghaus wanted to accomplish with his peculiar doctrine was to prove that victory over sin could be realized for every believer directly through Christ. However, neither the doctrine of organic reconciliation nor any other doctrine could prove such an "un-Lutheran and unbiblical belief."[122] Paul Fleisch made the criticism that Jellinghaus's doctrine of reconciliation only stated that Jesus' death and resurrection would also break the power of sin; however, he did not show how and why this would be the case. Even the claim that Jesus' resurrection was part of the sacrifice did not really convince, because the resurrection did not add anything to the sacrifice. Jellinghaus believed that both Christ's death and resurrection corresponded to both,

118. Ibid., 47–48.

119. Ibid., 48.

120. Ibid., 21–22. Although there seem to be parallels between Jellinghaus's doctrine of organic reconciliation and Irenaeus's doctrine of recapitulation, nowhere does Jellinghaus refer to Irenaeus or quote him. However, there might be indirect influences through his teachers. The influence of his teachers will be discussed below.

121. Ibid., 22.

122. Cremer, *Das vollkommene gegenwärtige Heil in Christo*, 28–30.

redemption from guilt and from the power of sin. The only differentiation made was that the death of Christ referred "negatively to the removal of sin" and that the resurrection referred primarily "positively to the emergence of virtues."[123] Fleisch argued that this playful dissection was a perfect demonstration that Jellinghaus's doctrine of reconciliation did not create a basis for a unity between justification and sanctification, and even not for a teaching of direct deliverance from the power of sin which was added to a doctrine of justification. Even Jellinghaus's argument that his doctrine of reconciliation would safeguard against any substantial or magic-sacramental teaching of regeneration was not compelling.[124] The greatest strength of his teaching, according to Fleisch, was that it fitted perfectly with Jellinghaus's emphasis on a personal relationship of the believer with Jesus Christ.[125] The focal point here was the teaching of the "experience of the death and resurrection of Christ" by the believer by faith, which actually was a summary formula of the process of the reception of salvation including moral regeneration. However, even here, Jellinghaus used terms with a "certain carelessness" which could lead to a magic-physical misunderstanding of salvation, especially when he referred to the "power of the blood" and the "resurrection powers" of Christ.[126] In addition, Paul Fleisch observed that Jellinghaus's doctrine of reconciliation was positively received by some modern theologians; however it had not taken root in the *Gemeinschaftsbewegung*. This was owing to two facts: first, Jellinghaus objected to the traditional doctrine of reconciliation, which was upheld in traditional Pietist circles. Second, Jellinghaus argued technically and elaborately. Not many laypersons could follow his arguments. That became clear when the doctrine of the atonement was discussed at a conference of the *Gemeinschaftsbewegung*, Jellinghaus was not mentioned, and his teaching was deliberately ignored. Fleisch wrote that "Jellinghaus was dropped."[127] This was probably due to the fact that this conference took place in 1909 at the climax of the crisis within the *Gemeinschaftsbewegung*, when Jellinghaus was in a psychiatric hospital. Nevertheless, it is significant that Jellinghaus's teaching had not gained any substantial rootedness within the *Gemeinschaftsbewegung* although he was considered one of their best theologians.

Warfield felt that any good foundation for Jellinghaus's teaching had been stripped from him in his theological studies under Johann Christian

---

123. Fleisch, *Heiligungsbewegung,* 2:106–7.
124. Ibid., 107–8.
125. Ibid., 108.
126. Ibid..
127. Ibid., 363.

Konrad von Hofmann. He stated that von Hofmann deprived Jellinghaus of the Protestant doctrine of the penal satisfaction on the atonement without giving him a positive doctrine. This could not lead to a good end for all of the teachings of Jellinghaus.[128] Warfield correctly saw lines of influence on Jellinghaus; however, his interpretation and final assessment is obviously quite extreme and shaped by his personal theological position on the atonement (penal satisfaction theory) which would leave no room for any other viewpoints.

CONCLUSIONS

Jellinghaus's attempt to build his doctrine of redemption on a strong doctrine of reconciliation must be commended. He was well aware that formulating doctrine had not been one of the marks in the Pietist tradition, especially in the nineteenth century. This was one of the reasons why Pietism was disregarded or at least not taken seriously by many of the Protestant theologians in Germany. Jellinghaus wanted the connection to the established churches, because he felt that one of the reasons for the existence of Pietism (and especially the *Gemeinschaftsbewegung*) was the revival of the established Protestant churches in Germany. With his theology, especially his doctrine of reconciliation, he aimed at making those connections.[129] At the same time, he filled a vacuum of formulated doctrine within the Pietist tradition. This made him vulnerable and sometimes even aroused suspicion, as can be seen by some of the reactions within the Pietist circles to his book and his approach. But the book was a tremendous tool for his efforts to train lay people for leading Bible studies, prayer meetings, and other small groups within the Pietist circles. It was actually one of the reasons why the *Heiligungsbewegung* was beginning to be established in Germany after the *Triumphreise* of Robert Pearsall Smith in 1875.

It must be noted that the so-called Anselmic ecclesiastical doctrine focused primarily on justification. Jellinghaus was aware that sanctification also must be based and rooted in the doctrine of reconciliation. Therefore, his attempt should be praised, because that is what he accomplished. He presented a doctrine of reconciliation which not only looked at what had been done wrong (actual sins committed), but also at the being of sinfulness. According to Jellinghaus, Christ in his death and resurrection took

---

128. Warfield, *Studies in Perfectionism*, 1:348–49.

129. See his efforts in establishing the *Eisenacher Konferenz* and his interest in contemporary biblical and theological debates.

care of both the actual sins and the sinful state humanity was in since Adam.[130] Biblically and theologically he worked hard to formulate a doctrine that would reflect not only the Pietist tradition but also pave the way for new insights he had gained through the Anglo-American holiness movement, which he felt needed to be heard in Germany as well. Actually, it was his doctrine of redemption that was the beginning point for his doctrine of reconciliation. This becomes clear not only from the fact that in the first edition of *Das völlige Heil* he did not yet have his own doctrine of reconciliation, but also by the statements he made. He stated that he wanted to build a strong foundation for his doctrine of redemption, which was already formulated.[131] Therefore, it could be argued (which one of his critics, Paul Fleisch,[132] did) that he built the foundation after he had already built the house. That is why Fleisch felt that his doctrine of redemption did not flow out of his doctrine of reconciliation, but vice versa.[133] This may not be entirely true, because as noted before, the influences on his doctrine of reconciliation were early in his life and career. Jellinghaus's doctrine of reconciliation may not have been present extrinsically (it was not fully formulated yet); but it was present intrinsically. Nevertheless, it seems also to be true that Jellinghaus's final formulation of his doctrine of reconciliation aimed at suiting his doctrine of redemption.

Another critical point is his almost superficial dealing with historical persons and their doctrines. The primary example is Jellinghaus's use of Luther as an authority. Jellinghaus quoted and used Luther rather randomly. When he needed him, he quoted him as a defender of his own thoughts.[134] On the other hand, where he disagreed with Lutheran thoughts, he would make statements like, "This is where the Reformation has not thought it all through. We need to bring it to completion."[135] This was criticized rightly and did not help his cause. Regarding his criticism of the traditional doc-

---

130. Noble makes the important point in his book, *Holy Trinity: Holy People. The Historic Doctrine of Christian Perfecting* in chapter 6, "Christian Holiness and the Atonement," 128–57, that a Wesleyan doctrine of sanctification must be based in the atonement.

131. Jellinghaus, *Das völlige Heil*, xii, 20–21.

132. Alwin Gottlieb Paul Fleisch (1878–1962) studied theology in Greifswald (strongly influenced by Hermann Cremer), in Erlangen and Göttingen. Most of his active ministry he was involved in various positions at the Protestant Seminary in Loccum. Later he held various offices in the administration of the Lutheran church of Hannover. See Ohlemacher in the introduction to the book by Fleisch he edited: Fleisch, *Heiligungsbewegung*, 2:xxi–xxv.

133. Ibid., 105–6.

134. Jellinghaus, *Das völlige Heil*, xii, 220, 258, 306–7, 400.

135. Ibid., 395.

trine of the atonement he considered primarily what he called the Anselmic ecclesiastical doctrine and contrasted it with his own understanding. In discussions in recent years on the doctrine of the atonement it has been said that the Scriptures use various metaphors to describe the work of Christ.[136] Jellinghaus did not see the whole scope of metaphors or models, but rejected particularly one (although that one incorporated various metaphors) and presented one, which also incorporated various metaphors, but it did not look at the whole scope of biblical metaphors. This is connected also to the next point.

A last critique of Jellinghaus's doctrine of reconciliation concerns its objectivity, namely that the center of his doctrine seems to be the salvation of the individual. Jellinghaus was aware of this criticism and tried to answer it by stating that the objectivity of the doctrine did not lie in a formula or doctrine, but rather in the person and work of Jesus Christ. That sounded good and conclusive. But was it conclusive? Jellinghaus's formulation of the doctrine of reconciliation was rather narrow. He used certain biblical passages and gave a sketch of doctrinal formulations in the history of the church. But he did not dig deeper! Jellinghaus used some key passages in the Old Testament, but not the whole scope of the Hebrew Bible. He was more detailed regarding the teachings of the New Testament. But again, he used the passages mainly to prove his point. Of course, the objective of the book was not to be a highly academic work of biblical-theological research. It was to be the textbook for the *Heiligungsbewegung*.[137] Nevertheless, he claimed that his doctrine should replace the old traditional doctrine of the atonement. That was quite ambitious. Since Jellinghaus did not take into account the whole scope of biblical metaphors and teachings, it could be argued that he presented a narrow view of a doctrine with the primary purpose of serving his doctrine of redemption. That, of course, had an important bearing on the objectivity of the doctrine.

In conclusion, Theodor Jellinghaus needs to be noted for his attempt to formulate a doctrine of reconciliation for his own theological system as well as for his tradition. It was not a fully formulated doctrine and had some weaknesses; nevertheless it constituted his distinct theological persuasion.

---

136. See Noble, 133 where he refers to John McIntyre, *The Shape of Soteriology* as identifying thirteen models that have been used historically: ransom, redemption, salvation, sacrifice, propitiation, expiation, atonement, reconciliation, conflict and victory, punishment or penalty, satisfaction, example, and liberation.

137. Jellinghaus, *Das völlige Heil*, vi–vii, xiv.

5

Doctrine of Salvation II
Doctrine of Redemption

DOCTRINE OF REDEMPTION: JUSTIFICATION AND SANCTIFICATION THROUGH FAITH IN CHRIST ALONE

Theodor Jellinghaus's doctrine of reconciliation (Christ as our organic representative) constituted the foundation on which he built his doctrine of redemption. Because of his doctrine of reconciliation he believed that God was at work in every human being even before their conversion. Therefore, every human being would have an awareness of God and guilt.[1] That would not mean that a human being was able by himself or herself to understand and apprehend God's offer of reconciliation. However, God's being at work enabled every human being to come to a decision of the will between faith and unbelief when he or she heard the gospel and the Holy Spirit worked in his or her heart.[2] "What turns the balance in salvation is not reason but rather the moral religious awareness, the heart and the will."[3] For the doctrine of redemption this meant that for sinful humans to be saved they must, when the gospel was being proclaimed in the power of the Holy Spirit,

---

1. Jellinghaus, *Das völlige Heil*, 1–4.
2. Ibid., 4 and 56.
3. Ibid., 4.

...acknowledge in penitent recognition of their horrible sin Jesus' reconciliatory death and totally yield by faith to Christ (urged by the great grace and love of God in Christ) and die and be raised with him. He who dies to the world and himself with Christ enters into a fellowship of faith with the risen Christ from death to life. He will have righteousness, sanctification, love, light and eternal life in the Risen One through the Holy Spirit.[4]

That means that Jellinghaus understood redemption as participation by faith in the death and resurrection of Jesus Christ. He summarized his doctrine of redemption from a Christological viewpoint by stating that Jesus was both object and subject of salvation in the sense that "Jesus, the Son of God, through suffering, death and resurrection and by sitting at the right hand of God as the high-priest king, has become salvation for all who in repentance and faith have died to sin with him and have been raised to new life and purity in him."[5] In the appropriation of the benefits of the work of Christ by faith Jellinghaus differentiated between participation in the "powers of the death of Christ" and the "powers of the resurrection of Christ."[6] He taught that abiding in the powers of the death of Christ meant redemption from all guilt of sin, power of sin and ego-centricity, worry, legalism, spiritual death, the devil, and from sufferings and temptations.[7] Constant participation in the powers of the resurrection by faith in Christ brought about a bestowal "with the Holy Spirit and with Him true love, peace, joy, patience, long-suffering, humility, courage, light, wisdom, righteousness, sanctification, eternal life, kingdom of heaven and a sure hope of Him who will come again as king and bridegroom."[8] Jellinghaus added that the powers of the death of Christ and the powers of the resurrection of Christ cannot be experienced separately by the believer because they are linked to the person of Christ with whom the believer is related through faith.[9] In his commentary on Romans (in reference to Rom 1:6) Jellinghaus described redemption similarly as "salvation from the guilt of sin, power of sin, distress in selfish conduct, law, world, death and devil through the powers of the death of Jesus" and as "life, love, light, purity, righteousness, holiness, hope, peace and joy through the powers of the resurrection of Jesus."[10]

4. Ibid., 36.
5. Ibid., 54.
6. Ibid., 55.
7. Ibid., 54–55.
8. Ibid., 55.
9. Ibid.
10. Jellinghaus, *Römerbrief*, 27.

It can be concluded that Jellinghaus tried to link justification and sanctification in his doctrine of redemption based upon his doctrine of reconciliation by trying to differentiate between what he called the powers of the death of Jesus and the powers of the resurrection of Jesus. For him they were both linked indivisibly in their effect in justification and sanctification. He differentiated between the emphasis on justification and sanctification when it comes to the proclamation of the gospel. When the gospel was being preached to non-believers emphasis must be put on the forgiveness of the guilt of sin, becoming a child of God and receiving eternal life in Jesus Christ (justification). On the other hand he felt that the "fullness of the powers of the death and resurrection of Jesus"[11] appertained best to believers in their growth in holiness (sanctification). That seemed also to be the approach by Paul, Peter and John in their New Testament epistles.[12] The distinction was made for practical reasons "in order to differentiate between the doctrine of justification and practical sanctification according to the standard of the Reformers which helps us to understand the organic and inner coherence of both."[13] That is the reason why he divided his book into two parts: *Rechtfertigung allein durch Christum* (Justification through Christ Alone)[14] and *Heiligung allein durch Christum* (Sanctification through Christ Alone).[15] However, the reference to the person of Christ in both justification and sanctification held both doctrines indivisibly together. This is what he called *heilistische Erlösungslehre* (salvific doctrine of redemption).

As Theodor Jellinghaus developed his doctrine of redemption he was convinced that the future of the church depended on a biblical and theologically sound doctrine which expressed the victory of Jesus over sin. He believed in total depravity of human nature. However, at the same time he was persuaded that the Scriptures taught full redemption from the power of sin and a cleansing of the heart for those who follow Jesus.[16] This message could and should be proclaimed to all Christians or they would get stuck in legalism and could not live a victorious life. Furthermore, if the church would not live out what she was called to and given through Jesus Christ, she could not reach the lost and could even be in danger of losing

---

11. Jellinghaus, *Das völlige Heil*, 436.
12. Ibid.
13. Ibid.
14. Ibid., 1–382.
15. Ibid., 383–730.
16. Ibid., 385–88. Jellinghaus even mentioned various Bible passages talking about sanctification in heart and life (John 15:5,10,14; 14:21; 17:19; Rom 12:1; Phil 2:14–15; 2 Cor 7:1; 2 Tim 2:19; he said that it was the heart of the sermon on the mount).

her own youth, because she could not offer any real change to them.[17] If the church wants to win the masses, from intellectuals to common factory workers, then she needed a "revelation of the presence of God (Jer 3:17), being permeated by the Holy Spirit and receiving from him new visions for the greatness of the power of redemption of Jesus."[18]

Jellinghaus seemed quite enthusiastic in his argument when he suggested that "as highly elevated as the fathers of the Reformation are, we must not think that their way of teaching about sanctification would be unsurpassable, as if the apostles' teaching and life were not higher than the Reformers."[19] The task of the Reformers was first of all to lift up a healthy doctrine of justification to become a sound base for a biblical doctrine of sanctification.[20]

> Therefore, we should not describe the times of the Reformers as an unsurpassable ideal. If we want to have victory, we not only must attain the strength of mind of the Reformation, but we must strive for a higher strength. In the kingdom of God there is no stagnation, no wholesome going back to past times; only by moving forward in the knowledge of the Son of God and in actuating the powers of the Holy Spirit can the kingdom of Christ have victory.[21]

Although this statement would invite disapproval of Jellinghaus and his doctrine, for him it was a consequence of his doctrine of redemption. The approach of a practical distinction between justification and sanctification was vehemently criticized by Lutheran and Reformed theologians. Ludwig Clasen[22] complained early that Jellinghaus' teachings would "destroy the right relationship between justification and sanctification."[23] Paul Gennrich formulated his criticism of Jellinghaus's doctrine of redemption by stating that the basic question of the Reformation focused on how a believer can be assured of a merciful God. The basic question of Jellinghaus and the *Heiligungsbewegung* however focused on how a believer can get rid of sin.[24]

17. Ibid., 391–93.
18. Ibid., 394.
19. Ibid., 395.
20. Ibid.
21. Ibid.
22. Ulrich Ludwig Clasen (1843–1907) studied theology in Halle, Tübingen, Erlangen, and Berlin. Clasen, except for a brief term as hospital chaplain (1870) served as minister in different parishes until his retirement in 1903.
23. Clasen, "Heiligung im Glauben," 473.
24. Gennrich, *Wiedergeburt und Heiligung*, 34–35.

He felt that the first question addressed the heart of the gospel which the Reformers had rediscovered in the doctrine of justification by faith. The second question was leading back to Roman Catholic attempts to please God.[25] Ernst Rietschel[26] felt that Jellinghaus did not want to destroy the Lutheran doctrine of justification but rather wanted to complement it with his doctrine of sanctification.[27] However, this would raise the question whether the Lutheran doctrine of justification could be complemented without being flawed. For Rietschel it was clear that Jellinghaus created a different doctrine, because the Lutheran doctrine of justification included the doctrine of sanctification.[28] Ernst Cremer argued in a similar way by stating that in this system justification will become a "lower level" of salvation which must be completed by the "higher level" of sanctification.[29] In addition he contended that Jellinghaus tried to create the possibility of transfer of Christ's moral acquisition (victory over sin) to the believers. However, this was not possible with any doctrine or theory, because it could not be lived out owing to the moral nature of humanity. Therefore, this teaching was both "morally objectionable" and an "impossible conception."[30] Another theologian who agreed with this basic critique was Ludwig Ihmels.[31] He reasoned that by differentiating between justification and sanctification as Jellinghaus did, sanctification must be more and above justification and that would destroy the basic reformation heritage of the doctrine of justification by faith.[32] Paul Fleisch commended Jellinghaus's attempt to keep justification and sanctification together. However, he questioned that this would be possible by leaving the Lutheran foundation and creating a different understanding of both justification and sanctification by faith. He believed that Jellinghaus would not get beyond a mere parallelism of justification and sanctification which in fact would disprove his attempt that a separate doctrine of sanctification was necessary.[33] B.B. Warfield agreed with that assessment when he

25. Ibid., 53.

26. Johannes Ernst Rietschel (1872–1960) served as private tutor, minister in different parishes in Saxony, superintendent in Oschatz/Saxony, and secretary of the central board of the *Gustav-Adolf-Verein* in Leipzig. Information from *Landeskirchenarchiv, Bestand 2, Evangelisch-Lutherisches Landeskirchenamt Sachsen* in Dresden.

27. Rietschel, 8.

28. Ibid.

29. Cremer, *Das vollkommene gegenwärtige Heil in Christo*, 13.

30. Ibid., 28–30.

31. Ludwig Heinrich Ihmels (1858–1933) was professor for church dogmatics at the University of Leipzig and later bishop of the Lutheran Church in Saxony.

32. Ihmels, "Zur Lehre von der Heiligung bei Theodor Jellinghaus," 103–4.

33. Fleisch, *Heiligungsbewegung*, 2:107–8.

stated that Jellinghaus succeeded so perfectly in showing that sanctification and justification belong together inseparably that a "second act of faith" to obtain sanctification is actually unnecessary.[34] Warfield ascribed that flaw in Jellinghaus to his "mediating theology" (as Warfield put it) which taught that if the believers entered into a "mystical union" with Christ they received "in Him all that He is and has, all at once."[35] What Jellinghaus did in his understanding of the relationship of justification and sanctification was trying to incorporate the teachings he had received in Oxford with the mediating theology he had been taught in his studies in Germany.[36] That understanding, Warfield argued, led to an artificial separation between justification and sanctification; the two were only parts of the same general experience, namely that of "participation in the Christ-life."[37] In fact, Jellinghaus did not really treat justification and sanctification doctrinally "but rather the experience of deliverance which the Christian has through faith in Christ, viewed, we might say, now from the point of sight of its inception, now from the point of its completion, though that would be to speak far too strongly in terms of chronological sequence."[38]

Warfield made some important observations. First of all, he was absolutely correct in stating that Jellinghaus's doctrine of redemption was built on his doctrine of reconciliation and that he was trying to integrate what he had experienced and learned in England into his basic theological convictions. This led, as Warfield rightly pointed out, to some unresolvable statements, especially regarding the relationship of justification and sanctification in Jellinghaus. Warfield basically agreed with Fleisch, whose works he had read and used, in that Jellinghaus did not succeed in demonstrating a unity and a distinction between justification and sanctification.

Justification in Christ Alone

One of the basic teachings of Jellinghaus's doctrine of justification was its instantaneous character. Since humanity existed in a depraved and lost condition, which meant that humanity was spiritually dead, the change from death to life must be rather sudden. The very nature of salvation was the faith relationship to Christ in which the believer died to the old life and was raised with the Savior to new life. New birth, therefore, was rather sudden

---

34. Warfield, *Studies in Perfectionism*, 1:355.
35. Ibid., 364.
36. Ibid., 373.
37. Ibid., 353.
38. Ibid., 353–54.

and instantaneous.[39] At the same time Jellinghaus also emphasized the importance of Christian education and instruction. He believed that it was the best preparation for becoming a Christian if a young person had been raised in the Christian faith. Nevertheless, even for children of Christians there normally was a certain turning point and instantaneous decision in which they experienced Christ as their personal Savior.[40] The nature of conversion as an instantaneous experience had an important implication for the order of salvation, namely that the different terms describing the experience cannot be understood as different stages of salvation which a repentant sinner had to go through. They were rather terms describing salvation from different perspectives.[41] Jellinghaus classified the different terms in three groups. First, actions of God which prepared conversion: call, enlightenment, awakening.[42] Second, processes and activities in the sinner through which he turned from sin and embraced Christ: repentance and faith.[43] And third, terms for the experience of salvation through repentance and faith in Christ: justification and forgiveness of sins, conversion, regeneration, sanctification.[44] The different terms in this third group described for him the same state of grace, just from different perspectives.[45] Jellinghaus explained the terms in each group in more detail.

Actions of God preparing conversion: call, enlightenment, awakening

Jellinghaus understood call as "God's strong call of grace"[46] through the gospel by which he called the sinner to repentance and faith. In the call God gave the sinner the ability to listen. It was a "life giving call of God" to the sinner which was powerful to convert the sinner.[47] Enlightenment was, according to Jellinghaus, the work of the Holy Spirit through the Word by which he gave insight to the sinner about the state of his or her soul, being impure, wretched and lost. At the same time the Spirit gave light to recognize the glorious redemption in Christ. This was more than intellectual en-

39. Jellinghaus, *Das völlige Heil*, 82–83.
40. Ibid., 85 (footnote).
41. Ibid., 85.
42. Ibid., 86.
43. Ibid.
44. Ibid.
45. Ibid.
46. Ibid., 87.
47. Ibid.

lightenment. It was a spiritual enlightenment which humans by themselves were not capable of. It was the work of the holy God in the heart of people.[48] When speaking about awakening, Jellinghaus claimed that this word did not appear in Scripture for sinners. Theologically it meant the same thing as enlightenment to the sinner, namely the awareness through the Holy Spirit of the state of lostness before God and the need of salvation in Jesus Christ. The word awakening was used for a believer to signify a revival of spiritual powers already at work and cooperation with God in the life of a believer.[49]

Processes and activities to experience salvation in Christ: repentance and faith

Jellinghaus taught that repentance and faith were the "God-ordered unique means to participate in Christ's redemption."[50] He defined repentance as a "realization about one's sin and damnation, a conviction of the error of the present life and the sense of being worthy of death and a concession to damnation before God according to his holy law."[51] This realization was not only happening on an intellectual level but was especially a perception of the heart which would lead to a serious intention to turn away from sin, accept Christ and be willing to serve him.[52] Therefore, he defined the New Testament term *metanoia* as "change of mind," "true stocktaking of oneself" and "thinking differently."[53] He argued that repentance and faith belong together. They were almost simultaneous and always related effects of the proclamation of the gospel through the work of the Holy Spirit in the hearts of people.[54] Repentance could be described as the "last act of the unconverted man," faith the "first act of the converted man."[55] Jellinghaus also gave some pastoral counsel on what to avoid when people sought repentance. On the one hand he was critical of the so-called "penitential struggle"[56] which was quite common in some Pietist circles. Here people were often misled to believe that they had to go through a long period of repentance in

---

48. Ibid.
49. Ibid., 88.
50. Ibid., 95.
51. Ibid., 101.
52. Ibid.
53. Ibid., 100–101.
54. Ibid., 106.
55. Ibid., 112.
56. Ibid., 126.

order for it to be "true repentance"[57]. He rejected this practice as unbiblical and making the grace of God dependent on a certain condition a person must experience. This would make repentance the key to salvation and not faith, and that is works-righteousness.[58] On the other hand, he also warned against underemphasizing repentance, which could happen with preachers who urged people to accept Christ without having them understand why and them being unaware of their sinfulness. He called these "pseudo-conversions" which could not lead to a victorious Christian life.[59]

Jellinghaus addressed the Lutheran teaching of daily repentance by stating that this has been misunderstood especially in the Lutheran tradition. He rejected an understanding of Christians having to sin and therefore needing to repent every day. Daily repentance would rather mean remaining in repentance, which was the humble realization that without remaining in Christ one can have no salvation and was utterly lost and cannot but sin. Therefore, it was important to differentiate between the repentance of unbelievers and the repentance of believers. The former was a converting experience (by faith) and the latter a spirit of humbly remaining in Christ and depending on him every moment for salvation.[60] Even if a Christian sinned, repentance was possible and should be sought immediately. This was the work of the Holy Spirit to bring people into relationship with God through Christ and to help them to remain in that relationship. In that sense, repentance was related to the human will, which was enabled by the Holy Spirit to react to God's gracious offer of salvation. Not being willing to respond to God was mistrust of the Holy Spirit which was one of the greatest sins.[61] Jellinghaus believed that faith was the only means to have a relationship with God and to participate in the "powers of the death of Christ" and the "powers of the resurrection of Christ."[62]

This understanding of repentance was criticized by Ernst Rietschel. He felt that there were two paradoxes in the Lutheran understanding of justification by faith which Jellinghaus tried to dissolve.[63] However, in the attempt to dissolve the paradoxes there was the danger to destroy the doctrine. The first paradox was that "God justifies sinners"[64] and the second

---

57. Ibid.
58. Ibid., 127.
59. Ibid., 128.
60. Ibid., 125.
61. Ibid., 114–15.
62. Ibid., 129.
63. Rietschel, *Lutherische Rechtfertigungslehre*, 11 and 14.
64. Ibid., 11.

was that believers were justified at once and yet this justification must be renewed every day.⁶⁵ This had to do with the Lutheran understanding of baptismal regeneration and the everyday walk of the Christians. Luther kept the paradoxes; however, both the orthodox Lutherans and Pietism tried to dissolve them in different directions.⁶⁶ Both traditions were wrong, and Jellinghaus followed Pietism.⁶⁷ Only when both paradoxes are kept can the Christian life, in its paradoxes of ups and downs, temptations and falling into sin be understood as being secure in God's gracious hands, because that does not depend on our works but only on his gracious act of having justified us as we are.⁶⁸ Fleisch's critique of Jellinghaus's understanding of repentance aimed at his understanding of repentance (and faith) primarily as an act, where the question and danger was that sin was understood quite narrowly and superficially.⁶⁹

In Jellinghaus's explanation of faith he argues that the primary Old Testament term for faith, *aman*, was best translated as faithfulness, trust and obedience. The New Testament terms *pistis, pisteuein, pistos* could be translated similarly as convincement, faithfulness and trust.⁷⁰ Therefore, he defined the Christian faith as trusting in Jesus Christ as Redeemer by being convinced that one was lost in sin and that Jesus could and wanted to save, by trusting in Jesus as Savior and in surrender to Jesus to be faithful and obedient.⁷¹ He believed that these three aspects of the Christian faith corresponded to the "powers of the soul" with its intellect (being convinced), feeling (trusting) and will (faithfulness or obedience).⁷²

Paul Fleisch assessed this understanding of faith as an act of the will.⁷³ Jellinghaus's understanding of "being faithful and obedient" raised questions because for him it was not clear what was meant and included in that, since they described primarily an act or a permanent performance ("remaining in Christ").⁷⁴ That was a narrow understanding of faith for Fleisch.

---

65. Ibid., 14.
66. Ibid., 24–25.
67. Ibid., 25.
68. Ibid., 28–29, 31.
69. Fleisch, *Heiligungsbewegung*, 2:118–19.
70. Jellinghaus, *Das völlige Heil*, 138.
71. Ibid.
72. Ibid., 139.
73. Fleisch, *Heiligungsbewegung*, 2:112.
74. Ibid., 113–15.

Jellinghaus followed the basic Protestant teaching that "natural man"[75] by himself cannot really trust in God. All that natural man can do, like in all other religions, was believe in some kind of fate. From a Christian standpoint it was not faith that saves humanity, but rather Jesus Christ. Christian faith then was both the object of faith (Jesus Christ), and the believer's apprehension of the object. Faith without the object of trust, according to Jellinghaus, could never be Christian faith.[76] This faith can only be evoked by God through the gospel. It was in the gospel that through God's grace, both the content or object of faith (Jesus Christ) and the ability to believe was offered as a gift to humanity. Since this gift of God is offered to all human beings through the work of the Holy Spirit, everyone who hears the gospel can respond to it.[77] This includes that faith must be experienced. However, experience must be understood in God's order of salvation. Jellinghaus described that order as first, knowledge of the fact that Christ was the full and present Redeemer; second, faith as surrender and trusting in Christ; and third, faith as experience of the power of redemption in Christ and the witness of the Holy Spirit. This order should not be reversed.[78] However, all three points in the order are important. Without experience faith can become legalistic and works-righteousness, and experience by itself can lead to fanaticism and enthusiasm.[79]

Ernst Cremer criticized this understanding of faith from a Lutheran viewpoint. He argued that the faith which God gives us is experience in itself. By this he meant that for Luther justification was always also experience, a daily experience of what God had done in baptism.[80] It would be wrong to say faith depended first on knowledge of facts; faith rather depended on God's gracious act of forgiveness and as such was a gift from God which would bear fruit.[81]

In relation to faith, Jellinghaus made important statements regarding election and predestination. He believed that the "old Calvinism"[82] with its double predestination was receding in all denominations in America, England and continental Europe. It was rather Methodism which was gaining influence everywhere, because in it an inner fusion of Reformed, Lutheran

---

75. Jellinghaus, *Das völlige Heil*, 144.
76. Ibid., 146, 149.
77. Ibid., 151–52.
78. Ibid., 165.
79. Ibid., 169.
80. Cremer, *Das vollkommene gegenwärtige Heil in Christo*, 32–33.
81. Ibid., 33.
82. Jellinghaus, *Das völlige Heil*, 176.

and Arminian spirit and character had taken place.[83] He rejected double predestination and believed that the relationship of human freedom and divine providence, of human accountability in faith and divine election, will forever be a mystery, because nobody can know why some people believe and others do not believe.[84]

Personal faith in biblical terms was characterized by a double witness, the witness of the human spirit and the witness of the Holy Spirit. Both witnesses were important, because the witness of the Holy Spirit (given by the grace of God) informed the human spirit of being a child of God. Therefore, Christians can really know that they are Christians. It was important that this witness was based on the fact that the believer had a personal faith relationship to Jesus Christ and continually remains in Christ.[85]

Consequences and results of repentance and faith: justification and forgiveness of sins, conversion, regeneration, and assurance of salvation

According to Jellinghaus, the consequences and results of the experience of salvation through repentance and faith in Jesus Christ have different aspects which are all connected to each other: justification and forgiveness of sins, conversion, regeneration and assurance of salvation. There is actually one more, which will be mentioned here, but dealt with separately: sanctification.[86]

Jellinghaus defined justification as "proclaiming righteous," "declaring righteous" and "bringing in order or rectifying."[87] At the same time he rejected what he called "Roman teaching" of justification as "infusion of righteousness" which claimed that sinners could only be righteous before God by faith and good works.[88] Justification and forgiveness of sins were the same for Jellinghaus. He declared that "forgiveness of sins and the removal of judgment is a declaration of righteousness, and the declaration of righteousness includes a cancellation of guilt and forgiveness of sins."[89] However, this must be closely connected to understanding that the Christian participates through faith in Christ's death and resurrection. This meant that forgive-

83. Ibid.
84. Ibid., 178.
85. Ibid., 191–94.
86. Ibid., 249.
87. Ibid., 250.
88. Ibid., 251.
89. Ibid., 253.

ness of sins was more than an imputation of the cancellation of guilt and the merit of Christ, but it signified that the dominion of sin was broken and that the believer had died in Christ and had been raised in Christ and therefore was united with God and rectified.[90] That would imply that Christ himself was the righteousness of believers; it could not be a righteousness in believers that was separated from a personal faith relationship to God in Christ. Jellinghaus opposed any understanding that separated salvation in Christ from the person of the Savior. Salvation was possible only through a participation in Christ and what he had done, by "dying with Christ" and "being raised with Christ" through faith.[91] Therefore, Jellinghaus believed that the justified person in himself remained sinful. Justification and sanctification were effective as long as the believer was in relationship to God through Christ and participated by faith in Christ's death and resurrection. Through the faith relationship with Christ, the Holy Spirit was at work and the believer could "bear God-honoring fruit."[92] Jellinghaus summarized his understanding in the following way.

> Justification happens immediately based on the redemption of Christ which happened in history and is available through repentance and faith in Christ by which a person is in relationship to Christ. Justification and forgiveness of sins abide as long as the Christian through surrendering faith in Jesus, the Redeemer, remains in his arms of grace as one who has died with Christ and has been raised with Christ.[93]

Theodor Jellinghaus understood conversion as a completed experience that had happened in the life of the believer; it was not an ongoing experience.[94] As such conversion included the acceptance of Christ in a moment in history through repentance and faith.[95] Conversion was wrought through the work of the Holy Spirit and sinful humanity cannot by themselves do anything about it. However, if the sinners had been seized by the truth through the Holy Spirit, then they had been enabled to respond and therefore must respond in order to be saved. God had created humanity in his own image which implied that human will, after being enabled through the Holy Spirit, must respond to God. Conversion was therefore God's work which

---

90. Ibid.
91. Ibid., 254–57.
92. Ibid., 261, 265.
93. Ibid., 266.
94. Ibid., 277.
95. Ibid., 280–81.

humanity responded to through the grace of God by the enablement of the Holy Spirit.[96]

Regarding regeneration, Jellinghaus held that it meant "new birth," "becoming a child of God," "eternal life" and "transfer into the kingdom of God."[97] Regeneration correlated with justification and the forgiveness of sins because the "new life" was related to the person of Jesus Christ, to whom the believer was related through faith, which happened at justification. Therefore, Jellinghaus rejected any teaching of baptismal regeneration, because it would separate the benefits of the work of Christ from the person of Christ.[98] According to Jellinghaus there were three causes of regeneration: the Word of God (gospel), the Holy Spirit, and the blood of Christ (work of Christ in his death, resurrection and being in the presence of God as our mediator).[99] Jellinghaus listed seven marks of regeneration: faith in Christ, peace with God through the Holy Spirit, confessing Christ, the renouncing of all deliberate sin, loving God and Christ, loving the brethren in Christ, and humility before God and other human beings.[100]

The relationships that Jellinghaus tries to show between justification and forgiveness of sins, conversion and regeneration are strongly connected to his teaching of "dying with Christ" and "being raised with Christ" according to Fleisch.[101] Since all of this was to be accepted "simply by faith" and all of it was happening in the moment of believing, Jellinghaus in fact came close to a "mystical-magic" understanding which he actually rejected.[102] Because of the nature of salvation, it was possible for believers to be sure of their state of grace.[103] The assurance of salvation was important for the daily life in faith. Christianity without assurance of salvation would be weak, swaying and would hardly bear any fruit.[104] Only because of the assurance of salvation was it possible to love one's neighbor, to come boldly before the

---

96. Ibid., 285–86.

97. Ibid., 291, 296.

98. Ibid., 291–93. This will be explained in more detail in chapter 6, which deals with his understanding of baptism.

99. Ibid., 297.

100. Ibid., 327–35.

101. Fleisch, *Heiligungsbewegung*, 2:122–23.

102. Ibid., 126. This critique is supported by Ohlemacher, *Reich Gottes*, 175–76, by stating that it was difficult for Jellinghaus to claim that salvation is in Christ (outside of the believer) and yet, the believer must die and be raised with Christ in order for it to be effective, which suggests an active participation of the believer in Christ, which would bring about victory over sin.

103. Jellinghaus, *Das völlige Heil*, 344.

104. Ibid., 358.

throne of God, to have hope in times of temptation and tribulation or even in the face of death, to be a witness for Christ and be willing to lay down one's life for the Savior.[105] Jellinghaus claimed that the assurance of salvation was possible only by remaining in Christ, by nurturing the relationship with him by continually participating in the death and resurrection of Christ through the Holy Spirit—being dead to oneself and living in Christ.[106]

Sanctification in Christ Alone

As mentioned in the last section under justification in Christ alone, one of the consequences and results of the experience of salvation through repentance and faith in Jesus Christ was sanctification. The reason for that is that justification and regeneration are simultaneous. Just as with justification, faith, according to Jellinghaus, played a vital role in sanctification, because it was the only means by which the "powers of the death of Christ" and the "powers of the resurrection of Christ" can be appropriated by the believer.[107] As he expounded his doctrine of sanctification, Jellinghaus insisted that in Scripture it cannot be understood as "self-sanctification" or "works-righteousness" or "fighting sin by oneself" or "self-improvement."[108] It was rather participation in the holiness of Jesus by a personal relationship with him through the Holy Spirit.[109] Already the Old Testament taught that only God was holy and whatever was called or made holy was such through relationship with God. The phrase used to describe this was that the "altar sanctified the gift."[110] Sanctification, purification and victorious living could only happen in relationship to God himself in Jesus Christ, which happened by faith as a work of the Holy Spirit.[111] Since Jesus was the object and subject appropriated by faith, justification and sanctification cannot be separated.[112]

---

105. Ibid., 358–66.
106. Ibid., 374–81.
107. Ibid., 533.
108. Ibid., 535.
109. Ibid.
110. Ibid., 536. Jellinghaus is referring to Exod 30:29 (and Matt 23:19). This phrase has been popularized by Phoebe Palmer for the holiness movement.
111. Ibid., 537.
112. Ibid., 540.

Paul's epistle to the Romans, chapter seven

Early in his presentation of the doctrine of sanctification, Theodor Jellinghaus focused on Paul's epistle to the Romans and asked if in chapter seven Paul described the "normal state of a believing Christian."[113] He felt that this was a key passage dealing with the key issues of a New Testament understanding of the relationship between justification and sanctification. Jellinghaus started the section by giving a historical overview of the various interpretations of this passage. He began with the first four hundred years (until Augustine) and said they believed that Paul either spoke about a nonconverted person or a Christian who still was under the law and had not yet experienced the spiritual power available to him.[114] A change happened with Augustine who believed that Paul was referring to his personal situation. This position was later adopted by the Reformers of both the Lutheran and Calvinist confessions.[115] Since Spener, the Pietists taught that Paul described the condition before the new birth. Jellinghaus believed that John Wesley followed that position.[116] The majority of the German interpreters of the nineteenth century (with the exception of the Lutherans) argued that Paul was not referring to the state of a regenerate believer, but the condition of the "natural man" in his struggle against sin or the state of the person who has been awakened by prevenient grace before his conversion, justification and regeneration.[117] His former professor in Erlangen, von Hofmann, expressed the mediating position that Paul was speaking about his relationship to the law, disregarding his moral capability in Christ.[118] The same position was taken by William Boardman and Robert Pearsall Smith.[119] They believed that Paul was talking neither about the condition of an unconverted person nor about the normal state of a child of God. Paul was rather referring to Christians who fell again under the law and were experiencing in their legal

---

113. Ibid., 399.

114. Ibid., 399–400. To support this understanding he referred to John Chrysostom (c. 347–407), as he cites the German translation of his work *Vom jungfräulichen Stande*, chapter 84, which probably corresponds to his *Homily XIII* on Romans 7.

115. Ibid., 400.

116. Ibid.

117. Ibid.

118. Ibid.

119. Jellinghaus quotes Smith and Boardman in *Das völlige Heil*, 401, without giving any reference to a book or a sermon. Boardman teaches this in his book, *The Higher Christian Life*, 99–104.

striving for holiness that they were still in the flesh and that they might have hated the flesh but they could not have victory over it.[120]

After that Jellinghaus expounded his own exegesis of the seventh chapter of Paul's epistle to the Romans, which, he argued, had to draw on the entire Pauline and New Testament teachings on justification, conversion, regeneration and sanctification.[121] Jellinghaus then came to the following conclusions: first, Paul was not referring to the present experience of a believer. The entire letter (Rom. 6:6,11–12,18,22; 7:5–6; 8:1–11) as well as other writings by Paul (Phil. 4:13; Gal. 2:20; 1 Cor. 15:57; 2 Cor. 3:18) did not allow this standpoint. It would also collide with Jesus' Sermon on the Mount, where he spoke about a clean heart. The same was true for the teachings in 1 John, where the author was arguing that a sign of being a child of God was the awareness to be able to have victory over sin.[122] Jellinghaus argued that if Romans 7:7–23 was the condition of all believers which could not be changed, then it would only be right to admit that there was no difference between Christians and all unbelievers and followers of other religions.[123] Therefore, to teach that Romans 7 refers to the normal state of a Christian is dangerous and misleading not only for the Christian life but also for the Christian message.[124]

Second, Romans 7:7–25 did not describe the condition of the unconverted and unregenerate person who tried to sanctify him- or herself in legal terms. This would contradict the context of the entire epistle.[125] Therefore, Jellinghaus believed that Romans 7 described the experience of a child of God who fell again under the law by trying to sanctify him- or herself legally.[126] That was why Jellinghaus could not agree on the exegesis of this passage with Wesley, who argued that a person was portrayed, who was awakened by the law but not yet regenerated. This position, according to Jellinghaus, would necessarily lead to the understanding that assurance of salvation was only possible at a high level of the sanctified life.[127] He emphasized that Paul was describing a believer who fell under the law and experienced the power

---

120. Jellinghaus, *Das völlige Heil*, 401.
121. Ibid.
122. Ibid., 402.
123. Ibid., 402–3.
124. Ibid., 404.
125. Ibid., 406.
126. Ibid., 408.
127. Ibid., 409.

of inward sin. However, that was not the norm for Christians, because it was the condition of a painful and unsuccessful struggle.[128]

At that point Jellinghaus picked up the discussion on old man and new man in the life of the Christian. He said that both Luther and Arndt in his *Wahres Christentum* argued that the concepts of old man and new man described rather independent natures and that the entire Christian life consisted of the fight between those two natures within the believer.[129] This teaching would lead either to the belief that sanctification and holiness was only imputed and no ongoing victory over sin was possible; or it meant that a second stage of entire sanctification after regeneration was necessary with the eradication of the old man which would allow a victorious life.[130] Jellinghaus rejected that teaching. He believed that old man and new man were not independent natures. Old man rather described the person who was controlled by the flesh, the sinful world and the devil. If a person was converted through faith in Christ, he would give his old self into the death of Christ in order to live the life in relationship to the risen Christ and for Christ by the power of the Spirit. Through this personal faith relationship to Christ the self was in Christ and as such a new self. This new man however, was not independent, but could only be understood in relationship by faith with Christ. Therefore, it is not possible to "put off the old man" without "putting on the new man."[131] Jellinghaus defined the new man as Christ's mirrored image.[132] He concluded then that the new man only existed through the faith relationship and indwelling of Christ in the believer. Therefore, if Christ did not live in the believer and if the believer did not remain in Christ, the believer could have no victory over sin by himself.[133]

Jellinghaus' position on this Scripture passage was influenced strongly by the teachings of Robert Pearsall Smith and William Boardman, which he admitted. However, it also fitted with his theological background and influence by von Hofmann. As such he drew on different sources to explain and justify his own teaching. This is an approach which can be observed throughout his writings.

---

128. Ibid., 418.
129. Ibid., 421.
130. Ibid.
131. Ibid.
132. Ibid.
133. Ibid., 424–25.

Scriptural evidence for sanctification by faith

Jellinghaus claimed that sanctification by faith was clearly taught in the New Testament. He believed that in the Old Testament there was no fully revealed teaching of the final victory over the power of guilt and the power of sin, except for some promises for a victorious life.[134] In the gospels the doctrine was not yet fully developed, however, it was clear that salvation is centered upon Jesus Christ, the Son of God and in his death and resurrection.[135] The clear teaching of sanctification by faith was found in the epistles.[136] It was here that the foundation for any doctrine of sanctification must be found. He believed that the apostolic epistles were primarily exhortations for sanctification by faith because they were addressed to regenerate believers who already lived in a faith relationship to Jesus Christ. As such they were admonished to live a life of love.[137] The writers of the epistles did not doubt the state of grace of the recipients of the letters. On the contrary, they usually addressed them as saints, as persons who had experienced God's grace in their lives. It is important to the authors that sanctification and the life in righteousness did not happen as legal struggle in the believer's own strength, but rather through faith in Jesus Christ.[138]

Jellinghaus reviewed the different epistles in the New Testament to prove his point. The Galatians, he argued, made the error to think that they had to fulfill the law in their own strength in order to live the sanctified life. Paul did not write that they needed to be converted, but rather admonished them to continue their journey as they had started it by faith in Jesus Christ.[139] They had started their Christian life by faith but then wanted to complete it by works. But that would lead them back to a life under the law and in the flesh.[140] Paul was clear in Galatians that the promised Holy Spirit could only be received by faith and not by works of the law.[141] In Colossians Paul taught that the believer shared by faith in everything that Christ had provided, so that he was transferred through participating by faith in the death and resurrection of Christ into the heavenly kingdom of God.[142] In

---

134. Ibid., 573.
135. Ibid., 575–76.
136. Ibid., 557.
137. Ibid.
138. Ibid.
139. Ibid., 558.
140. Ibid., 561.
141. Ibid., 563.
142. Ibid., 570.

Hebrews special attention is given to the "believer's rest in faith" in chapters three and four.[143] At that point Jellinghaus asked if the passing of the people of God through the Red Sea could be compared to justification and conversion and the passing through the Jordan in the Promised Land after wandering in the desert for many years to sanctification and the believer's rest in Christ as Robert Pearsall Smith had done.[144] He felt that although Smith and the holiness movement in England and America had been criticized for that, some of these allegorical interpretations have been used by New Testament writers themselves. Nevertheless, the evidence for the life of holiness must be found in the New Testament.[145]

Regarding the doctrine of sanctification by faith in the gospels, Jellinghaus felt that is was clearly taught in John's gospel, especially in chapters six, seven and fifteen. In the synoptic gospels Jesus spoke about the content of a life of holiness. But that must be understood by its context that Jesus Christ first had to become the full redeemer through his death and resurrection before this could be realized in the lives of the disciples. Nevertheless, it was clear that the sanctified life was only possible by following Jesus and trusting fully in him.[146] Jellinghaus emphasized the fact that the New Testament also talked about fulfilling the law and being obedient. However, these were not to be understood as external and demanding laws, but rather as "evangelical laws"[147] as outward signs of the faith relationship to Jesus Christ. It was the gospel of Christ that brought the gift and the power to the powerless (love) and made possible to live the new life in Christ.[148] Therefore, Jellinghaus argued, it was possible for the believer through faith to fulfill the commandments of God and the duties of the Christian life and to do that with joy in order to do the will of God. It was actually the realization of the victorious life in Christ.[149]

It is interesting to see how Jellinghaus tried to avoid some of the pitfalls of scriptural evidence for the sanctified life. He did not really criticize some of the interpretations of the Old Testament by holiness teachers to which he alluded. Jellinghaus rather did not follow their example. He felt that the scriptural evidence could only be based on the teachings of the New Testament. Although he is correct that the full understanding of the

143. Ibid., 572.
144. Ibid., 572–73.
145. Ibid., 573.
146. Ibid., 575–76.
147. Ibid., 578.
148. Ibid., 578–79.
149. Ibid., 579.

way of salvation can only be found in the New Testament, it is important to note that any understanding of the holiness of God, which is the basis for any teaching of a sanctified life, is clearly taught in the Old Testament. For example the teaching of holiness in the book of Leviticus is foundational in this regard. Jellinghaus did not expound on that at all, which made his biblical argument weaker. Overall it can be stated that Theodor Jellinghaus's scriptural evidence for sanctification by faith, although he wanted to avoid allegorical methods which raised more questions than they answered, basically did not get beyond proof-texting. His doctrines were already finalized before he got to the scriptural basis. It is safe to say that it was not his exegetical work that led him to his teachings, but rather his teachings were already set and his scriptural evidence for sanctification by faith mainly affirmed his main doctrinal conclusions.

The experience of sanctification in Christ alone

The question that Jellinghaus found important to answer was: How did the Christian appropriate the holiness and the victory of Jesus more completely in his or her Christian life?[150] It was true that through justification the believer was in relationship with Jesus Christ and all that was his was available to the believer. However, the Bible, he argued, taught that there needed to be a deeper sanctification, a fuller experience and daily life in the "power of the death of Christ" and the "power of the resurrection of Christ" which was a victorious life.[151]

Jellinghaus taught that there were conditions for a deeper and more complete sanctification. These conditions were not to be misunderstood as self-effort, but rather as being open in faith for Christ to work through his Holy Spirit in the life of the believer. Therefore, the conditions could be summarized as a deep hunger for righteousness and holiness, a deep renouncing of sin and love for the world, a despair in one's own strength and one's own will and a full surrender of body and soul to the Lord to be his complete and sanctified possession.[152] This complete surrender was possible only through a love for God which the Holy Spirit poured into the heart of the believer. The believer must respond by faith to this love by surrendering completely his full will to God.[153] The full and complete surrender must remain constant. It was not just a moment in time, but rather surrender from

150. Ibid., 482.
151. Ibid.
152. Ibid., 483.
153. Ibid., 516.

moment to moment by faith in Christ. As such it was fully consecrating oneself to Christ.[154] Connected to the full consecration was unconditional and absolute obedience.[155] At the same time the consecration was not static, it was possible to grow as the believer's relationship to Christ grew.[156]

Paul Gennrich was one of the first to call this reasoning of Jellinghaus into question. Since regeneration and justification are simultaneous, he argued, why was a special doctrine of sanctification by faith necessary?[157] Gennrich felt that it was unnecessary.[158] In fact, this doctrine opened the door to excesses in later developments in terms of teaching sinlessness and absolute perfection, teachings which Jellinghaus wanted to avoid.[159] Ludwig Ihmels agreed with this assessment. He argued that if the personal relationship with Christ was established in justification by faith, which actually meant the regeneration of the believer as a child of God, and everything that was necessary to salvation was present in Christ—why was a second experience, a deeper or higher relationship necessary?[160] For him it seems that Jellinghaus wanted to integrate what he had learned in Oxford into his basic doctrine of redemption. For that he had to construct this doctrine, which actually was unnecessary in his basic understanding of salvation.[161]

Ernst Cremer criticized the understanding of the pouring out of the Holy Spirit in Jellinghaus. He argued that Jellinghaus spoke of the Holy Spirit as a *Lebenskraft* (life power) which was portrayed as empowerment almost as a *physische Kraft* (physical power) which meant a *gratia infusa*, a Catholic understanding of sanctification.[162] Paul Fleisch reasoned in the same direction. It seemed, according to Fleisch, that Jellinghaus distinguished between *Vergebungsgnade* (forgiveness grace) and *Heiligungsgnade* (sanctification grace). The second seemed to be poured as power into the believer, which made it a *gratia infusa*. Jellinghaus did not see it as such, but it was present.[163]

---

154. Ibid., 525.

155. Ibid., 526.

156. Ibid., 529.

157. Gennrich, *Wiedergeburt und Heiligung*, 29–30.

158. Among others Ernst Rietschel and B. B. Warfield followed this conclusion. Rietschel, 20 and Warfield, *Perfectionism*, 1, 355.

159. Gennrich, *Wiedergeburt und Heiligung*, 34–35.

160. Ihmels, "Zur Lehre von der Heiligung bei Theodor Jellinghaus," 94–96.

161. Ibid., 96.

162. Cremer, *Das vollkommene gegenwärtige Heil in Christo*, 50–51.

163. Fleisch, *Heiligungsbewegung*, 2:142–43.

Victory over sin

The consequence of the more complete sanctification according to Jellinghaus will be victory over sin. As he discussed this topic, he began with a definition of sin, because he claimed that much misunderstanding could be avoided when it was clear what sin was and what it was not. Jellinghaus defined sin basically as an action or a state in which a person rebelled against God with a heart which was separated from God and served evil lust, unrighteousness, the sinful world and therefore the kingdom of Satan. Therefore, it was a conscious and deliberate transgression of the law of God.[164] According to Scripture and experience, Jellinghaus continued to argue, it was also possible for a Christian who loved Jesus and wanted to be faithful to him and hate sin and who experienced the stirring of the "power of the old Adam"[165] not to live a consistently victorious life but give into temptation. This sin Jellinghaus called "sins of weakness" or "sins of precipitance."[166] He believed that these sins would not abolish the Christian's state of salvation. However, repentance and cleansing would be necessary.[167] The frequent manifestation of these sins and their power over the Christian were not the correct or normal state of the believers, but rather a sign of the inner weakness and unrest in their lives. The only remedy was faith in Christ and remaining in Christ through the work of the Holy Spirit.[168]

Next Jellinghaus discussed sin in the sense of the nature of sin or the flesh. Sin in this sense needed to be crucified with Christ by faith and kept on the cross so that it cannot rule in the life of the believer and pollute his or her heart. However, it cannot be removed; it will be with every human being until death, because we are part of a fallen world. Nevertheless, if kept crucified by faith in Christ, a Christian does not have to sin, but can live a victorious life.[169]

Third, Jellinghaus taught that there was sin in the sense of unconscious sins or actions which were erroneous and which were done with a good conscience and with good intentions. The New Testament would not term this sin. In fact, he felt that it is fatally wrong to believe that being human meant being a sinner. Most of these erroneous actions can be ascribed to original sin, because in the fallen nature of humanity their capacities to

---

164. Jellinghaus, *Das völlige Heil*, 603.
165. Ibid., 605.
166. Ibid.
167. Ibid., 605–6.
168. Ibid., 607.
169. Ibid., 608.

understand the will of God and in relation to good and bad had been weakened. However, some unconscious sins were due to lack of faith, indifference, luke-warmness and lack of love.[170] This, of course, was also connected to Christians living in a fallen world. Protestants, Jellinghaus felt, should avoid defining sin as individual acts, but define it primarily as a state of the heart. If this was used also to include unwitting mistakes and unconscious omission, then Christians cannot be sinless as long as they live in a fallen world.[171]

What does it mean then to have a "clean heart"?[172] For Jellinghaus it could not mean pure impeccable feelings and inclinations. In that sense it would not be possible for Christians to have a "pure heart" or even a "pure conscience."[173] In the Old and New Testaments heart was to be understood as will or intention. Therefore, when the Bible spoke of clean or pure heart it meant pure will or pure intentions.[174] This was possible only through participation in the holiness and righteousness of Christ by faith in the power of the Holy Spirit, who applied to the believers the "powers of the death of Christ" and the "powers of the resurrection of Christ."[175] Therefore, when temptations come, the Christian should intentionally turn by faith to Christ and ask for his help and deliverance. A pure heart was only possible in Christ.[176] And because it was possible only in Christ, victory over sin was possible for every believer.[177]

Paul Gennrich commented to this understanding of victory over sin that it mixed the religious and the ethical judgment of sin. Gennrich agreed that the power of sin was broken by the death and resurrection of Christ. However, the believers were only really free of sin if they were ethically impeccable.[178] Since Jellinghaus was aware of that he began to qualify the victory over sin, which actually was more confusing than clarifying. Because of this vagueness Jellinghaus's doctrine opened the door to a "mythical-catholic" understanding of sanctification, by which he meant the infusion of divine holiness by faith into the believers which actually created a new

---

170. Ibid., 609.
171. Ibid., 611.
172. Ibid., 614.
173. Ibid.
174. Ibid.
175. Ibid., 617.
176. Ibid., 617, 627.
177. Ibid., 667.
178. Gennrich, *Wiedergeburt und Heiligung*, 40.

substance.[179] Although Jellinghaus wanted to avoid that, he opened the door to this development.[180]

Ernst Cremer criticized the superficial understanding of sin basically in ascetic terms (attitudes and activities against the law). That led Jellinghaus to define victory over sin as avoiding and suppressing these attitudes and activities. However, that did not do justice to the nature of sin and the sinfulness of sin. Since Jellinghaus did not portray a real remedy to the basic problem of sin, his teachings would lead to enthusiasm and new legalism.[181]

Fleisch wondered in which ways a cleansing from sin and a pure heart were possible in Jellinghaus's system, since he rejected both Wesley's doctrine of sanctification and Luther's understanding of *simul iustus et peccator*.[182] Jellinghaus approached the question by stating that a pure heart basically meant pure will. That led him to different categories of sin and the claim that the sinful nature of Christians could be suppressed by faith. Because of the practical questions and challenges to live a victorious life, Jellinghaus elaborated the theme without being specific and clear. He wanted to avoid extremes on the one hand but also wanted to be faithful to the teachings he received in Oxford. The result was an unclear and superficial teaching of sin and an unsatisfactory description of a life in victory over sin.[183]

Stages in the Christian life

At the end of his book, Jellinghaus discussed the different stages of the Christian life. He argued that although this was taught in different epistles (Ephesians, 1 Thessalonians, 1 Timothy, Hebrews and 1 Peter); it was most clearly described in 1 John.[184] The main purpose of speaking of stages by the writers of the New Testament was to encourage the believers to continue in their walk with Jesus; the Christian life was not static, but rather progressive. Growth was imperative in the Christian life.[185] Jellinghaus followed the metaphor in 1 John and spoke of stages of children, young men, and fathers.[186] The stage of children described the children of God who had been born again through faith and who trusted and loved their heavenly Father

---

179. Ibid., 42–43.
180. Ibid., 44.
181. Cremer, *Das vollkommene gegenwärtige Heil in Christo*, 120–22.
182. Fleisch, *Heiligungsbewegung*, 2:148–49.
183. Ibid., 157–58.
184. Jellinghaus, *Das völlige Heil*, 700–701.
185. Ibid.
186. Ibid., 702.

and called on Him. However, they still needed to grow in understanding the Word of God and in living the Christian life in the daily challenges and temptations.[187] The young men had already grown in knowledge of the Word of God and knew how to have victory in Jesus. There is not only basic enthusiasm in their faith, but they had been trained in using the armor of God for their daily work and in living a victorious life.[188] The fathers were those who lived in continuous victory over sin, because of their constant abiding in Christ.[189]

At this point Jellinghaus criticized the Wesleyan understanding of the stage of fathers as Christian perfection. He could not agree with a teaching of cleansing of original sin. In fact he rejected any teaching of perfect holiness or entire sanctification because of the danger of perfectionism and teaching sinlessness. According to Jellinghaus, the victorious Christian life was one where the believer abided constantly in Christ and lived by the power of the Holy Spirit.[190] Although Jellinghaus wanted to avoid perfectionism, he believed in stages, which raised many questions theologically and practically. Ernst Rietschel asked what the real difference between the Christians in the different stages were both theologically and practically? He did not find clear answers in Jellinghaus, but felt that the stages opened the door to excesses and misunderstandings which actually took place in the first decade of the twentieth century.[191] Ludwig Ihmels wondered what was different for the Christian who was justified and regenerated by faith in Christ from the Christian who experienced a second surrender. If all victory was in Christ then it was available to every child of God (regenerated person) without any additional experiences. Therefore, any stages were actually not necessary. Jellinghaus's argument, according to Ihmels, was not conclusive at all.[192] Paul Fleisch followed that train of thought as well. The only difference between the different stages was the awareness that a pure heart was possible for the believer in Christ—a *völlige Übergabe* (full surrender) was not necessary but adapted from the teachers at Oxford.[193] The second surrender had primarily practical reasons for Jellinghaus (believers experiencing falling into sin); that is why he emphasized the will in his doctrine of sanctification. Fleisch concluded that this was actually

---

187. Ibid., 701.
188. Ibid., 703.
189. Ibid., 704.
190. Ibid., 706–13.
191. Rietschel, *Lutherische Rechtfertigungslehre*, 23–24.
192. Ihmels, "Zur Lehre von der Heiligung bei Theodor Jellinghaus," 121–22.
193. Fleisch, *Heiligungsbewegung*, 2:169.

the *vollendeter Selbstwiderspruch* (completed self-contradiction) in Jellinghaus. He argued that according to Jellinghaus all of salvation is available in justification through the faith relationship to Jesus Christ. Every form of self-sanctification was rejected. However, after the believers came to the awareness that a pure heart was possible an act of the will was necessary in the form of full surrender. How was this to be understood if it was not self-sanctification?[194] Fleisch felt that the relationship of faith and surrender as trust and obedience was not clear in Jellinghaus. He seemed to differentiate between a justifying faith and a sanctifying faith, but it was not clear what the difference was and how both were to be defined theologically.[195] Fleisch concluded that Jellinghaus actually failed to show the unity and substantial distinction between justification and sanctification which he had proposed to do. The two doctrines never got beyond a mere parallelism.[196]

CONCLUSIONS TO JELLINGHAUS'S DOCTRINE OF REDEMPTION

The influence of the Pietist tradition on Jellinghaus becomes quite obvious in his doctrine of redemption, especially in the emphasis of justification and sanctification primarily as subjective experience of individual believers and their personal relationship to God through faith in Christ. However, this general statement must be qualified. Although he was part of the Pietist tradition and did not deny it, he had a different approach. It was his attempt to put at the center of his theological concept not the individual and his or her salvation, but rather the person and work of Jesus Christ. That is why he felt it was important to have a biblically clear and theologically sound doctrinal foundation. This concern was the main reason why he wanted to bridge the gap between the *Gemeinschaftsbewegung* and biblical-theological scholarship within the Protestant church.[197] Nevertheless, he held on to the Pietist belief that the test for biblical-theological doctrine must be life experience. That is why he emphasized the objective truth of the person and work of Christ and the subjective personal relationship of the believers with Christ so that the objective truth of reconciliation is appropriated and actualized in their lives.

---

194. Ibid., 176–77.
195. Ibid., 178–79.
196. Ibid., 203–4.
197. See the discussion on Jellinghaus's attempt to bridge that gap by being one of the founders of the *Eisenacher Bund* in the third chapter of this work.

The greatest and most important influence on his doctrine of redemption (especially his doctrine of sanctification) came from his experiences in Oxford and through the teachings of William E. Boardman and Robert Pearsall Smith.[198] These influences are evident in the following teachings: instantaneous faith (now);[199] parallelization of justification and sanctification;[200] understanding of Romans 7 (living defeated life because of not abiding in Christ which leads to victorious life);[201] definition of sanctification by faith as dying and rising with Christ, "through death to life," not relying on self but remaining in Christ every moment;[202] defining sanctification not as "sinlessness" or "sinless perfection" but as "liberation from sinning" or not having to sin;[203] counteracting or suppressing tendency to sin;[204] and stages in Christianity.[205] It is obvious that Jellinghaus was greatly influenced by Smith and Boardman; he incorporated the main points of their teachings into his own *heilistisches System* (salvific system). Although he made some adjustments, he also took over the main weaknesses, which he did not resolve.

The Achilles' heel in his system was certainly the way in which Jellinghaus put justification and sanctification in parallel. Jellinghaus repeated many times the unity and connectedness of justification and sanctification in the person of Christ. However, why did he portray both doctrines in parallel form? Although Jellinghaus rejected the understanding of a "second work,"[206] he stressed the fact that for most believers there was a "second complete surrender."[207] Secondness was not imperative or compelling, but

---

198. The question of the influence of Keswick teaching on Jellinghaus can be raised at this point. There are many parallels and even points of contact. Jellinghaus visited one Keswick convention in 1896 and speakers at the Keswick convention spoke at the meetings in Bad Blankenburg (e.g., F. B. Meyer). The parallels can best be explained by the same sources (especially Smith and Boardman); however, there is no evidence of an ongoing exchange of ideas and teachings in relation to Theodor Jellinghaus.

199. Boardman, *The Higher Christian Life*, 40–41, 115. Smith, "Weg," 22–23; and Smith, *Wandelst Du in der Heiligung*, 4, 18; and Smith, *Heiligung durch den Glauben*, 126.

200. Smith, "Weg," 23; Smith, *Wandeln in Heiligung*, 3. Smith, *Geheimniß des Sieges*, 10–12. Smith, *Heiligung durch Glauben.*, xiii–xiv. Boardman, 38, 40–41, 115.

201. Boardman, *The Higher Christian Life*, 3, 227

202. Smith, "Weg," 26, 32, 33. Smith, *Wandeln in Heiligung*, 19–20. Smith, *Geheimniß*, 14–15, 17. Smith, *Heiligung durch Glauben*, xi–x.

203. Smith, *Heiligung durch Glauben*, vii, xi–xii.

204. Smith, *Geheimniß*, 14–15.

205. Boardman, *The Higher Christian Life*, 155–77.

206. Jellinghaus, *Das völlige Heil*, 421 and 505.

207. Ibid., 528.

that is how it was experienced by most Christians, because they realized that after conversion they experienced a lack of love and surrender and come to this point of "complete surrender."[208] According to his argumentation, the reason for that seemed to be practical and not theological, because full salvation was present in regeneration. Why did he still separate between "justification through Christ alone" and "sanctification through Christ alone"? Theologically, any "secondness" only makes sense if there is a theological need for it (as in Wesley and Palmer), where something significantly different happens than in justification by faith, namely the cleansing of inbred sin. Since Jellinghaus rejected that, he actually did not need to talk about a "deeper" and "more complete" experience (at least not theologically, which he seemed to mix with his practical concerns for the experience).

There are probably three reasons why Jellinghaus presented his system as he did. First, that is what he had heard and experienced in Oxford because both Robert Pearsall Smith and William Boardman taught it that way. Jellinghaus followed the same train of thought and tried to apply this teaching to the German situation. The second reason is closely connected to the first. Jellinghaus looked at justification and sanctification in parallel terms because of practical reasons and his pastoral approach. He was aware from his own ministry and even his own life that Christians struggle with sin. In fact the sanctified life had always been a central theme in Pietist teachings. Jellinghaus felt that in the teachings in Oxford he found a solution, a path breaking for a "victorious Christian life" which Pietism had been open to. The need for victory over sin and the awareness of its possibility usually happened after justification in the life of the Christian. In that sense, it was treated as a next step in the Christian life. Third, the parallelism fitted his theological system, his doctrine of reconciliation as well as his Pietist understanding of regeneration. In his doctrine of reconciliation he emphasized the participation in Christ's death and resurrection. The former he connected primarily to justification and the latter to sanctification (although neither of them exclusively so). The Pietist influence on his doctrine of regeneration had a perfectionistic tendency in its focus on renewal in the image of God to live a God-pleasing life. At the same time he did not want to give up his rather Reformed understanding of total depravity. Thus the doctrine of sanctification (as "victorious life" by "remaining in Christ") without any real change in the believer seemed to satisfy both the Pietist and Reformed concerns. Jellinghaus was quite unique in Germany in his doctrine of sin by using different categories. Although he wanted to be careful and avoid extremes (sin as "normal for all Christians" on the one hand and

208. Ibid., 693–94.

"sinlessness" on the other) he had to adopt these categories from Boardman and Smith in order to explain the possibility of victory over sin. But with the adoption of the categories and teaching he also adopted the problems; namely a superficial doctrine of sin both as original sin and actual sins.

Important is also his understanding of faith primarily as an act of the will. Although this was already present in Pietist tradition, it seems that Jellinghaus was influenced (consciously or unconsciously) by revivalist teaching from the United States as he referred to writings of Charles Finney.[209] He did not get beyond following this train of thought and developing an understanding of faith in a broader sense building on the rich tradition of the Reformation which he had wanted to be the basis for his theological teachings.

Although his theological system had many flaws which Jellinghaus did not resolve, it is also true that his doctrine of redemption was the result of both strong influences from different sources (Lutheran teaching, Reformed theology, Pietist tradition, Anglo-American holiness movement) and a distinct personal theological processing and development. That is what made him the most outstanding theologian of the *Heiligungsbewegung*.

---

209. Ibid., 89–94, 175–76. In these pages Jellinghaus quotes Finney extensively. He mentions *Lectures on Revivals of Religion*. He also refers to *Leben und Wirken des Rev. Charles G. Finney, evangel. Prediger und Professor zu Oberlin (Ohio) und die neuesten Erweckungen in den Vereinigten Staaten* which was the German translation of *Memoirs of the Rev. Charles G. Finney*, written by himself.

6

Church and Christian Life

AN IMPORTANT QUESTION ARISING out of the doctrine of redemption is how the life of victory over sin is to be lived out. Theodor Jellinghaus's doctrine of sanctification leads to his understanding of the church and Christian life. In the section *Der Christ mit reinem Herzen und Wandel erfreut sich nicht immer besonderer Gaben und Kräfte des Heiligen Geistes* (The Christian with a clean heart and walk does not always experience special gifts and powers of the Holy Spirit)[1] in *Das völlige Heil* Jellinghaus wrote that the gifts of the Holy Spirit were always given for the church and not as reward for the individual believer.[2] Because of the emphasis on love to God and neighbor, sanctification was never directed just to an individual but could only be properly understood in relationship to others. Jellinghaus believed that God dispensed gifts and powers (he mentioned especially miracle working prayer, healing of the sick, revivals) primarily for the "witness to the truth of redemption for the church and not as a reward for personal faithfulness in sanctification."[3] The church was for Jellinghaus the context of the Christian life. This chapter will have two main sections dealing with that context. First of all, the ecclesiological concept[4] of Theodor Jellinghaus will be exam-

---

1. Jellinghaus, *Das völlige Heil*, chapter 10, 646–52.
2. Ibid., 650.
3. Ibid., 651.
4. The term ecclesiological concept is chosen, because the author will demonstrate that Jellinghaus did not develop a new ecclesiology but accepted the ecclesiology of the established Protestant church in Germany and interpreted that from his own theological convictions. In the area of ecclesiology he followed the Pietist tradition but gave that a distinct interpretation.

ined. Second, the practical implications of his ecclesiological concept for the Christian life will be explored.

JELLINGHAUS'S ECCLESIOLOGICAL CONCEPT

Although Theodor Jellinghaus neither wrote a treatise on his ecclesiology nor a chapter on his understanding of the church in *Das völlige Heil*, an ecclesiological concept can be drawn from the sources of his literary work. Important in this regard are two articles in the *Mitteilungen aus der Bibelschule* from 1904 and 1905. The later article is more fundamental, therefore it will be considered first. It was called, *Das Verhältnis der Gemeinde der Gläubigen oder des Leibes Christi zum Reiche Gottes zur allgemeinen Christenheit und zu den einzelnen christlichen Kirchen und Gemeinschaften* (the relationship of the community of the believers or the body of Christ to the kingdom of God, universal Christianity and the particular Christian churches and fellowships).[5] This article helps to understand some basic terms and definitions that are important for his ecclesiological concept. Jellinghaus started out with the proposition that Luther translated the Latin term *ecclesia* not with the German term *Kirche* (church) but with the term *Gemeinde* (this word in German can be used for church, congregation, parish and community, depending on the context). In the article he used the term *Gemeinde* specifically to describe the community of believers which he also described as body of Christ and as being invisible.[6] On the other hand, the term *Kirche* was being defined as visible (e.g., historically developed visible Christian churches) and equated with visible Christianity and organized congregations.[7] In order to illustrate the meaning of *Kirche* (visible) and *Gemeinde* (invisible), Jellinghaus introduced a circle concept. Visible Christianity (*Kirche*) was a big circle with a visible line. The center point of the circle was Jesus Christ. Within the big circle there were the particular churches (*Kirchen*), which could be described as different smaller and larger circles. The *wahrhaft Gläubige* (true believers) were within the large circle of universal Christianity (*Kirche*) and within the smaller circles of the particular churches (*Kirchen*) and close to the center, Jesus Christ. He stated that it was not possible to draw visible lines for the true believers. However, what could be said was that whoever would not belong to visible Christianity could not belong to the community of believers. Therefore, it was

---

5. *MadB* 18:34–36. How Jellinghaus's ecclesiological concept fits into the Lutheran two kingdoms doctrine goes beyond the scope of this work.

6. Ibid., 35.

7. Ibid.

important to remain a baptized member of Christianity.[8] Jellinghaus then used another illustration, that of a temple. He stated that Christianity comprised the *sichtbarer Vorhof* (visible vestibule) and the believers (invisible *Gemeinde*) constituted the *Heiligtum* (holy of holies).[9] Therefore, nobody should despise the vestibule, because without it no community of believers could exist permanently and the Bible and Christian doctrine came to us through it.[10]

In the article Jellinghaus also spoke about the relationship of the kingdom of God (*Reich Gottes*) and the church (*Kirche*). The kingdom of God was not the same as visible Christianity or *Kirche*, and it was not the uncountable and unknown number of true believers.[11] The kingdom of God was present before the creation of the world. It became substantial (*wesenhaft*) especially in the person of Jesus Christ. It is through Christ that persons get into the *Himmelreich* (kingdom of heaven).[12] Jellinghaus claimed that the kingdom of God was supernatural, a transcendent kingdom, the "mother of all believers."[13] No church or community could claim to be the kingdom of God; however, the more the powers of the kingdom of God were present in a church or congregation in terms of faithfulness, love, righteousness, insight into Scripture, wisdom, purity, humility and courage for witness, the better she could be a servant of the kingdom.[14]

The earlier article was called *Gemeinschaften (ecclesiolae) und Kirchen (ecclesiae)* (fellowships and churches).[15] This article was Jellinghaus's response to developments within the *Gemeinschaftsbewegung* to leave the

---

8. Ibid.

9. This differentiation is not originally Jellinghaus's. He used current pictures and concepts within the *Gemeinschaftsbewegung*. The picture of the temple with sanctuary and vestibule was used by Graf von Pückler and Elias Schrenk at the first *Gnadauer Pfingstkonferenz* to describe the relationship of church and the fellowships of the *Gemeinschaftsbewegung*. See Pfleiderer, *Gnadauer Pfingstkonferenz 1888*, 134 and 140. The term historically developed Christian churches was used by Witt in his presentation at the second *Gnadauer Pfingstkonferenz* (1890). See Drechsel, *Das Gemeindeverständnis in der Deutschen Gemeinschaftsbewegung*, 29. Jellinghaus was present at both events and even criticized the presentation as being too idealistic in presenting the situation of the New Testament churches. Idealizing New Testament times and trying to reestablish a New Testament church would always lead to schisms and split-off organizations. See Drechsel, *Das Gemeindeverständnis in der Deutschen Gemeinschaftsbewegung*, 30–31.

10. *MadB* 18:35.

11. Ibid.

12. Ibid., 35–36.

13. Ibid., 36.

14. Ibid.

15. Ibid. 16:23–34.

Volkskirche (literally "peoples' church," better established Protestant church) "to gather a holy community/church" (*heilige Gemeinde*).[16] He challenged the *Gemeinschaftsbewegung* to stay within the established church and to seek her renewal and fulfill the mission of the church within the church.[17] Jellinghaus summarized his understanding in five principles:[18] First, the *Gemeinschaftsbewegung* could only enjoy God's blessing on the church (*Kirche*) when it remained within the church.[19] Second, in the history of the church there have always been those who looked for renewal of the church by promoting fellowship for those who were desirous of being Christians in earnest (*ecclesiolae in ecclesia*).[20] Third, the state church (*Landeskirche*) as the historically given form of the church of Jesus Christ for the people must demand from the fellowship (*Gemeinschaft*) to support the ministry of the church (*ecclesiolae pro ecclesia*).[21] Fourth, through the ongoing research of the Scripture and the confessions the state church provided protection against sectarian teachings for the fellowship (*ecclesia pro ecclesiolis*).[22] For the relationship of the church to the fellowship the apostolic admonition of carrying each other's burdens should be followed.[23]

From the content of these two articles and from the fact that they were the only written articulations of Jellinghaus's ecclesiological concept, at least two conclusions can be drawn. First, he accepted the basic ecclesiology of the established church. Jellinghaus did not want and not need to create a new ecclesiology. He rejected any attempts to create a new or separate church. On the contrary, he believed that the *Gemeinschaftsbewegung* could only follow God's guidance if it stayed within the *Kirche* (church). Second, he interpreted the basic ecclesiology of his *Kirche* from the viewpoint of his own theological system, which focused primarily on the individual believers. These two conclusions can be demonstrated by reviewing Jellinghaus's personal development and his theological system in regard to his ecclesiological concept.

---

16. Ibid., 24–25.

17. Ibid., 28–29.

18. Jellinghaus quotes here court chaplain Ohly, who stated these principles at a conference in Potsdam. Since Jellinghaus agrees with Ohly in all points, he adopted all five principles from him. *MadB* 16:34.

19. Ibid.

20. Ibid.

21. Ibid.

22. Ibid.

23. Ibid.

Personal Development

The personal development of Theodor Jellinghaus played a fundamental role in his ecclesiological understanding. Important elements had been his Pietist background, theological studies, work as missionary to India, pastoral ministry, participation at the holiness convention in Oxford and his participation in the German *Heiligungsbewegung* and *Gemeinschaftsbewegung* as described in chapter three. From these influences the following conclusions can be drawn regarding his ecclesiological concept.

First, his entire theological approach was basically characterized by Pietist tendencies with their basic focus on the individual. Distinguishing elements in a Pietist ecclesiology included a basic distrust, although not a basic rejection, of church organization in general, because of theological fights, political maneuvers, striving for power and other outward bickering.[24] By way of contrast, Pietism emphasized introspection and the individual experience of salvation and faith. Basic to salvation was the personal experience of the new birth. Only then a believer would be saved and be part of the body of Christ, the true church. The Christian life was then to be fostered by Scripture reading, a personal devotional life, prayer, fellowship with other believers and the evangelistic zeal to share this truth with unbelievers. This basic Pietist ecclesiology defined also Theodor Jellinghaus's ecclesiological concept. His theological education and his experience in ministry helped him to reflect on this basic Pietist understanding and to find his own expressions of his belief.

Second, his experience as missionary and minister helped to shape his pragmatic pastoral approach. That can be seen by his ongoing emphasis on the importance of the laity for ministry for the church to fulfill her mission (priesthood of all believers). His experiences in the *Gemeinschaftsbewegung* had confirmed his convictions and given him opportunity to participate in the equipping of the laity. Important in this regard is the content of the invitation to the first *Gnadauer Pfingstkonferenz*, especially since Jellinghaus was part of the committee which composed the invitation to the conference.[25] The invitation was addressed to persons who would share the following convictions:

> 1. That with all due respect for the regulations of the church, the collaboration in the kingdom of God is not only the privilege for

---

24. See Ulrich Gäbler's portrayal of Gottfried Arnold's ecclesiology, which would become a basic influence of Pietist tradition. Gäbler, "Geschichte, Gegenwart, Zukunft," in *GdP* 4, 30–33.

25. Pfleiderer, *Gnadauer Pfingstkonferenz 1888*, 16.

all believers but also their responsibility according to Protestant teaching;

2. That private spiritual formation in common prayer, Bible study and sharing of spiritual experiences is an important complement to what the church offers in public services; and that these events are often an indispensable support and wholesome protection for newly awakened Christians, and for all participants a stimulation to deepen the inner life and even a certain substitution for lacking church discipline;

3. That our established church (*Volkskirche*) is to be recognized as a divine blessing and that the influence of the order of ministry should be strengthened; that therefore all separatist tendencies and un-Protestant and enthusiastic and forcible methods of evangelism should be kept afar, since those methods cause much harm to the power of faith and love.[26]

Theodor Jellinghaus shared all three convictions in his entire life and ministry and he advocated them constantly. In this framework, Jellinghaus felt that he was called to help in the training of laypersons as people who would be able to lead Bible studies and share the gospel within the established Protestant church in Germany or in missionary service. He did not intend to provide a full academic educational programme for ministers. His students came predominantly from the *Gemeinschaftsbewegung* and some from other church organizations from outside of Germany. In his addresses at conferences and in his publications he challenged "un-Protestant and enthusiastic and forcible methods of evangelism."[27] Jellinghaus believed that the Pietist organization of the *Gemeinschaftsbewegung* was ordained by God to renew the established Protestant church in Germany and to share the gospel of Jesus Christ through missionary service in nations with no or little Christian witness. The overall context for the Christian life and all church ministries was the kingdom of God established in Jesus Christ.

Theological Foundation

Following his personal development, it is possible to identify ecclesiological implications of Theodor Jellinghaus's doctrines of reconciliation and

---

26. Ibid., 14.
27. See his attacks on Darbyite tendencies within the *Gemeinschaftsbewegung* (especially in regard to the *Allianzhaus* in Blankenburg), but also his warnings against extreme teachings like in the case of Jonathan Paul as discussed in chapters 3 and 7 of this work.

redemption as theological foundation for his understanding of the church. There is a twofold purpose in that: first, it can be demonstrated that his ecclesiological concept was based on his doctrines of reconciliation and redemption. Second, it will become evident that his ecclesiological concept was distinct within the *Gemeinschaftsbewegung*.

Christocentric approach

Joachim Drechsel tried to provide evidence that the basic biblical-theological concept of the early *Gemeinschaftsbewegung* followed a pneumatological approach, which led to the belief that it was important at all times for the church to fulfill a New Testament ideal.[28] This was especially strong among groups within the *Gemeinschaftsbewegung* which followed Darbyite traditions. Jellinghaus was critical of this approach, because it concentrated too much on the individual and the structure and diverted from the actual center of the church, Jesus Christ himself.[29] He followed a Christocentric approach. In his doctrines of reconciliation and redemption this approach was most clearly demonstrated. Reconciliation can only be understood, according to Jellinghaus, with Christ as second Adam and new head of humanity. To participate in his reconciliation the believer must be organically related to Christ.[30] Christ was also the center of Jellinghaus's doctrine of redemption. The center was neither justification nor regeneration nor sanctification, either in doctrine or experience. The center was Christ himself. Jellinghaus taught that justification, regeneration and sanctification became reality for the believer only in Christ. In other words, Jellinghaus wanted to demonstrate that at the center of his theology was Christ himself who would bring about salvation, not faith or an act of the will.[31]

On the basis of this theological approach the question for Jellinghaus's ecclesiological concept was not: What constituted the church? The question was rather: How can a person become part of the *Gemeinde der Gläubigen* (community of believers)? An important key can be found in his temple illustration mentioned earlier in this chapter. In this temple he differentiated between the *Gemeinde der Gläubigen* (community of believers) or

28. Drechsel, *Das Gemeindeverständnis in der Deutschen Gemeinschaftsbewegung*, 29–31 and 198–202.

29. See Fleisch's comment on the critical assessment of Darbyite tendencies in the *Gemeinschaftsbewegung* and Jellinghaus's opposition to it. Fleisch, *Gemeinschaftsbewegung*, 1:497 and 484.

30. See chapter 4 of this work.

31. See chapter 5 of this work.

Heiligtum (sanctuary), which he felt was more invisible than visible, and the *geschichtlich gewordenen sichtbaren christlichen Kirchen* (historically developed visible Christian churches) or *Vorhof* (vestibule).[32] Crucial for Jellinghaus's ecclesiological concept was that believers were both members of a church (*Kirche*), and then had a personal faith relationship to Jesus Christ, the center, and therefore were members of the body of Christ or community of believers. The second aspect, however, was the more important one, because mere membership did not mean being saved. Salvation was only possible through a personal relationship to Jesus Christ. Therefore, his ecclesiological concept could be defined as Christocentric.

Sacraments and the church

The sacraments were important in Jellinghaus's theology, although his understanding was different from that of the Reformers. He did not give them the central function and place as the Reformers did. However, the sacraments played a vital role in his ecclesiological concept.

BAPTISM

Jellinghaus distanced himself from the Lutheran understanding of baptismal regeneration. With that he rejected a basic Lutheran ecclesiological conviction, which held that through regeneration in baptism a person was embodied in Christ (*Einleibung in Christus*). Because of this embodiment baptism became constitutive for the church, in that the sacrament would not only express an outward incorporation into the church, but an inner incorporation into the body of Christ.[33] In his rejection of this Lutheran doctrine he referred to his Reformed convictions, however he did that selectively.[34] The Reformed doctrine of baptism cannot be disconnected from the doctrine of predestination, which Jellinghaus rejected completely.[35] Baptism in the Reformed tradition differentiates strongly between outward and inward event (outward sign of inward grace) and is primarily to be understood as God's promise to the person being baptized and only secondary as confession. Since faith and baptism cannot be disconnected, one is being baptized unto faith even if that should be experienced in the future. In this

---

32. *MadB* 18:35.
33. Sommerlath, "Taufe. IV. Dogmatisch. 1. Luth. Lehre."
34. Jellinghaus, *Das völlige Heil*, 75–77.
35. Ibid.

Reformed understanding the person being baptized is adjudicated the fruit of the sacrifice of Christ on the cross and the incorporation into Christ's body and the person is being sealed (covenant of grace).[36] Therefore, in the Reformed tradition baptism is also understood as constituting the church.

A certain proximity to Schleiermacher's understanding of baptism is discernible in Jellinghaus. The great nineteenth century theologian did not believe that baptism would accomplish anything in the inner life of the Christian. He viewed it just as an outward sign (entering the church), if it was not considered in the context of God's salvation plan, the other influences of the church and the inner developments of the person to be baptized until regeneration.[37] There might be certainly influences of Schleiermacher on Jellinghaus, directly and indirectly through some of his teachers; however, there are serious differences which exclude a simple adoption of Schleiermacher's position. The main differences are in the doctrines of reconciliation and redemption as has been shown earlier. Important for this study is that Schleiermacher and the tradition following him renounced the doctrine of baptism taught by the Reformers and therefore opened the door for new interpretations.[38]

What was Jellinghaus's understanding of baptism? Which role did baptism play in the order of salvation? These questions must be answered in a twofold way: first in regard to his ecclesiological concept, and second in regard to his doctrines of reconciliation and redemption. In regards to his ecclesiological concept the differentiation between the community of believers (sanctuary) and the historically developed Christian churches (vestibule) is important. Baptism could be understood in terms of constituting the church if church was understood as a historically developed Christian church. Through baptism one became a member of the historic church, or in terms of the temple illustration, a person entered the vestibule which then could give access to the sanctuary. That was the main reason why he endorsed baptism (especially baptism of small children) and gave this sacrament an important status in the life of the believers and the church. However, he also held on to his other conviction, namely becoming a member of the community of believers (entering the sanctuary) was only possible by regeneration through a personal faith relationship to Jesus Christ. Holding on to the necessity of both (vestibule and sanctuary) constituted

---

36. Kreck, "Taufe. IV. Dogmatisch. 2. Ref. Lehre"; and Beintker, "Baptism. IV. Dogmatics. 3. Protestantism. b. Reformed."

37. Schleiermacher, *Der christliche Glaube*, §136–38, 2:318–340. See also Kettler, "Taufe. III. Dogmengeschichtlich."

38. See also his teachings on the church in *Der christliche Glaube*, § 3–6, 1:14–47 and §115–25, 2:215–48.

Jellinghaus's strongest weapon against separatist tendencies within the *Gemeinschaftsbewegung*. He made clear that the community of believers can only be found within the historically developed Christian churches. He argued that one can only get to the sanctuary through the vestibule. The relevance and importance of the vestibule can be seen in two aspects: in the guarantee of a permanent and stable community of believers in a hostile world (protective function of the church) and being the bearer of the biblical witness and Christian doctrine.[39] In other words, without the church there can be no community of believers.[40] Nevertheless, Jellinghaus did not believe that baptism was necessary unto salvation, which leads to the second point, his doctrines of reconciliation and redemption.

Jellinghaus wanted to ward off the danger of individual subjectivity in his teaching by emphasizing the objectivity of the Christian faith in the person of Jesus Christ. In his view it was Jesus Christ himself who constituted the community of believers (sanctuary) in his person and work. In the redemption of the believer the object of the Christian faith (Jesus Christ) becomes subjectively experienced both for the individual believer as well as for the community of believers. Being one in Christ means both personal renewal (through dying and rising with Christ) and the constitution of the community of believers (body of Christ), where Jesus Christ himself is the head. Although this understanding gave a good and solid foundation against an overemphasis on the individual, at the very core of his ecclesiological concept Jellinghaus gave more importance to the subjective experience of salvation than the objective nature of the church.

Lord's Supper[41]

Theodor Jellinghaus's understanding of the Lord's Supper must also be viewed in the light of his doctrines of reconciliation and redemption. In his sparse remarks regarding the Lord's Supper he primarily obtained a Reformed standpoint. That becomes clear in three points: first of all, his understanding of the presence of Christ in the sacrament followed the Reformed tradition that "the believers shall be uplifted in the Spirit to Christ in heaven (*sursum corda*), being made one with him in his mystical body and

39. *MadB* 16:34.

40. This is, of course, an understanding of the church found in John Calvin who taught that one must be a member of the visible church in order to belong to the invisible church, the church of the elect. See Ritter, "Church. 2.2. Historical Constructs and Theories. 2.2.7. The Reformation. 2.2.7.2. John Calvin."

41. Jellinghaus uses the Lutheran term *Abendmahl* (literally evening meal), which will be translated in this work as Lord's Supper.

through the same Spirit being fed with the powers of life from the flesh of Christ."[42] This teaching differentiated between outward action and inward spiritual occurrence, which are still connected since the former was the visible deposit and sign or pledge for the latter.[43] Jellinghaus never made an explicit statement regarding the presence of Christ in the elements of the Eucharist. Nevertheless, he rejected the Lutheran teaching of consubstantiation, because of its danger (in Jellinghaus's understanding) that one could receive grace without having a personal relationship with Jesus Christ.

Second, because of Reformed influences, Jellinghaus believed that only believers (converted persons) should be admitted to the Lord's Supper, because it only could have an effect on those who have a "faith relationship to Jesus Christ."[44] This position gave him a strong argument to differentiate between converted persons (persons in Christ) and unconverted persons (persons outside of Christ in the flesh).[45] While this differentiation in Reformed teaching was grounded in the doctrine of predestination, Jellinghaus argued that it followed the biblical teaching of regeneration. His understanding of regeneration, of course, was based on his doctrines of reconciliation and redemption. This meant for his ecclesiological concept that not all members of the historically developed Christian churches should participate in the Lord's Supper but rather only those who belong to the community of believers, because it can only be a means of grace for those who believe and are related to Christ by faith.

Third and last, although the Lord's Supper did not have the same function for Jellinghaus as for the tradition of his church, he believed that it must be valued and esteemed as strengthening believers and supporting them in their faith. This, of course, was based on the belief that the Lord's Supper can only be effective in believers. Jellinghaus pursued this understanding in two directions. On the one hand he believed that the purpose of the Lord's Supper was to be found in "bringing the souls to an assurance of their position in grace and to lead them and keep them in a deeper experience of sanctification."[46] Second, Jellinghaus declared that his doctrine of salvation had shed new light on the understanding of the Lord's Supper, because he saw in it a "preservation of the great mystery of 'Christ in us.'"[47] With that

42. Graß, "Abendmahl. II. Dogmengeschichtlich."
43. Wolters, *Der Heidelberger Katechismus*, questions 75, 78, 79. See also Kreck, "Abendmahl. III. Dogmatisch. 2. Ref. Lehre."
44. Jellinghaus, *Das völlige Heil*, 232–33 and 676–77.
45. Ibid., 233.
46. Ibid.
47. Ibid., 481.

he meant two things: on the one hand, because of the "lack of visibility of Christ" the Lord's Supper could help the believers to believe "like children in his real divine and human presence" and to expect joyfully his return.[48] Jellinghaus interpreted the Lord's Supper here in a Reformed way as outward sign of an inward grace. The real presence he was talking about was not to be understood in a Lutheran, but rather a Reformed way as spiritual presence in the life of the believers through the Holy Spirit. On the other hand, Jellinghaus concluded that "true Christianity" could only be found in the "awareness of the presence of the blood of Christ in the heart of the believer."[49] The constituting element of the community of believers was, therefore, only Christ himself, who became real in the life of the believer by faith in regeneration.

It could be argued that by his reference to the person of Christ in the Lord's Supper, Jellinghaus represented a modern position in the Protestant understanding.[50] However, it is also clear that Jellinghaus did not want to develop a new theology of the Lord's Supper; he rather wanted to interpret this rite of the church from his doctrine of redemption. Therefore, he concluded that this sacrament was significant for the church and the believer; however, it was secondary in experience and order of salvation. The new birth was primary, and the Lord's Supper signified the faith relationship to Jesus Christ, the union with Christ, and it supported that relationship and strengthened it. But it cannot produce it; this was only possible by a personal encounter by faith.

It is clear that Jellinghaus's teaching of baptism and the Lord's Supper represented a vast devaluation of the significance of the sacraments compared to the teachings of both Luther and Calvin. Although he wanted to emphasize a continuation of his theology with the theology of the Reformers, in this central understanding there was a clear break. He seemed to accept that, because he clearly believed that any doctrine of the sacraments must be subordinate to the doctrines of reconciliation and redemption.

48. Ibid.

49. Ibid.

50. This statement is referring to the interpretation of Gerhard Ruhbach in connection to two important ecumenical documents (*Leuenberg Agreement* of 1973 and the *Lima–Document* of 1982), both of which also deal with the understanding of the Eucharist. Ruhbach wrote: "For many centuries, the presence of Christ was interpreted substantially 'under the bread and the wine' either as real or spiritual change. For about one hundred years a new category of interpretation has unfolded, namely that of the 'person' instead of substance." Ruhbach, "Abendmahl. b) theologiegeschichtlich."

Kingdom of God and the church

Jellinghaus exhibited his understanding of the kingdom of God and the church in *Das völlige Heil* as well as in his *Mitteilungen* always in connection to his doctrines of reconciliation and redemption.[51] As Ohlemacher has pointed out, Jellinghaus did not present a new detailed historical theological concept of the kingdom of God.[52] The before mentioned article in the *Mitteilungen* is key to his understanding.[53] For Jellinghaus, the kingdom of God was part of the invisible world, although it must not be identified with the invisible community of believers, i.e. the body of Christ. The kingdom of God comprised the entire invisible reign of God; the community of believers was part of it. That means that humanity can only be part of the kingdom of God through a personal faith relationship to Jesus Christ, which happens in regeneration.[54] It is interesting to note that Jellinghaus described the kingdom of God as the "mother of all believers."[55] It was Cyprian who introduced the terminology of mother for the church, which was later picked up and reinterpreted by Calvin.[56] Based on his doctrines of reconciliation and redemption, Jellinghaus could not arrive at this description. It is not clear why Jellinghaus applied this phrase to the kingdom of God; however, one could argue that the kingdom of God, which came to humanity through Jesus Christ, could be described as mother of all believers because the believers have their "true home in heaven."[57]

Christ himself represented the coming to reality of the kingdom of God on earth. In and through Christ all believers participated in the kingdom of God and were related to each other across all kinds of human boundaries. This relationship was not only to be understood spiritually but also "organically"[58] in Christ. That meant this relationship was real and

---

51. Jellinghaus, *Das völlige Heil*, 43–46, in the section "Reconciliation and redemption through the sacrifice of the new head of humanity" and in *MadB* 18:34–36.

52. Ohlemacher, *Reich Gottes*, 170. He wrote about Jellinghaus's understanding of the kingdom of God: "He tries to relate biblical structures to single statements. In a rugged contrast of kingdom of God and world his interest is focused on the impact of the kingdom of God on the individual."

53. *MadB* 18:35–36.

54. Jellinghaus, *Das völlige Heil*, 43; *MadB* 18:36.

55. *MadB* 18:36.

56. This understanding is embedded in Calvin's doctrine of predestination. See Ritter, "Church. 2.2. Historical Constructs and Theories. 2.2.7. The Reformation. 2.2.7.2. John Calvin."

57. *MadB* 18:36.

58. Regarding the "organic" relationship with Christ, see the explanation in chapter 4 in this work.

universal through Jesus Christ. The universality of the church is realized through the kingdom of God, which pointed to another important aspect of the ecclesiological concept of Theodor Jellinghaus, the unity of the church.

Unity of the church

The unity of the church was a central theme in Jellinghaus's ecclesiological concept. For Jellinghaus unity had three basic attributes: first, the unity of the church was constituted through Jesus Christ. The doctrines of reconciliation and redemption demonstrated that Jesus Christ was the foundation of the unity of the church. At the same time, the Son of God was also the life-giving power of the church; through his presence the church was made possible. And in Christ the church also had her goal as she approached the "groom" as the "bride."[59]

Second, the unity of the church was made effective through the renewal of the individual Christian. This effectiveness had two sides. On the one hand the personal renewal came by the union with Christ by faith. It could be stated that the personal renewal manifested the vertical dimension of the unity (between the individual believers and Christ). The effectiveness of this vertical unity also has an effect on the horizontal dimension of the unity, i.e. the unity of believers with each other. The individual believers must have a relationship (unity) to other believers in order to grow in their relationship to Jesus Christ and to fulfill the mission of the church in the world. It is at this point where the church as institution received its significance. The adoption of the understanding of invisible and visible church allowed Jellinghaus to protect the institutional character of the church (visible church) without neglecting the spiritual (invisible) character. Since the church has a visible dimension, institution is part of her nature. This becomes clear in his articles in the *Mitteilungen*. On the one hand, although he believed in the ordained ministry, Jellinghaus rejected any teaching of a special class of priests (who were necessary to mediate between God and humanity) on the basis of the Reformation and Pietist tradition.[60] On the other hand, he endorsed the necessity of church constitution. However, church constitution (visible) had a subordinate role. If church constitution contradicted objectives of the kingdom of God (invisible), it must not be followed.

The tensions that classical Pietism faced in its relationship to the established church come to the surface at this point. The *Gemeinschaftsbewegung* was part of the historically developed Christian churches and therefore

---

59. Jellinghaus, *Das völlige Heil*, x–xi.
60. *MadB* 2:13.

visible church; at the same time it emphasized the priority of the invisible community of believers. Therefore, the *Gemeinschaftsbewegung* must be ready to confront the established church, when it came to conflicts relating to the kingdom of God. The tensions were therefore twofold. On the one hand the *Gemeinschaftsbewegung* itself was both visible (as an institution) and invisible (as fellowship of the community of believers). Furthermore, it was part of the visible established church which herself had visible and invisible dimensions. Jellinghaus was not only aware of these tensions, he argued that the *Gemeinschaftsbewegung* must live in these tensions in order to have a *raison d'être*. The tensions must be preserved, because both dimensions (visible and invisible) were part of the nature of the church. At the same time unhealthy tensions between the visible *Gemeinschaftsbewegung* and the visible church must be avoided.[61] Jellinghaus saw himself as a mediator between the established church and the *Gemeinschaftsbewegung*.

This leads to the third attribute of the unity of the church: unity must also be pursued organizationally. This was necessary for the strengthening of the believers and for the witness to the world.[62] This is where his support for the *Evangelische Allianz* came into effect. In the *Evangelische Allianz* Jellinghaus saw an ideal instrument to demonstrate visibly and practically the unity of the body of Christ. On the one hand, the *Evangelische Allianz* was not about unifying denominations but rather about the unity of the true believers, those who were part of the body of Christ. On the other hand, the *Evangelische Allianz* demonstrated a global understanding of church. It was not primarily about Christians in Germany or any other nations, but rather about the redeemed from all denominations and nations.

Bible and the church

Theodor Jellinghaus believed that any Christian life and therefore any church life depended on the witness of the apostles, the Scriptures (Bible). This means that any Christian life must be lived according to the Scriptures. Jellinghaus viewed the Bible for believers as the "Bearer of Christ and his light and the guideline for their lives" by which they can differentiate between true and false teaching.[63] He believed, that in its totality the Bible is

---

61. That is why Jellinghaus criticized and tackled any separation tendencies within the *Gemeinschaftsbewegung*, which were present especially in the Darbyite groups.

62. In the visible fragmentation of the believers in so many denominations and parties within the churches, Jellinghaus saw one of the greatest hindrances for the kingdom of God. See Jellinghaus, *Das völlige Heil*, 396.

63. Ibid., 533.

> ...the reliable document of the divine history of salvation and brings to us the full Redeemer to our heart and conscience, so that we can confidentially get to know and experience the full Christ and the true way of faith. The particular words, stories and teachings of the Bible do not benefit much and even seem contradictory if we do not experience the Jesus of the Bible. But we cannot know and own Jesus and the kingdom of heaven, if we do not have a reliable report of the incarnated Christ who had died and was raised and how the apostolic Christians have experienced him as the way of salvation, if we did not have the Bible.[64]

The influence of von Hofmann on his view of Scripture is obvious. Like von Hofmann, Jellinghaus rejected both the verbal inspiration of the Bible and the historical criticism of the Tübingen School. In addition, his understanding of inspiration is similar.[65] What Jellinghaus continued to develop beyond von Hofmann was his view that it was not Scripture which constituted the formal principle of Christian doctrine, but Christ himself.[66] If Christ himself was the content of our faith, who constituted both personal salvation through the new birth and the body of believers, then any doctrine of the inspiration of Scripture cannot be made a fundamental doctrine of faith. As a guideline for life the Bible can only be beneficial for believers, because only believers can perceive and perform the will of God through the work of the Holy Spirit. Therefore, the Bible played a decisive role in the life of the individual believer and in the community of believers. The Bible must be read, interpreted and applied under prayer in the power of the Holy Spirit.

JELLINGHAUS'S ECCLESIOLOGICAL CONCEPT AND THE CHRISTIAN LIFE

Jellinghaus's ecclesiological concept had practical implications for the Christian life. For him the redemption of humanity was the goal of the gospel and therefore the content of the mission of the church, which must

64. Ibid., 63.
65. *MadB* 16:13–14. See also Swarat, "Johann Christian von Hofmann."
66. Jellinghaus, *Das völlige Heil*, 533. In the preface to his book he discusses the "material principle" and the "formal principle" of the Protestant church. He felt that both principles have been understood most of the time as two separate principles (justification as material principle and the Holy Scriptures as formal principle). Jellinghaus believed that both the content and the goal of both principles were constituted in the person of Christ. In him there are not two separate principles but rather one. See also *MadB* 14:33.

determine the ministry of the church. Based on his ecclesiological concept five aspects in the practice of the Christian life can be discerned in Jellinghaus's teaching.

The Church as the Frame for Ministry and the Christian Life

For Jellinghaus the church (historically developed Christian churches) represented the frame for all church ministries and the Christian life. He could not and did not want to detach himself from the church. Neither the church structures nor the central content of church life (worship service with preaching of the Word of God and the administering of the sacraments) were discarded by Jellinghaus. He criticized theologically how the Word was preached and how the sacraments were administered, but he did not cast off the activities themselves. On the contrary, as it was shown in the previous sections, Jellinghaus challenged believers to stay in their churches and support their pastors, because he believed that this was how they could participate in the fulfillment of the mission of the church. According to Jellinghaus, the church had the responsibility, through her structure and her ministry, to fulfill the biblical mission, i.e., to proclaim to humanity redemption through Jesus Christ. Because this was partly neglected by the church or was even rejected because of theological aberrations, the *Gemeinschaftsbewegung* through its different societies and associations needed to help fulfill the mission of the church; however, this should never happen isolated or detached from the church.

Jellinghaus actually never commented on the church structures or the liturgy. He saw his sphere of activity in the *Gemeinschaftsbewegung* in supporting the church to fulfill her mission. Any influence on the structures or the liturgy was only possible indirectly, namely, if pastors and other leaders of the church collaborated with the *Gemeinschaftsbewegung*. Jellinghaus pursued this collaboration on two levels: first, in theological dialogue (see his involvement in the *Eisenacher Bund*) and second, in mentoring theology students and candidates for ministry through his Bible school. However, it must be observed that Jellinghaus did not expect a renewal of the church through its structures and liturgy. Based on his ecclesiological concept it can be concluded that a true renewal (awakening) was conceivable for him only through Christ himself and through the awakened believers. Since the *Gemeinschaftsbewegung* shared his theological understanding (emphasizing personal regeneration, which was the prerequisite for any spiritual renewal) he got involved structurally in the visible church through the *Gemeinschaftsbewegung*. He felt that this organization could become the vehicle of renewal within the established church. It can be concluded that Jellinghaus did not concentrate his ministry on the structures of the church but rather used the church as a frame for his ministry. The key aspects of his ministry (and for any church ministry) were evangelism and community building (*Gemeinschaftspflege*), because the renewal of the church (and therefore the continuation of the reformation) could only happen that way.

Evangelism

Following basic Pietist convictions, Jellinghaus believed that the goal for evangelism must be the proclamation of the truth of the gospel and the invitation of people to experience personally that truth through regeneration, by being united with Christ by faith and therefore becoming part of the kingdom of God. This task was to be fulfilled within the historically developed Christian churches, to guide people from the vestibule to the sanctuary (community of believers), to make believers out of unbelievers. The evangelistic task was at the same time a global task, because God called all people to repent and believe. Therefore, Jellinghaus believed that this task was to be fulfilled through missionary activities in different parts of the world and to be supported through prayer, financial resources and readiness to prepare and send people for missionary service.[67]

The practice of evangelism happened primarily through the proclamation of the Word. Ideally this would happen in the Sunday worship service or in biblical teaching. However, since this did not always happen or it was neglected, the *Gemeinschaftsbewegung* organized various evangelistic events and campaigns to invite people to personal faith in Jesus Christ. It could also happen in personal conversations or Bible studies. An important and effective method of evangelism in the *Gemeinschaftsbewegung* became the distribution of evangelistic literature. Jellinghaus found it important that any evangelistic activity should never fall prey to false human pressure which could result in more damage than blessing. He felt that it was important to depend on the work of the Holy Spirit when sharing the good news of Jesus Christ, to work both in the person evangelizing and in the person who was evangelized.[68] Although Jellinghaus never viewed himself as an evangelist,[69] he supported these basic concerns of the *Gemeinschaftsbewegung*, as shown in previous chapters. Many of the alumni of his Bible

---

67. This point will be discussed later in this chapter under the heading "Global Missionary Involvement."

68. Jellinghaus, *Das völlige Heil*, 283.

69. *MadB* 8:3–4.

school ministered as evangelists in different societies and associations of the *Gemeinschaftsbewegung*.[70]

Community Building (*Gemeinschaftspflege*)

Community building (*Gemeinschaftspflege*) must be mentioned as inseparable from all evangelistic activity, because it focused on the gathering of believers for edification and spiritual formation through Bible study and prayer.[71] While evangelism concentrated on the justification of the sinners, community building emphasized the sanctification of believers. This was important to Jellinghaus in order for the believers to remain in Christ and to fulfill the mission of the church. The fostering of the vertical and horizontal relationships of believers (vertical to Christ and horizontal to other believers) was to happen in the different meetings and events centering on community building. In this regard the *Gemeinschaftsbewegung* was indispensable within the church.[72] It was in the gathering of believers that they were strengthened in their faith relationship to Christ through the reading and interpretation of Scripture, prayer and teaching. For Jellinghaus this was basic for the sustainability of any renewal and awakening of the church.[73] Actually this was probably the key motivation for Jellinghaus to found and operate his Bible school, because through that ministry he was preparing men and women for this task within the *Gemeinschaftsbewegung*. In addition, Jellinghaus supported the founding and sustaining of Bible studies and prayer groups personally and practically in Berlin but also in different cities in Germany where he spoke at conferences or conducted courses for his Bible school as has been shown in previous chapters. Jellinghaus supported the development of community building (*Gemeinschaftspflege*) theoretically and practically locally and nationwide, because it was a key factor in fulfilling the mission of the church.

---

70. Ibid., 10:1–3. This is just one example where Jellinghaus points out this fact.

71. Jellinghaus practical involvement and support of community building is explained in more detail in previous chapters. See *MadB* 13:28–29.

72. See the invitation to the founding and first meeting of the *Gnadauer Pfingstkonferenz* which was signed by Jellinghaus. See Pfleiderer, *Gnadauer Pfingstkonferenz 1888*, 19.

73. *MadB* 18:35–36.

Education of Believers to Fulfill the Mission of the Church

In order for community building (*Gemeinschaftspflege*) and evangelism to happen, believers must be educated for these ministries. Jellinghaus believed that pastors (professional ministers) could not and should not be responsible alone for fulfilling the mission of the church.[74] On the one hand, they had to fulfill other important tasks, which only ministers could fulfill (e.g., administering the sacraments, officiating at church services and ministries reserved for the ordained ministry). On the other hand, the education of laypersons conformed to the Reformation teaching of the priesthood of all believers.[75] In other words, there were two main reasons for the education of laypersons: organization and theology. Jellinghaus appreciated the ordained ministry and at the same time never intended to provide a full academic theological education for ministers through his Bible school or seminary. The reason for that was his understanding of the person and role of the minister. People who felt a call to the ordained ministry in Germany needed to fulfill the qualifications specified by the church,[76] this would exclude many believers. Nevertheless, the mission of the church could only be fulfilled by the involvement of all believers. In addition, there were services in the church which could and should be fulfilled by laypersons; for that they needed also to be educated. Evangelists and Bible study leaders should ideally be viewed as helpers of the pastors in the ministry of the local church.[77]

Although the education of ministers and laypersons was different, Jellinghaus did not view the structures as being opposed or independent from each other. He never viewed his Bible school as unacademic or even opposed to academics. On the contrary, he wanted to build bridges between academic studies and lay training as he wanted to build bridges between the Protestant churches and the *Gemeinschaftsbewegung*.[78] It was this basic understanding and orientation which shaped his Bible school. His goal was

---

74. Jellinghaus experienced the limitation of the pastoral office personally. See also Pfleiderer, *Gnadauer Pfingstkonferenz 1888*, 19; and Drechsel, *Das Gemeindeverständnis in der Deutschen Gemeinschaftsbewegung*, 8.

75. Jellinghaus, *Das völlige Heil*, 361 and 650.

76. Jellinghaus accepted the structures of the Protestant churches in Germany as long as they would not disagree with the basic principles of the kingdom of God (from his viewpoint). See Jellinghaus, *Das völlige Heil*, 318–26.

77. See *MadB* 2:13–14. This article was also published in the *Evangelisches Allianzblatt*, vol. 10, issue 13, 100–101. See also Pfleiderer, *Gnadauer Pfingstkonferenz 1888*, 167; and Martin Brecht, "Pfarrer und Theologen" in *GdP* 4, 211–26.

78. Even from critics from the established Protestant churches Jellinghaus was not viewed as opposing the church, but rather as a sober-minded representative of the *Gemeinschaftsbewegung*. See Gelshorn, 890.

exclusively to prepare men and women to be engaged in evangelistic work and the edification of believers in small groups.

At this point it is important to highlight the fact that in 1895 Jellinghaus began to offer courses for women. The goal of these courses was to help women hold women's Bible studies and to be prepared for ministry as deaconesses.[79] Since the first half of the nineteenth century deaconesses' homes and ministries had been a vital part of the Protestant church and many had connections to Pietist circles and allowed women to be involved more prominently in the ministry of the church.[80] In the history of the *Gemeinschaftsbewegung* new deaconesses' homes were founded and became an important part of its ministry.[81] Ohlemacher made an important observation when he stated that from the last quarter of the nineteenth century ministries by women and to women became popular also in Germany through the influence of the American Holiness Movement and the ministry of Hannah Whitall Smith.[82] The education of the believers should strengthen the *Gemeinschaftsbewegung* to help the church fulfill her mission, so that many people would experience a personal regeneration and would be added to the community of believers.

Global Missionary Involvement

Jellinghaus's ecclesiological concept had a global dimension beyond the mission of the church in Germany. The good news of the redemption of humanity through Jesus Christ was to be proclaimed to all people. The mission of the church was a global mission. The ecclesiological concept of Jellinghaus also served this understanding. He believed that the goal of Christianity must be to invite as many people as possible into the community of believers (the sanctuary) so that they could be part of the kingdom of God through union with Christ through faith. That was actually the great commission of Jesus to his disciples in Matthew 28:18–20. Christians in all eras and at all times have participated to fulfill this mission. It also has been an important factor in the development of the different Pietist groups and

---

79. See the discussion regarding the Bible school and the different Bible courses from 1895 to 1898 in chapter 3.

80. Kruczek, *Theodor Fliedner*. Nightingale, *The Institution of Kaiserswerth*. Stempel-de Fallois, *Von den Anfängen bis zur Gründung des Diakonissenmutterhauses Neuendettelsau*.

81. Lüdke, *Diakonische Evangelisation*. Krawielitzki, *Carl Ferdinand Blazejewski*. Mund, *Theophil Krawielitzki*.

82. See Ohlemacher, *Evangelikalismus und Heiligungsbewegung*, 374. See also the discussion on women in the *Gemeinschaftsbewegung* in chapter 3 of this work.

traditions in Germany and beyond.[83] Jellinghaus himself felt an obligation to global missionary involvement when he served as a missionary to India. His ministry there had been to proclaim the gospel and to help indigenous people to develop the church and participate in the fulfillment of the mission of the church.[84] It is at this point that the global importance of the unity of the church in his ecclesiological concept has an effect. Because the church was constituted through the person of Jesus Christ it has a global character and therefore must have a global ministry and interest in the advancement of the kingdom of God into all countries.

CONCLUSIONS

Jellinghaus did not intend any basic changes to the structures, the liturgy or the basic ecclesiology of the established church he was a part of. His ministry has to be understood within the given framework of the church. However, it is remarkable and his unique contribution to the history of the *Gemeinschaftsbewegung* that Jellinghaus developed a practical ecclesiological concept that grew out of his theological system, especially his doctrines of reconciliation and redemption. He even believed that he continued to develop the structures as they were intended by the Reformers and the early Pietist leaders. He did that within the framework of the church and thus followed early Pietist tradition.

In his ecclesiological concept, any questions regarding structure, liturgy and ecclesiological formulations would be secondary. The consummation and perfection and the goal of the church was to be found in Jesus Christ. For this reason the kingdom of God had come in Jesus to humanity. Even when all structures and forms and liturgies would come to an end, the kingdom of God will remain forever, because Jesus Christ remains forever. It is within this framework that the Christian life needs to be viewed and understood.

---

83. See Wellenreuther, "Pietismus und Mission" in *GdP* 4, 166–93.

84. On his understanding of this point see Jellinghaus, *Das völlige Heil*, 314–16, 320–26, and 398–99.

7

Assessment of Theodor Jellinghaus's Recantation

Toward the end of his life, when Theodor Jellinghaus looked back at more than forty years of ministry, he was rather dissatisfied. He felt responsible for the deep crisis and schism within the *Gemeinschaftsbewegung* in the first decade of the twentieth century and published a recantation of his teachings, *Erklärung über meine Lehrirrungen* (statement on the errors of my teachings), in 1912. The echo to this devastating self-assessment turned out to be quite divided. For some it was a late but clear realization of different aberrations in his theological understanding. For others these were utterances by an old and ill man, who had been suffering from depression for many years and spent five of the last seven years of his life in closed psychiatric institutions and who was trying pathologically to destroy his life-work, which could and should not be taken seriously.

How was it possible that this father of the *Heiligungs-* and *Gemeinschaftsbewegung* was evaluated so diversely? Is a true assessment of his life and ministry found in one of the two positions? Or does his life need to be viewed in certain ambivalence with contradictions and inconsistencies? From these questions it becomes clear that the teachings of Jellinghaus, as well as his life and ministry, can only be truly appraised if this last episode of his ministry is taken into account. Therefore, in this assessment the circumstances of his recantation will be examined and final conclusions will be drawn.

THEODOR JELLINGHAUS'S RECANTATION

In this section we will examine the circumstances leading to Jellinghaus's recantation and then review and assess his *Erklärung über meine Lehrirrungen*.

Circumstances Leading to Jellinghaus's Recantation

Although it was especially the last eight years (1905–1913) of his life that Jellinghaus was very ill, physical as well as psychological afflictions seem to have been part of his entire life. In retrospective reflection on his youth Jellinghaus wrote about his "sanguine-melancholic temperament," which had given him often the "feeling of being unskillful and useless."[1] During all of his working life, beginning in India until the end of his life, he had to deal with self-doubts and dispiritedness. Later this would develop into a "nervous disease" as he put it himself that led to his early retirement of parish ministry.[2]

During his missionary service in India Jellinghaus experienced an enormous amount of stress which led to his first reported breakdown. There were two reasons for that: first, he suffered under the controversy among the missionaries of the Gossner Mission, and second, he was absolutely devastated by the tragic death of his first wife and two children. The doctors in India recommended that he return to Germany in 1870. Another similar setback seemed to have been the sudden death in infancy of his third child Martin in 1874. At the end of his pastoral ministry in Rädnitz (1892–1893), he experienced a major breakdown. He wrote about this time: "In the years 1892 and 1893 I suffered under a terrible nervous disorder, accompanied by anxiety attacks and losing weight, which led to my retirement."[3] Nothing was mentioned about a trigger or reason for the nervous disorder.

Nothing is known of illnesses or setbacks within the following ten years. On the contrary, the years 1893–1903 seem to have been the most productive time in his life. However, it is also clear that these years were draining on him both physically and psychologically with all the travel, engagement, and worries about his ministry. September 1903 seemed to have been a turning point in his health. Jellinghaus was sixty-two years old when he spent some time at a sanatorium, together with his daughter Anna, for rest and convalescence after a strenuous time of ministry. During that time he fell and dislocated his arm. Although it did not seem like a serious injury,

---

1. *MadB* 8:1.
2. Ibid. 1:3; 18:10.
3. Ibid., 18:10.

he developed a life-threatening pneumonia and pleurisy after his return to Berlin. The situation was so serious that his son Paul returned home because it was not clear how the illness would develop. After a brief recovery he suffered a relapse, which affected him emotionally.[4] Jellinghaus himself wrote about this time: "When I awoke from fearful and wild dreams, I was glad that the nurse could comfort me."[5] Although he was able to teach the next session of the Bible school (January until May 1905), he never fully recovered and continued to suffer from "chronic intestinal trouble, sleeplessness, nervous disorder, and haunting depression."[6]

His health deteriorated so that Paul Jellinghaus had to take over as editor of the *Mitteilungen* in August 1906 as well as teaching all the courses for his father.[7] In September of that year Paul succeeded Theodor Jellinghaus in leading the Bible school.[8] Paul Jellinghaus summarized the situation in the following way: "His only occupation during this time seemed to be to compose long letters with nebulous confessions of sins which he had never committed. The more we tried to persuade him that he had not committed any of these sins, the worse the situation and the bigger his sins became."[9] The family tried to take care of Jellinghaus; however, the situation worsened until Johannes Seitz, a friend and early companion of Theodor Jellinghaus, offered to take him for some time to his Christian Convalescence Home in Teichwolframsdorf in Saxony.[10] No improvement could be discerned; on the contrary his situation deteriorated so that the family decided to admit Jellinghaus to a private psychiatric hospital in Lichtenrade on December 10, 1906.[11] About a year later (November 2, 1907) Jellinghaus was transferred to the *Evangelische Heil- und Pflegeanstalt für Gemütsleidende Tannenhof* in Lüttringhausen (close to Remscheid).[12] Jellinghaus spent a total of five

---

4. Ibid., 15:2, 33. See also ibid. 49:2.

5. Ibid., 16:2.

6. Ibid., 49:2. See also Jellinghaus, *Erklärung*, 2, 3, and 9.

7. Ibid., 23:10.

8. Ibid., 24:8–9.

9. Ibid., 49:2.

10. Ibid., 24:8.

11. Ibid., 25:1 and 27:3. The cost for the stay was covered by friends. From the first page of the medical chart of Theodor Jellinghaus at the *Evangelische Heil- und Pflegeanstalt für Gemütsleidende Tannenhof* in Lüttringhausen (close to Remscheid), where Jellinghaus was transferred to after his stay in Lichtenrade, it is mentioned that the "private hospital" was the *Sanatorium für Gemüts- und Nervenkranke* of Dr. Anker in Lichtenrade.

12. Theodor Jellinghaus was admitted as no. 1898 (class II). As diagnosis the doctor remarked: "Atypical illness, mental weakness and state of excitement with subtle traits of mental exhaustion and confusing physical illnesses." Under "external behavior at

years (until 1911) in closed institutions. Theodor Jellinghaus remained in a state of self-accusation and began to draft letters about his "erroneous teachings"[13] which he sent to leading men of the *Gemeinschaftsbewegung*. However, those who received the writings acknowledged his health situation and talked him out of publishing these thoughts.[14] The relationship between Jellinghaus and his son suffered during this period. Paul tried to persuade his father to refrain from these negative thoughts and self-accusations and from writing letters; however, Theodor felt that this was the only way to save the movement and himself.[15]

Paul Fleisch actually made the observation that in the beginning stages of Jellinghaus's illness (1903–1906) the attacks from within the ranks of the *Gemeinschaftsbewegung* played an important role:

> The older groups (of the *Gemeinschaftsbewegung*) put pressure on Jellinghaus and his Bible school since he objected to Darbyite thoughts and Jonathan Paul's teachings, while these were on the move forward . . . in addition to that Jellinghaus had a nervous breakdown so that he . . . had to be admitted to a closed institution. He was haunted by the idea that he had spread heresies with his "salvific theory." It is rather difficult to differentiate between what was due to his illness and what was not. . . . However, it was sad that now his enemies from within the movement took

---

admittance" the remark was: "Accompanied by his caregiver, very restless, bewildered and indignant, cannot observe the proprieties." Under "anamnesis" the following remarks were made: "Earlier institutions—Dr. Anker in Lichtenrade (10.12.06–2.12.07)" and "Cured?—No." Under "heredity" it stated: "Father was very old and hypochondriac." This information has been made available to me by Dr. Windgassen and Rev. Martin Wolff of the *Evangelische Stiftung Tannenhof*.

13. Jellinghaus, *Erklärung*, 9.

14. Ibid., where he wrote: "Because I was so excited about each error I discovered in my teachings and the sins I had committed, that I did not have the moral strength of mind to expound the false teachings of my 'salvific system' and to demonstrate the right beliefs. The brothers, to whom I turned, convinced me that before I had found peace of mind and that my nervous system was calmer, such writings could do more damage than good." One example of such advice can be found in the correspondence within the *Gnadauer Verband* (organization of the *Gemeinschaftsbewegung*) of summer 1907, which Ohlemacher refers to (Vorgang GAV, Ordner 1907): "He (Jellinghaus) wanted to publicly recant from his teachings and recall all his writings from publishers and book sellers. His initiative and his correspondence was received by the chairman Michaelis and referred to Rev Heinatsch for review (who himself followed Jellinghaus's teachings). Any further action became unnecessary since Jellinghaus was very ill and needed to spend time in a closed psychiatric hospital." Ohlemacher, "Gemeinschaftschristentum," 435.

15. *MadB* 49:2–3.

the opportunity to accuse him and his work, although many of them had never read him nor even understood him.[16]

These attacks continued in the following year.[17] In summer 1907 Jellinghaus was "exposed to various suspicions and persistent allegations" so that his son in August 1907, "after long silence" reacted in an issue of the *Mitteilungen*.[18] Besides an article he also printed the doctor's certificate which attested to Jellinghaus's "mental illness."[19] It also happened that he received visitors, which was not helpful for his recovery. This was one of the reasons why he was transferred on November 2, 1907 to another sanatorium which was kept a secret.[20]

Until 1910 no changes could be observed in his condition.[21] The medical record of Jellinghaus at Tannenhof confirmed this assessment. It stated that he did not even participate regularly in church services, which only changed in April 1911, when other improvements were observed.[22] On May 8, 1911 he asked for a leave-of-absence to be able to visit his daughter Anna, who was terminally ill. Based on the promise that he would return after five days, the request was granted. However, he never did return. The medical record states for May 12, 1911, "released based on request of care-giver" with the remark "withdrawn, condition has ameliorated."[23] The care-giver has not been identified. Anna passed away on July 28, 1911, at the age thirty-two. She was the fourth child who died during his lifetime. Paul Jellinghaus remarked that his father seemed to do better and the family decided "against

---

16. Fleisch, *Gemeinschaftsbewegung*, 1:497 and 484.

17. *MadB* 25:22.

18. Ibid., 27:2–3. In the article Paul Jellinghaus asks the leaders of the *Gemeinschaftsbewegung* to consider the health situation of his father and refrain from continued accusations.

19. Ibid.

20. Ibid., 28:4.

21. Ibid., 36:7; 37:3.

22. The following entries were found in the medical record: "The overstatements that all of Christianity is doomed because of him are not mentioned anymore; only that the world is getting worse and that Christianity is not much better" (entry of February 1). "Attends church services more regularly, is more calm, it is possible to have a conversation, does not make any abstruse statements anymore, is still weighed down by sorrow; has gained 28 pounds, sleeps better" (entry of April 5). "Repeats of and on the old statements, sleeps quite well, regrets that he does not have more conversations—especially people who want to listen to him when he repeats the same stories" (entry of May 1). *Medical record* of Theodor Jellinghaus in the archives of the *Evangelische Stiftung Tannenhof* (made available by Dr. Windgassen and Rev Martin Wolff).

23. These entries can be found on the first page of the medical record of Theodor Jellinghaus at the *Evangelische Heil- und Pflegeanstalt für Gemütsleidende Tannenhof*.

the advice of the doctors"[24] to keep him at home. However, "he was still obsessed with some compulsive ideas," but the family hoped that "people would recognize that and respond accordingly."[25]

After the funeral of Anna, Theodor Jellinghaus decided to stay for six weeks (in August and September 1911) with Friedrich Hahn in Markt Alvesleben[26] and worked with him on the first draft of his recantation.[27] In October this draft was discussed at the center of the *Christlicher Verein Junger Männer (CVJM)* in Berlin with the following persons being present: Friedrich Hahn, Graf Pückler, Asmus Christiansen[28] and Friedrich Blecher.[29] A second draft was produced, which was an abridgement of the first. The changes were justified with the explanation that "some earnest souls could be misled in their state of grace by what Jellinghaus wrote regarding 'flippant faith', 'false assurance of salvation' and the 'absolute necessity of living according to the commandments of Christ."[30] This second draft was never published.[31] However, excerpts of it appeared in a couple of magazines, *Licht und Leben* and *Glaubensgrüße*.[32] This fueled the discussion, which went only in one direction: Jellinghaus and his teachings were judged as direct preparation for both the sinlessness doctrine of Jonathan Paul[33] and the *Pfingstbewegung*, since that was how Jellinghaus assessed himself as well. It needed another revision until the final version of the recantation was ready for publication. Theodor Jellinghaus met again with Friedrich Hahn

24. *MadB* 49:4.

25. Ibid. 44:1–2 and 49:3.

26. Friedrich Gustav Johannes Gotthold Hahn (1859–1950) was minister at Markt Alvesleben (Sachsen-Anhalt) from 1906–1917. He was director at the Deaconess-Mother-House Salem in Lichtenrade (where Jellinghaus's Bible school was located) for two different periods: from 1904–1906 and from 1917–1924.

27. Jellinghaus, *Erklärung*, 4–5. Paul Jellinghaus was upset about that, since that is what they were afraid would happen. See *MadB* 49:3–4.

28. Rev. Asmus Jessen Christiansen (1867–1949) served among other places as director at the Deaconess-Mother-House Salem in Lichtenrade from 1906–1913 and from 1926–1934. His second wife was Hilda Jellinghaus (1931), daughter of Theodor Jellinghaus. See *Evangelisches Pfarrerbuch für die Mark Brandenburg seit der Reformation*, 123; and Fleisch, *Gemeinschaftsbewegung*, 1:523.

29. Friedrich Blecher (1866–1936), was founder of the German branch of the *Christian Endeavour* in 1894 and worked for most of his life with that organization. The organization has been part of the German *Gemeinschaftsbewegung*. See Bautz, "Friedrich Blecher."

30. Jellinghaus, *Erklärung*, 4.

31. The manuscript did not survive. It is known only by being referenced in the *Erklärung* and *MadB*.

32. *MadB* 44:2.

33. See discussion on Jonathan Paul in chapter 2.

and this time also with Friedrich Brucks, an evangelist from Lichtenrade. They revised the second draft by putting back in much of what the first draft contained. With the publication of the recantation Jellinghaus withdrew all copies of his former publications from the publishers and booksellers and prohibited them from being republished. Many of the copies were destroyed. All of this happened against the wishes of his family.[34] In that same year he wrote letters to different theologians (among who were Ernst Cremer, Ludwig Ihmels,[35] Johannes Gensichen,[36] Ernst Bunke[37] and Paul Fleisch) and asked them to support him in his recantation. Later Jellinghaus affirmed his recantation in an article in the magazine *Licht und Leben*.[38]

At the same time he arranged the sale of the property and facilities of the Bible school in Lichtenrade, which were his personal possession. He had already planned the sale during his stay at Tannenhof.[39] This decision brought about the move of the Bible school. In December of 1912 his brother Karl passed away, who was also a minister and with whom he had a close relationship. In the course of the following year Jellinghaus became weaker physically as well. In September 1913 he fell ill to influenza. Paul Jellinghaus wrote later that his father "did not have to suffer for long" and passed away on October 4, 1913 in Lichtenrade.[40] Four days later, October 8, 1913, he was buried by Rev. E. F. Klein (Lichtenrade), Rev. Schmidt (Berlin) and his son-in-law Rev. Richard Horst (Liebenzell).[41]

34. Jellinghaus, *Erklärung*, 4–5. See also Paul Jellinghaus's assessment of the whole process and situation in *MadB* 44:1–3 and *MadB* 49:4.

35. Ludwig Heinrich Ihmels (1858–1933) wrote the article "Zur Lehre von der Heiligung bei Theodor Jellinghaus," 89.

36. Hermann Johannes Renatus Gensichen (1841–1918) was a minister in Treppeln/Oder (1866–1881), which belonged to the parish of Crossen II. See *Evangelisches Pfarrerbuch für die Mark Brandenburg seit der Reformation* 2, no. 1 (1941) 239. It seems that the two knew each other from that time since Theodor Jellinghaus served from 1873 in 1882 in Rädnitz/Oder, which was part of church parish Crossen I. Gensichen, "Jellinghaus—und seine Erklärung über seine Lehrirrungen."

37. Bunke, "Jellinghaus gegen Jellinghaus," 183.

38. Jellinghaus, "Ist 'Gnadau' und Heiligungsbewegung eins?," 487–90.

39. See the remark in his medical record of February 1, 1911: "Worries about the sale of his property; is afraid that the sales tax will rise if it is not sold at once."

40. *MadB* 49:1.

41. A report of the funeral has been written by Heinrich Dallmeyer and printed in the magazine *Auf der Warte* 44 (November 2, 1913) 5–6. Obituaries were printed in *Lichtenrader Zeitung* 192 (October 7, 1913) 1; *Heilig dem Herrn*, 4:683–84; *Licht und Leben*, 25:668; *Philadelphia*, 23:175.

Content of Recantation

Theodor Jellinghaus's recantation (*Erklärung über meine Lehrirrungen*) was designed to be the final verdict on his life and work. Did this last publication by him meet the desired goal? How does it need to be classified in his life and work?

General observations

In the first preface and in the epilogue of the *Erklärung* the two helpers (Friedrich Hahn and Friedrich Brucks) commented that they had supported Jellinghaus in preparing this publication. Both stated that Jellinghaus was in good health when he composed the piece of writing. Their help was primarily focused on historical coherency, but they did not want to be responsible for the full content. They wanted to clarify that he "was definitely clear in his head and reasonable in his expression and behavior"[42] and that they could "clearly see" that "Jellinghaus did not suffer from any idiosyncratic ideas, and that what he had recognized as right or wrong, accurately correlated to the truth."[43] Brucks even wrote that those who reckoned that Jellinghaus was still ill were wrong. "It is rather true that the constant breaking out of a stanched nervous disorder (especially due to unfounded objections which also conflicted with the Bible) had its cause in the fear over the misery caused by his teachings."[44]

In the second preface Jellinghaus commented himself about his mental condition. He repudiated any criticism that the letters he had sent out to theologians asking for help to write against his teachings were circulated and labelled as "the product of the acuteness of thoughts of an insane person."[45] Jellinghaus assessed his own mental and physical condition in such a way that he had "a weak memory regarding names and coherencies" and that he felt he was "mentally incapable" to "express clear and incontrovertible thoughts, statements and events."[46] Therefore, he was dependent on help from others. He was especially thankful for Friedrich Brucks who would help him in the future to compose more writings to refute his teachings "...as long as no spiritually experienced academic theologian was willing to

---

42. Jellinghaus, *Erklärung*, 3–4.
43. Ibid., 48.
44. Ibid.
45. Ibid., 5.
46. Ibid.

assume this role."⁴⁷ Jellinghaus added that he was "continually painfully reminded of his errors" and that "now" he had "clear insight" that everything "did not agree with the Bible or what the best Christians of all times had taught."⁴⁸ Brucks formulated it similarly in the epilogue when he wrote that it was "painful and wistful" to help Jellinghaus in "admitting his heresies."⁴⁹

Both prefaces and the epilogue spoke to the immediate circumstances of the writing and publishing of the recantation of Jellinghaus. Because they were written by Jellinghaus himself and those who helped him, they are important in understanding and assessing the document. The rather unconventional assessments of the mental and physical condition of Jellinghaus seem quite surprising. It is understandable that his health situation was presented as good, because the credibility of the document depended on it. Although the comments sounded impartial they were rather subjective and highly dubious. It must be stated as strongly as this because both helpers exclusively relied on their own observations and not on professional judgment. Actually the circumstances of the discharge from the psychiatric hospital and the rather arbitrary presentation and assessment of the author and his helpers made clear why the question regarding the mental condition of Jellinghaus stood at the center of the discussions and assessments of the recantation.

Beyond these circumstances, certain formulations of the document gave reason to believe that the mental problems (at least some of them) which caused Jellinghaus to be detained in a psychiatric hospital were still present and were the main motivation to compose the document. In the entire text it was repeatedly stated (actually eight times) that "fear" and "anxiety" caused Jellinghaus to write this recantation.⁵⁰ In addition, terms like heresies and sins were used for Jellinghaus's teachings which needed to be combated. These formulations not only seem to be exaggerated but actually express a certain obsessiveness which was one of the characteristics of his illness. These were probably some of the important reasons why he could not find "spiritually experienced academic theologians" to support him to competently formulate his *Erklärung*.⁵¹ His mental and physical condition needs to be given due weight in assessing the recantation of Jellinghaus. However, that does not necessarily mean that the document can be discard-

47. Ibid., 7.
48. Ibid., 6. Jellinghaus repeats this point three times on pages 7, 9, and 45.
49. Ibid., 47.
50. Ibid., 7, 9, 21, 40–41, 42–43, 44, 45, 48.
51. As presented in the previous sections, many of the theologians who wrote comments and assessments of his work expressed these reservations. Their evaluations were done independently from him and his objectives.

ed. The content needs to be reviewed and evaluated to make a final assessment. Nevertheless, the circumstances of the writing play an important role.

Description of the eight main errors

Jellinghaus began to describe his "main errors" by a generally negative total assessment of his teachings.

> I acknowledge before God that it is my duty to present briefly the errors of my teachings and to indicate the correct beliefs. As I can see after long years of reflection, my writings are misleading in a superficial and unbiblical understanding of sin, world, lust of the flesh, law, holiness, justice, wrath of God, judgment, seriousness of eternity, sacrificial death of Christ, watching, praying, struggle, self-awareness, self-judgment, repentance and faith, justification and sanctification and cleansing. . . . I have established a new doctrinal system and called it 'salvific' (*Heilismus*). The seemingly simplicity and clarity have deceived so many."[52]

Then he pointed to the theme which was the foundation for his teachings: "1. Fact: The present and full Redeemer in the Word. 2. Faith. 3. Redemption."[53] He concluded that "it was clear that in this system the doctrine of sin, the law, crucifying the old man and strengthening the inward man, the struggle between spirit and flesh, the kingdom of God, the narrow road, repentance, etc. would not be emphasized correctly."[54]

This formulation, which should introduce the main errors of his teachings, raises some important questions. First, what did Jellinghaus mean with long years of reflection which have led him to this conclusion? He was talking about the years 1906 until 1912, which he spent in closed institutions and where he was treated because of his mental condition. Why did he emphasize this? Second, the theme on which his teaching was founded was indeed mentioned in *Das völlige Heil*. However, the three-point-formula was used to explain faith in Christ. He used it to demonstrate that the hope of faith is based on Christ alone and his "word of grace" and not on feelings and experiences.[55] That means it was a sub-theme, but certainly not a main theme which was the foundation for his teachings. In addition, it is

---

52. Jellinghaus, *Erklärung*, 9–10.
53. Ibid., 10.
54. Ibid.
55. Jellinghaus, *Das völlige Heil*, 162–65.

not clear why this theme should suppress all the other doctrines Jellinghaus mentioned. No attempt is made to explain these statements more clearly.

These inaccuracies and ambiguities did not fit Jellinghaus, at least not the healthy Jellinghaus, who carefully explained his teachings in *Das völlige Heil*. The critical question needs to be raised if Jellinghaus was aware of the breadth of his teachings and that he only focused on a single or sub-theme, which he actually used totally out of context? This must have been one of the reasons why both Modersohn and Fleisch raised the question: how many of those who criticized Jellinghaus (and even those who helped him write this document) had actually read and understood Jellinghaus's teachings?[56] In many of the reactions to his recantation the questions raised by Jellinghaus were treated, however, there was no comparison with the actual teachings (e.g. as presented in *Das völlige Heil*). Jellinghaus himself criticized points totally out of context and in a false correlation to his teachings. This practice can be observed throughout the document as well as in the reactions to his writings. On thirty-five pages Jellinghaus summarized his so-called main errors in eight points:

1. Holiness, justice, and wrath of God were not expressed appropriately

Jellinghaus wrote that Christ was also prophet and judge and that the New as well as the Old Testament aimed at "bringing people to a holy awe and adoration of God and to trepidation before God, the consuming fire."[57] The Bible portrayed God as holy; however, his own books "did not master" the first commandment.[58] He continued: "If these warnings are not mentioned in all severity together with the message of salvation for sinners, then evil human nature does not take it seriously but believes that one can be a child of God without being totally broken through thorough penitence."[59]

Jellinghaus was correct that he never wrote or taught this way. However, in this critique he actually did not address any teaching in *Das völlige Heil*. He only mentioned that his books "did not master" the first commandment[60]; however, he did not explain what he meant by that. In *Das völlige Heil* Jellinghaus actually dealt with the holiness of God and the sinfulness of

---

56. Modersohn, ed., *Heilig dem Herrn*, 4:683–84. Fleisch, *Gemeinschaftsbewegung*, 1:484.
57. Jellinghaus, *Erklärung*, 11.
58. Ibid.
59. Ibid., 12.
60. Ibid., 11.

humanity.⁶¹ Why did he not criticize that part of his book directly, if it did not fulfill the standard he then used? Jellinghaus did not seem to be aware of this discrepancy.

2. Severity of Death, Judgment, and Eternity are not present

He felt that his teaching was pressing for assurance of salvation rather than "deep repentance and working out one's salvation with fear and trembling, living faith with the fruits of a heavenly disposition, a constant prayer life and a walk in love."⁶² This criticism did not actually correspond with *Das völlige Heil*. Jellinghaus actually warned against human pressure in evangelism and advocated a "thorough and sound repentance."⁶³ Jellinghaus actually emphasized "necessary marks of repentance" and the importance to differentiate between converted and unconverted persons in his writings.⁶⁴ However, it is also true that Jellinghaus did not teach the "severity of death, judgment and eternity" in the way he advocated these teachings in his recantation. Nevertheless his self-criticism is deficient and unclear.

3. Decisive Insistence on Self-Denial, Devout Living in God's Presence and Renunciation of the World are not present

This third point was actually quite ambiguous. Although Jellinghaus stated that he did not insist enough on self-denial, in *Das völlige Heil*, he actually dealt with that topic because it was foundational for a sanctified life.⁶⁵ In the recantation he did not pick that up, especially if he might have felt that this section was not thorough enough. The ambiguity of the third point continued in his criticism that his definition of sin was obscure and misleading. It is certainly true that the doctrine of sin was one of the weak points of his teachings. Many other writers had pointed out the weaknesses concerning his hamartiology; however, he did not go into more detail where and why

---

61. Jellinghaus, *Das völlige Heil*, 8–10, 29–32.
62. Ibid.
63. Ibid., 283.
64. Ibid., 327–36.
65. Ibid., 519–22, where Jellinghaus deals with "true denial of the world by God-devoted Christians."

his doctrine of sin was "obscure and misleading"[66] (he only mentioned that his definitions were imprecise and vague). Actually this could have been a main point in the so-called main errors, but it was only treated as a subpoint regarding self-denial and denunciation of the world.

4. Alteration of the Biblical-Reformation doctrine of reconciliation

This fourth point of criticism does not only take most of the space of his recantation (twelve pages), but Jellinghaus actually aimed here at the center of his *heilistisches System* (salvific system). This point actually is formulated clearly and correctly, in contrast to the first three points. However, there are some ambiguous assertions which need to be analyzed.

It started with the statement that he "realized after 1906" that "when I attended the holiness convention in Oxford in 1874, I had neither experienced nor understood the Lutheran-Pietist doctrine of reconciliation in which I had been raised."[67] This actually means that he had the realization during the time of his illness, and raises the question why he had clearer insights in a condition of illness (especially attested mental illness) than when he was healthy. The argumentation is ambiguous. More importantly, the weakness of this section is in the presentation of the different doctrines of reconciliation rather than in the criticism of his so-called salvific doctrine. He described it as "contradictory in itself," because it taught a "mystical putting to death of self and reviving of self" as "effort of self."[68] He continued to write: "It is impossible for me to expound all the harmful changes to the traditional doctrine of salvation through the alteration of the biblical-ecclesiastical doctrine of reconciliation; many pages would need to be written."[69]

This rather shallow criticism is essentially not adequate for his doctrine of reconciliation. Actually he had founded his rejection of the so-called Anselmic ecclesiastical doctrine on a long list of arguments,[70] which he never began to refute in the recantation. Why not? Because too "many pages would need to be written"[71]? Why did he not write many pages since he had the time to do it? It seems clear that he was not able to do that. Therefore, the critique is primarily polemical, unbalanced and ambiguous.

66. Jellinghaus, *Erklärung*, 14.
67. Ibid., 15–16.
68. Ibid., 18–19.
69. Ibid., 19.
70. See especially Jellinghaus, *Das völlige Heil*, 15–73.
71. Jellinghaus, *Erklärung*, 19.

5. Erroneous Teaching on the Relationship of Law and Gospel

After writing about the Reformation teaching of the relationship of law and gospel, he remarked: "In my books the sinners and seekers for salvation are not sternly admonished that they only can come to God if they earnestly desire to do the will of God."[72] This is certainly not a Reformation teaching, but rather what he used to describe and denounced as "poor-sinner-Christianity of Pietist tradition."[73] It is actually remarkable that earlier Jellinghaus had warned against "such legal, half-evangelical Pietism" which "always summoned believers to mourn over the salvation of their soul and asks them to sanctify themselves by mourning over sins and by putting sin to death by themselves. This must have a ruinous effect especially on persons with nervous disorders."[74] It appeared like a self-fulfilling prophecy that he seemed to describe his own future! In other words, Jellinghaus certainly did not return to the Reformers in this point, but rather takes the position which he took during his time of illness and which stood in a reciprocal relationship to his illness.[75] Therefore, at this point it is important to allude to his mental condition over many years and its consequences which tremendously weaken his argumentation at this point.

6. Differentiating between Awakening, Repentance, Faith, Conversion, and Regeneration as Different Processes

In this critique we have again a variation of good reflection on his teachings and inaccuracies and superficialities. Right at the beginning of this section there was a rather blunt mistake, when he wrote that "with many others I differentiate between awakening, repentance, faith, conversion and regeneration as different processes."[76] It is true that this was one of the accusations against him; however, he never held this position. In his Bible school newsletter, *Mitteilungen aus der Bibelschule*, he wrote in 1903: "What is important in our Reformation doctrine is that our confession is clear, which might seem marvelous to some: Conversion, justification,

---

72. Ibid., 29–30.
73. Jellinghaus, *Das völlige Heil*, 126–28, 504, 550–53.
74. Ibid., 490.
75. That means that this understanding was reinforced by his illness and it reinforced itself the symptoms of the illness. This becomes clear in his medical records.
76. Jellinghaus, *Erklärung*, 30.

forgiveness of sins, regeneration, and sanctification are all terms of the same standing in Christ."[77] How could he have forgotten or overlooked that? He never divided his understanding of redemption in this way. He had rather presented the processes quite meticulously, but never as different processes. Again, it becomes clear that Jellinghaus in his recantation, although some had contended that, did not return to the Reformation teaching of Luther and Calvin, but rather presented some kind of Pietist penance as ideal. In the document he continued to stress the "struggle" and "battle" against the "dominion of the flesh."[78] He claimed: "Jesus demands painful and deep repentance in sackcloth and ashes, revealing a deep inner pain. Repentance is a biting and painful salt in the sinful heart. . . . Not trusting in God's grace but rather the fear of the Lord is the beginning of wisdom."[79] His new position is especially noticeable in the following statement:

> The Pietists were correct when they became suspicious with a man who had not deeply regretted his sins, who had not become humble, who had not agonizingly put away all sin, who had not rectified all wrong, who did not show great solemnity in getting better and who did not earnestly struggle for salvation, but rather believed that he could attain forgiveness and life through faith in Christ.[80]

It is true that he did not hold this belief, but it is also true that this was not the teaching of the Reformers. Jellinghaus was clear in presenting what he then understood by living the Christian life, but quite ambiguous with what he then called biblical and Reformation teaching.

7. Weaknesses in the Teaching of Faith

In this section Jellinghaus criticized specifically his doctrine of faith, especially his emphasis on human will. This understanding was probably already existent before his visit to Oxford and was certainly reinforced there. However, what Jellinghaus was providing as an alternative in this document was certainly not the teaching of the Reformers, but rather again the Pietist penance faith which bordered on works-righteousness (battle, struggle, prayer, "soaring" to God, development of character).[81] In addition, he then

---

77. *MadB* 14:17.
78. Jellinghaus, *Erklärung*, 36.
79. Ibid., 35.
80. Ibid., 32.
81. Ibid., 37.

presented the "mystically substantial" understanding of regeneration as "biblical doctrine,"[82] which he had opposed before. In his criticism he did not reflect on the arguments of his book (refuting the mystical substantial teaching), but rather gives just a brief presentation of his new views. Jellinghaus repeatedly emphasized that he did not "invent" these doctrines, but that he adopted them from "English-American circles."[83] These statements made his arguments even more ambivalent. On the one hand, it seemed that he did not want to assume full responsibility for his "erroneous" beliefs, but rather argues "nationalistically" that these doctrines would "not fit German nature"[84] (whatever that meant). On the other hand, he had argued throughout the document that he felt personally responsible for what were considered maldevelopments in the *Gemeinschaftsbewegung*. This is another example of rather sketchy and superficial and polemical argumentation with little or no substance, especially when compared to *Das völlige Heil*.

8. False Teaching Regarding the Love of God

Jellinghaus argued in this section that the Bible included both law and gospel, but that he had formerly only taught gospel. According to his former teaching it was possible that "someone believed that he could rest in perfect love who still sought carnal security without true fear and love for God, the brothers, the lost and the enemies."[85]

> Therefore it is a severe error if the Word of God is only understood as gospel and not as law and gospel. This leads easily to a faith without deeds, to a revolutionary detachment from divine and human regulations.[86]

What Jellinghaus was actually referring to in his former teaching was not clear. In *Das völlige Heil* he discussed under the heading "main marks of conversion and regeneration" about love and the different aspects of love to God, God's Word, the Christian brothers, and humility before all humans.[87] He had never taught a faith without deeds or from detachment from divine and human regulations. On the contrary, these were important aspects in his teaching. Again, there were inaccuracies and superficialities in his ar-

---

82. Ibid., 39, 41. Regarding his former view, see Jellinghaus, *Das völlige Heil*, 304–5.
83. Jellinghaus, *Erklärung*, 37, 38, 39, 43.
84. Ibid., 22, 30.
85. Ibid., 44.
86. Ibid.
87. Jellinghaus, *Das völlige Heil*, 332–35.

gumentation in the recantation. In addition, his understanding of law and gospel was rather opposite to the teachings of Martin Luther, who might have called his teachings works-righteousness.

At the end of the presentation of the eight main errors Jellinghaus exhorted his readers rather emphatically: "It is very difficult for the best to save themselves, but it is possible through humble repentance and self-denial and faithfulness until death."[88] Actually, it is this sentence which could be used as an explanation for the entire document, because it is quite revealing that Jellinghaus was actually not invoking the Reformation heritage but rather a narrow Pietist tradition in which he sought refuge.

Closing Remarks to Jellinghaus's Recantation

To be sure, with the so-called recantation we are not dealing with utterances of an insane person which should not be taken seriously. Even when he was assisted, Jellinghaus was the initiator and driving force behind this document; it expressed his new insights. At the same time it is quite obvious that we are dealing with another (or later) Jellinghaus than the writer of *Das völlige Heil*, speaker at many conferences, and founder and leader of a Bible school. This means that the later Jellinghaus was strongly influenced by his mental and physical condition, which left its mark in the recantation.

From a personal and a historical background two catalysts for the document can be detected: on the one hand, there was the crisis within the *Gemeinschaftsbewegung* and on the other hand, Jellinghaus's illness. Both catalysts must be considered separately but also in relation to each other. The crisis in the *Gemeinschaftsbewegung* can be observed in the context of the emerging *Pfingstbewegung*. Both the occurrence of new phenomena (e.g., speaking in tongues, prophecies, dancing, laughter, crying, shouting, etc.) and the teachings of Jonathan Paul (sinlessness debate) played central roles in this crisis. The reactions to the phenomena and the teachings were not uniform in the *Gemeinschaftsbewegung* but finally culminated in a schism within the movement. The crisis affected friends and colleagues of Jellinghaus on all sides. The *Heiligungsbewegung*, which was initiated among others by Jellinghaus, played an important role in the formation of the *Gemeinschaftsbewegung* (with its roots and relations to Pietist traditions in different parts of Germany) as well as of the *Pfingstbewegung*. The *Pfingstbewegung* emerged for the most part within the circles of the *Heiligungsbewegung*. Although Jellinghaus raised a voice of warning early on about extreme developments (especially regarding the sinlessness debate),

---

88. Jellinghaus, *Erklärung*, 46.

he felt responsible because the historical and theological relationships were obvious.

In addition to these exogenous factors came the mental and physical breakdown of Jellinghaus. The impact of the illness on the composition of the recantation becomes obvious in the following points: first, the circumstances of the writing and publishing of the document indicate the effects of the illness. Perhaps the illness did not necessitate a never-ending residence in closed institutions; nevertheless Jellinghaus continued to be haunted by fear and obsessive thoughts. This had implications on the motivation and goal, as well as on the content and style of the document. Second, the language and quality of the recantation was affected. In comparison to *Das völlige Heil* and other publications of the former Jellinghaus, a discrepancy can be observed. Part of that is due to the fact that there were no experienced academic theologians available for help. However, already the fact that he needed help, because he felt himself incapable of this project, is an indication of the discrepancy between the former and the later Jellinghaus. Third, it is obvious that the eight main errors (according to Jellinghaus) have been selected almost arbitrarily. On the one hand, he could not clearly demonstrate his points convincingly, especially in regard to his doctrines of sin, faith and reconciliation. On the other, he did not even consider other important and more crucial themes, especially the parallelism of justification and sanctification, where he was not successful in presenting them in unity without parallelism. Fourth, it becomes apparent that he took a position which he used to describe (and to oppose!) as Pietist penance. He did not identify it as a Pietist variation, but rather spoke of his new insight as biblical and Reformation doctrine, which was obviously a misjudgment.

The new theological position actually matched the clinical picture of his illness, because it corresponded to the fears and compulsive thoughts he experienced. This is actually the point where the circle seems to close: from the circumstances to the language and quality and the selection of main errors to the new theological position, the influence of the illness on the recantation becomes clearly obvious. This leads to the conclusion that the so-called recantation should not be considered the final verdict of the entire life and work of Jellinghaus. Therefore, it should not be used as an argument against himself. Nevertheless, the recantation is part of his life and work. One can only do justice to the life and work of Theodor Jellinghaus when a differentiation is made between the former (healthy) and the later (ill) Jellinghaus. Both phases were part of his life. However, both should be viewed and assessed separately. They should not be mixed. The so-called recantation is a crucial document for the later Jellinghaus and helps to demonstrate this important aspect of his life. Beyond that, the importance and significance of the recantation can be found in the following points: first, the document expressed discontent and critique against theological developments which could not be tolerated within the *Gemeinschaftsbewegung* at least since the publication of the *Berliner Erklärung* in 1909. The salvific system (*Heilismus*) of Jellinghaus did not match the direction which the *Gemeinschaftsbewegung* had taken. Because Jellinghaus was recognized as a formative teacher of the *Gemeinschaftsbewegung*, his judgment was valued greatly, even if it was expressed rather weakly and vaguely. He formulated in the recantation what many ultimately believed and what had become common opinion by the opponents of the *Pfingstbewegung* since the *Berliner Erklärung*.

Second, the recantation also played an important political role in the debate between the different and opposing groups of the *Gemeinschaftsbewegung*, especially, many of the prevailing group (of those who had not left the movement) used this document to demonstrate that they were right. The origin, propagation and the critique of the recantation must be viewed from this background. Third, the recantation put an end to the *Heiligungsbewegung* in Germany. After the founding of the *Gnadauer Verband*, the influence of the German *Heiligungsbewegung* on the development of the *Gemeinschaftsbewegung* was limited; its main protagonist had been Jellinghaus. Through his main book and his Bible school he safeguarded a certain presence for the *Heiligungsbewegung*; however, it never had any crucial or decisive influence. From among the early representatives of the *Heiligungsbewegung* (e.g., Otto Stockmayer, Ernst Modersohn, Jonathan Paul) there was no deep theological agreement or even conformity, which caused every one of them to develop differently. Jellinghaus was the only representative of the "old *Heiligungsbewegung*" (as Paul Fleisch formulated it). Because he could not find a theological successor the old movement came to an end with his death. Clear outwards signs of this collapse of the *Heiligungsbewegung* were the recall of all of Jellinghaus's publications by himself as well as the demise of the Bible school, which was finally closed with the beginning of the Great War.

CONCLUSIONS TO LIFE AND WORK OF THEODOR JELLINGHAUS

The following final conclusions regarding the life and work of Theodor Jellinghaus can be made: Jellinghaus, theologian and leader of the *Heiligungsbewegung* and one of the fathers of the German *Gemeinschaftsbewegung* had acquired a distinctive theological profile within the Pietist tradition in nineteenth-century German Protestantism. In many things he remained faithful to the Pietist tradition and practices within the *Gemeinschaftsbewegung* and was hardly distinguishable from the other fathers of the movement. Where he was different and distinct was his peculiar and specific theological system (*Heilismus*), which determined both his personal life and his practical ministry. To conclude this work the following points can be recognized:

The key event for the life and work of Jellinghaus was his participation in the convention on Christian holiness in Oxford in 1874. He wanted to bring the new insights he gained there to revive the Protestant and Pietist traditions in the land of the Reformation. He believed that the doctrine of sanctification by faith in Jesus Christ which he had heard in England was an indispensable consequence of and necessary accompaniment to a clear doctrine of justification by faith in Jesus Christ.

The primary achievement of his life was his theological system (*Heilismus*), which he delineated in different publications, especially in his *magnum opus, Das völlige, gegenwärtige Heil durch Christum*, which went through five editions between 1880 and 1903. His doctrines of reconciliation and redemption constitute the foundation for his theological system. It has been demonstrated in this work that his teachings were a distinctive treatment of different, direct and indirect, conscious and unconscious influences in his life and learning.

Through his theological system, Jellinghaus tried to develop for Pietism in Germany a distinctive doctrine of sanctification which should flow out of a Pietist doctrine of justification. He tried to demonstrate that they belonged intrinsically together, in doctrine and experience, and yet were different in that sanctification went beyond justification in a higher Christian life. Although he tried hard, especially through the repeated reference to the person and work of Jesus Christ as both objectivity and subjectivity of both doctrine and faith experience, Jellinghaus did not succeed in this endeavor. In the end, he did not get beyond a mere parallelism of justification and sanctification because no real change happened in sanctification (ethical change) that went beyond justification (change in relationship to God). Throughout his ministry, Jellinghaus had to defend and explain his theological system which never found full acceptance in German Pietism, the *Gemeinschaftsbewegung*. At the end of his life, in light of developments within the *Gemeinschaftsbewegung* through the emergence of the *Pfingstbewegung*, which brought about a schism in German Pietism and because of his mental illness, Jellinghaus recanted his theological system and actually brought it and the German *Heiligungsbewegung* to a close.

Regarding the church and Christian life, Jellinghaus stayed faithful to the basic ecclesiology of his church. On that basis he developed an ecclesiological concept based on his theological system. In this regard he was unique among the fathers of the *Gemeinschaftsbewegung*. In all his doctrinal formulations on reconciliation and redemption and in his ecclesiological concept Jellinghaus wanted to demonstrate that the objectivity and subjectivity of both, belief system and faith experience, needs to be found in the person and work of Jesus Christ. His involvement in the *Gemeinschaftsbewegung* must be interpreted from the viewpoint of his ecclesiological concept, which is portrayed in light of his understanding of the kingdom of God in indissoluble relation with the Protestant state churches of Germany. His special concern in his involvement in the *Gemeinschaftsbewegung* was the education of laypersons for work in the kingdom of God. He not only found personal fulfillment in his ministry at the Bible school, it also helped him to spread his theological convictions.

Jellinghaus neither created new structures nor initiated new approaches to church work. He assumed the present structures as given. This was true in relation to church structures as well as the development of the *Gemeinschaftsbewegung* with its different organizations and associations and the *Evangelische Allianz* which all fitted very well his understanding of the kingdom of God. Even the structures of the Bible school were not developed autonomously. As has been shown in this work, Jellinghaus drew on other models and adjusted them to his own needs and goals.

His personal life as well as his ministry involvement was subordinated to his theological convictions. The last phase of his life has to be understood in this light, which actually led to a discrepancy in his life. This time was characterized by crisis and illness which were related to each other directly and indirectly. The climax of this time of illness was his so-called recantation (*Erklärung*). Although it cannot be used as the final verdict of his life and ministry, it is part of his story. We can only do justice to the overall persona of Jellinghaus if we differentiate between the former (healthy) and later (ill) Jellinghaus. Theodor Jellinghaus has to be viewed in the contradictions and tensions within the development of this movement as well as his theological teachings. Without doubt he was one of the distinctive theologians in German Pietism at the turn of the nineteenth to the twentieth century.

Appendix
Biographical Timeline of Theodor Jellinghaus

Year	Events
1841	Birth on June 21 in Schlüsselburg
	Baptism on July 30 in Schlüsselburg by his own father, Rev. Karl Heinrich Franz Florens Jellinghaus (1799–1876)
1861	Theological studies at *Vereinigte Friedrichs-Universität Halle-Wittenberg* in Halle (until 1862)
1862	Theological studies at *Friedrich-Alexander-Universität Erlangen-Nürnberg* in Erlangen (until 1864)
1864	First theological exam at the Royal Consistory in Münster (October 18)
1865	Second theological exam at the Royal Consistory in Münster (May 27)
	Ordination at the St. Matthäikirche in Berlin (September 24)
	Sending service for missionary ministry of the Gossner Mission association to India (October 7)
	Departure by ship to India (October 9)
1866	Arrival in Kolkata, India (February 18) and begin of missionary service in Ranchi and Burju (Jharkhand)
1867	Marriage to Mary Prochnow (November 4), daughter of chairman of Gossner Mission association Dr. Johann Dettloff Prochnow (1814–1888)
1868	Birth of son Emil (September)

Year	Events
1870	Death of son Emil (March 20) because of cholera Birth of daughter Martha (March 22) Death of wife Mary (March 27) due to childbed fever Death of daughter Martha (April 24) Theodor Jellinghaus departs from India (May) and returns to Germany Stays with his father-in-law in Berlin and serves as curate (until 1873)
1871	Publication of *Sagen, Sitten und Gebräuche der Munda Kolhs in Chota Nagpore* (Legends, customs and conventions of the Munda Kolhs in Chota Nagpore)
1873	Publication of *Die deutsche Kolhsmission* (The German Kolhs' Mission) Marriage to second wife Karoline Sluyterman van Langeweyde in Berlin (April 29) In spring of this year Jellinghaus takes charge of the parish in Rädnitz (county of Crossen at the Oder). He serves there until 1882.
1874	Publication of articles in the *Allgemeine Missionszeitschrift* Birth of son Martin (March 18) Death of son Martin (July 30) Participation at the Union Meeting for the Promotion of Scriptural Holiness at Oxford (August 29 to September 7)
1875	Publication of articles in the *Allgemeine Missionszeitschrift* Birth of daughter Frieda Participation in the so-called triumphant journey of Robert Pearsall Smith and his wife Hannah Whitall Smith in Germany and Switzerland (April 1 to May 3) Participation at *Heiligungskonferenz* in Gernsbach, organised by Baron von Gemmingen
1876	Death of father Rev. Karl Jellinghaus in Wallenbrück (January 14) Birth of son Paul Max Nathanael (October 12)
1878	Participation at *Heiligungskonferenz* in Gernsbach, organised by Baron von Gemmingen
1879	Birth of daughter Anna Participation at *Heiligungskonferenz* in Gernsbach, organised by Baron von Gemmingen
1880	Publication of first edition of *Das völlige, gegenwärtige Heil durch Christum*
1882	Begin of pastoral ministry at parish in Gütergotz, close to Potsdam. He serves there until 1893.
1883	Participation at founding meeting of *Christlicher Verein Junger Männer (CVJM)* in Berlin

Year	Events
1884	Birth of daughter Hilda
1885	Start of Bible school (*Jahresbibelschule für Laien bzw. Stundenhalterschule*) in Gütergotz
1886	Bible school in Gütergotz Publication of 2nd ed. of *Das völlige Heil*
1887	Bible school in Gütergotz Participation at meeting of *Deutscher Evangelisationsverein* (April 13–14) and signs invitation to first *Gnadauer Pfingskonferenz*
1888	Bible school in Gütergotz Death of his mother (April 12) Participation at first *Gnadauer Pfingstkonferenz* (May 22–24)
1889	Bible school in Gütergotz
1890	Bible school in Gütergotz Publication of first edition of *Der erste Brief des Johannes für gläubige Bibelforscher aus allen Ständen* Participation at second *Gnadauer Pfingstkonferenz* (May 27–30) Publication of 3rd ed. of *Das völlige Heil*
1891	Bible school in Gütergotz
1892	Bible school in Gütergotz Participation at third *Gnadauer Pfingstkonferenz* (June 7–9) Participation at seventh *Allianzkonferenz* in Blankenburg
1893	Bible school in Gütergotz Participation at eighth *Allianzkonferenz* in Blankenburg
1894	Bible school in Gütergotz (last time) Retirement as pastor (October 1) Jellinghaus family moves from Gütergotz to Potsdam Co-editor of *Evangelisches Allianzblatt* (October), a position he held until May 1904
1895	Bible courses in Hamburg (January—March) Participation at the tenth *Allianzkonferenz* in Blankenburg Bible course in Blankenburg (September)
1896	Bible course in Hamburg (January—March) Five week stay in England to participate at fiftieth anniversary of the Evangelical Alliance in London and at the twenty-second Keswick convention (July 25 to August 3) Bible course in Wiesbaden (autumn)

Year	Events
1898	Bible school in Berlin begins at the facilities of the *CVJM* (January—March)
	Publication of first edition of *Auslegende Erläuterungen zum Römerbrief für gläubige Bibelforscher*
	Participation at the thirteenth *Allianzkonferenz* in Blankenburg
	Publication of fourth edition of *Das völlige Heil*
1899	Bible school in Berlin (January—March)
	Participation at believers' conference in Düsseldorf
	First edition of *Mitteilungen aus der Bibelschule* (April/May)
	Participation at *Gnadauer Pfingstkonferenz* (July 24–27)
	Participation at fourteenth *Allianzkonferenz* in Blankenburg
	Participation at conferences in Nakel, Wernigerode, Stettin, Königsberg, Wiesbaden, Halle and Stuttgart
	Bible courses in Magdeburg, Halle, Blankenburg, Wernigerode and Wiesbaden
	Publication of 2nd ed. of *Der erste Brief des Johannes*
1900	Bible school in Berlin (January—March)
	Participation at *Gnadauer Pfingskonferenz*
	Participation at fifteenth *Allianzkonferenz* in Blankenburg
	Participation at conferences and meetings in Frankfurt/Oder, Wallenbrück, Bielefeld, Nakel, Vandsburg, Blankenburg, Hersfeld, Chrischona, Wernigerode, Stettin, Stolp, Kolberg, Wiesbaden and Düsseldorf
	Bible courses in Staßfurt, Berlin-Westend, Chrischona, Wernigerode, Wiesbaden and Dortmund
	Appointment to board of governors of the *Deutsche Orientmission* (December)
1901	Bible school in Berlin (January—March)
	Sixtieth birthday (June 21)
	Participation at sixteenth *Allianzkonferenz* in Blankenburg (August 26–30)
	Starting Christian Convalescence Home with his son-in-law Rev. Horst in Soislieden
	Participation at conferences in Wernigerode and Wiesbaden,
	Bible courses in Mühlheim/Ruhr, Wernigerode and Wiesbaden

BIOGRAPHICAL TIMELINE OF THEODOR JELLINGHAUS

Year	Events
1902	Bible school in Berlin (January—March)
	Participation at *Allianzkonferenz* in Blankenburg
	Participation at first *Eisenacher Konferenz* (May 26–28)
	Participation at conferences in Frankfurt/Oder, Kiel, Meiningen, Wernigerode and Wiesbaden
	Bible courses in Blankenburg, Wernigerode, Neumünster, Wiesbaden and Düsseldorf
	Publication of 2nd ed. of *Auslegungen zum Römerbrief*
	Publication of fifth edition of *Das völlige Heil*
1903	Bible school in Berlin (January—March)
	Participation at second *Eisenacher Konferenz* (June 8–10)
	Delivering official address at the laying of the foundation stone for the new *Evangelisches Allianz-Gemeinschaftshaus* in Charlottenburg
	Participation at eighteenth *Allianzkonferenz* in Blankenburg
	Participation at conferences in Gnadau, Meiningen and Wernigerode
	Bible course in Wernigerode
	Publication of fifth edition of *Das völlige Heil*
	Health problems (September and November)
1904	Bible school in Berlin (January—March)
	Opening of *Bibelschulseminar* in Lichtenrade
	Resignation from board of *Allianzkonferenz* in Blankenburg due to theological differences (Darbyite tendencies in Blankenburg)
	Resignation as co-editor of the *Evangelisches Allianzblatt*
	Participation at Evangelists' conference in Stargard
	Resignation from board of governors of *Deutsche Orientmission*
	Participation at dedication service for *Evangelisches Allianz-Gemeinschaftshaus* in Charlottenburg
	Participation at conference in Wiesbaden
	Bible courses in Wiesbaden and Wallenbrück
1905	Bible school in Berlin (January—March)—last time in Berlin
	Bibelschulseminar in Lichtenrade
	Health (psychosomatic) problems (sleeplessness, depression, nervous disease, gastric problems)

Year	Events
1906	Bible school in Lichtenrade (January—March)
	Teaching last time at *Bibelschulseminar* (May)
	Jellinghaus ill. His son (Paul Jellinghaus) becomes editor of *Mitteilungen* (August)
	Paul Jellinghaus takes over leadership of Bible school (September)
	Jellinghaus at convalescence home in Teichwolframsdorf
	Jellinghaus admitted to private psychiatric hospital in Lichtenrade (December 10)
1907–1911	Jellinghaus in two different psychiatric hospitals (Lichtenrade until November 1907) and then at *Evangelische Heil- und Pflegeanstalt für Gemütsleidende Tannenhof* in Lüttringhausen near Remscheid (1907–1911)
	Jellinghaus writes letters to different leaders of the *Gemeinschaftsbewegung* to help him recant from his teachings
1911	Dismissal from psychiatric hospital in Lüttringhausen (May)
	Death of daughter Anna (July 28)
	Jellinghaus spent time with different people to work on his recantation (August—October)
	Sale of property in Lichtenrade (Bible school needs to move)
1912	Publication of recantation, *Erklärung über meine Lehrirrungen*
1913	Death on October 4 in Lichtenrade
	Funeral on October 8 in Lichtenrade

Bibliography

PRIMARY SOURCES

Unpublished Sources

Archives of the *Evangelische Kirche von Westfalen* in Bielefeld.
Archives of the *Evangelische Stiftung Tannenhof*. Medical Records of Theodor Jellinghaus, made available by courtesy of Professor Dr. Windgassen and Rev. Martin Wolff.
Archives of the *Evangelischer Diakonieverein* Berlin-Zehlendorf, files H 753 and H 754
Documents in the private archives of Mr. Sigmar Jellinghaus in Heidelberg
Student records in the archives of the Martin-Luther-Universität Halle-Wittenberg in Halle.

Published Sources and Contemporary Literature

Account of the Union Meeting for the Promotion of Scriptural Holiness, held at Oxford, August 29th to September 7th, 1874. Chicago: Revell, 1874.
Baur, Wilhelm. *R. Pearsall Smith in Berlin*. Berlin: Evangelischer Verein für kirchliche Zwecke, 1875.
Boardman, William E. *The Higher Christian Life*. Boston: Hoyt, 1858.
Böhme, Alwin. "Wie ist der Widerruf von Pastor Jellinghaus zu beurteilen?" In *Bausteine: Monatsblatt für Innere Mission. Organ des Landesvereins für Innere Mission und des Gesamtverbandes für Innere Mission der Evangelisch-Lutherischen Kirche in Sachsen*, edited by Pastor Wendelin. Volume 46, no. 547. Dresden: n.p., 1914.
Buddeberg, Ernst. "Die Heiligung durch den Glauben." In *Licht und Leben*, edited by Joseph Gauger. Volume 24, issues 16–21 and 44–45. Elberfeld: Licht und Leben, 1912.
Bunke, Ernst. "Jellinghaus gegen Jellinghaus." *KJ* 39 (1912) 182–83.
Clasen, Ludwig. "Heiligung im Glauben. Mit Rücksicht auf die heutige Heiligungsbewegung." *ZThK* 10 (1900) 439–88.

Cremer, Ernst. *Das vollkommene gegenwärtige Heil in Christo: Eine Untersuchung zum Dogma der Gemeinschaftsbewegung.* Gütersloh: Bertelsmann, 1915.

Fleisch, Paul. *Die gegenwärtige Krisis in der modernen Gemeinschaftsbewegung.* Leipzig: Wallmann, 1905.

———. *Zur Geschichte der Heiligungsbewegung: Erstes Heft: Die Heiligungsbewegung von Wesley bis Boardman.* Leipzig: Wallmann, 1910.

———. *Die Heiligungsbewegung. Von den Segenstagen in Oxford 1874 bis zur Oxford-Gruppen-Bewegung Frank Buchmans.* Edited by Jörg Ohlemacher. Gießen: Brunnen, 2003.

———. *Die innere Entwicklung der deutschen Gemeinschaftsbewegung in den Jahren 1906-1907.* Leipzig: Wallmann, 1908.

———. *Die moderne Gemeinschaftsbewegung in Deutschland.* Vol. 1, *Die Geschichte der deutschen Gemeinschaftsbewegung bis zum Auftreten des Zungenredens (1875-1907).* 3rd ed. Leipzig: Wallmann, 1912.

———. *Die moderne Gemeinschaftsbewegung in Deutschland.* Vol. 2, *Die deutsche Gemeinschaftsbewegung seit Auftreten des Zungenredens. I. Teil: Die Zungenbewegung in Deutschland.* 3rd ed. Leipzig: Wallmann, 1914.

Gelshorn, Karl. "Die moderne Gemeinschaftsbewegung." *ChW* 19, no. 38 (1905) 854-97.

Gennrich, Paul. *Wiedergeburt und Heiligung mit Bezug auf die gegenwärtigen Strömungen des religiösen Lebens. Eine dogmatische Beleuchtung der modernen Gemeinschaftsbewegung in ihrer neuesten Entwickelung.* Leipzig: Deichert, 1908.

Gensichen, Johannes. "Jellinghaus—und seine Erklärung über seine Lehrirrungen." In *EKZ.* Volume 86. Berlin: Oehmigke, 1912.

Godet, Frédéric. *Studies on the New Testament.* Edited by W. H. Lyttelton. London: Hodder & Stoughton, 1876.

Hardeland, Theodor. *Die Evangelisation mit besonderer Rücksicht auf die Heiligungsbewegung.* Leipzig: Deichert, 1898.

Heinatsch, Ernst. *Die Krisis des Heiligungsbegriffes in der Gemeinschaftsbewegung der Gegenwart (Theodor Jellinghaus): Eine biblisch-dogmatische Studie.* Neumünster: Ihloff, 1913.

Horst, Richard. *Jesus unsere Heiligung.* Kassel: no publisher, no date.

Ihmels, Ludwig Heinrich. "Zur Lehre von der Heiligung bei Theodor Jellinghaus." *NKZ* 27 (1916) 89-128.

Jellinghaus, Paul. *Zum 25 jährigen Bestehen der Bibelschule.* Lichtenrade: no publisher, no date.

Jellinghaus, Theodor. *Auslegungen und Erläuterungen zum Römerbrief.* Berlin: Thormann & Goetsch, 1898 and 1903.

———. *Des Christen Glaubensweg: Blätter zur Weckung und Förderung des christlichen Leben.* Basel: Spittler, 1875-76: "Lebens-Erfahrung," 1, no. 2 (1875) 38-40. "Buße und Glauben: Buße," 2, no. 4 (1876) 74-79. "Buße und Glauben: Glauben," 2, no. 5 (1876) 87-91. "Gewissheit der Sündenvergebung und der Gotteskindschaft," 2/1, no. 9 (1876) 165-71. "Gewissheit der Sündenvergebung und der Gotteskindschaft," 2/2, no. 10 (1876) 192-97. "Gewissheit der Sündenvergebung und der Gotteskindschaft," 3/2, no. 11 (1876) 215-20.

———. *Die deutsche Kolhsmission.* Berlin: Buchhandlung der Goßnerischen Mission, 1875.

———. *Erklärung über meine Lehrirrungen.* Lichtenrade: Prack, 1912.

———. *Der erste Brief des Johannes für gläubige Bibelforscher aus allen Ständen.* Basel: Spittler, 1890 and 1898/1899.
———. *Erst Glaube, dann Erfahrung. Rede bei den Oktober-Versammlungen zu Gernsbach 1878 über 2. Chronik 20,1–30.* Lichtenthal: Kolportage Verein, 1899.
———. *Evangelisches Allianzblatt für diejenigen, welche mit allen Kindern Gottes Gemeinschaft haben.* Blankenburg: Evangelisches Allianzhaus: "Neues Dogma oder volleres Evangelium," 3, no. 3 (1893) 21–22. "Alter Adam und Neuer Adam," 3, no. 5 (1893) 35. "Wahre Buße und Glaube sind immer zusammen," 3, no. 13 (1893) 99. "Laodizea und Du?—Völlige Übergabe," 3, no. 19 (1893) 146–47. "Worin besteht die völlige Übergabe," 3, no. 21 (1893) 161–62. "Nichtsündigen und Sündigen," 4, no. 4 (1894) 195–96. "Biblische Ausdrücke über die Heiligung," 5, no. 1 (1895) 4–6. "Zeit und Ewigkeit," 5, no. 8 (1895) 57. "Blick in die Maulwurfsarbeit der modernen Theologie," 5, no. 9 (1895) 66–67. "Jesus unsere Heiligung," 5/1, no. 14 (1895) 109–10. "Jesus unsere Heiligung," 5/2, no. 15 (1895) 114–15. "Ewigkeit," 5, no. 16 (1895) 123. "Pfingsten," 5, no. 17 (1895) 129. "Addition oder Subtraktion?," 5, no. 19 (1895) 146. "Rechte Schriftauslegung" volume 5, no. 21 (1895) 162. "Die Arbeiter im Weinberg," 6/1, no. 10 (1896) 75. "Die Arbeiter im Weinberg," 6/2, no. 11 (1896) 84. "Die 22. Keswick-Konferenz. 25. Juli—3. August 1896," 6, no. 23 (1896) 178–79. "Redet von niemand Böses!," 6, no. 24 (1896) 188. "Evangelisches Allianzhaus. Was haben wir in Christo?," 7, no. 2 (1897) 9. "Evangelisches Allianzhaus. Taufe mit dem Heiligen Geist," 7, no. 3 (1897) 17. "Evangelisches Allianzhaus. Über das Wesen der gründlichen Bekehrung," 7, no. 5 (1897) 33. "Ueber den Methodismus," 7, no. 10 (1897) 78–79. "Die Heilsbotschaft vom völligen Erlöser," 7, no. 20 (1897) 156. "Die Bedeutung des Opfers in der Völkerwelt und in der Bibel," 7, no. 21 (1897) 162–63. "Entschlafen. Zum Tode von R.P. Smith," 9, no. 3 (1899) 23. "Wassertaufe," 9/1, no. 3, S (1893) 19–20. "Wassertaufe," 9/2, no. 5 (1899) 27. "Schwärmerei," 9, no. 5 (1899) 34. "Die Heiligungskraft des Blutes Jesu," 9, no. 11 (1899) 85. "Tote und Lebende," 9, no. 12 (1899) 92. "Das Gottesbewusstsein der Heiden," 9/1, no. 16 (1899) 125. "Das Gottesbewusstsein der Heiden," 9/2, no. 16 (1899) 134. "Ist das Unterschiedmachen von Geistlichen (Klerikern) und Laien biblisch?," 10, no. 13 (1900) 100–101. "Erwiderung. Zu S. Kellers Artikel 'Antienglische Plaudereien'," 10, no. 15 (1900) 116–17. "Durch Tod zum Leben," 10, no. 23 (1900) 184. "Der chinesische Krieg und die erzwungene Opium-Einfuhr in China," 11, no. 1 (1901) 4. "Die Abhängigkeit der Heidenmission von den geistlichen und sittlichen Zuständen der heimischen Christenheit," 11, no. 2 (1901) 14–15, 19–20. "Ist die Rechtfertigung und die Wiedergeburt eine substantielle Umwandlung der Menschennatur?," 11, no. 9 (1901) 71–72. "Friede auf Erden," 12, no. 6 (1902) 47. "Offene Antwort," 12/1, no. 8 (1902) 58–60. "Offene Antwort," 12/2, no. 9 (1902) 69–70. "Gemeinschaft mit Gott," 12, no. 23 (1902) 181. "Ist die Bibel in jedem Satze untrügliches Wort Gottes oder ist Gottes Wort in der Schrift?," 13, no. 6 (1903) 46. "Wo lag das Galiläa, in welchem der Auferstandene Seinen Jüngern erschien?" 13, no. 7 (1903) 55. "Die psychologische Möglichkeit des Unglaubens," 13, no. 9 (1903) 67.
———. *Die Heiligungskraft des Blutes Jesu.* Gernsbach: Kolportage Verein, 1882.
———. "Ist 'Gnadau' und Heiligungsbewegung eins?" In *Licht und Leben*, edited by Pfarrer Gauger, 487–90. Volume 24, no. 31. Elberfeld: Licht und Leben, 1912.

———. "Die Kolhs in Ostindien und ihre Christianisierung." *AMZ* 1 (1874) 24–35, 104–12, 167–84, 203–14, 253–70, 290–95, 341–50.

———. "Die Missions-Conferenz in Allahabad." *AMZ* 2 (1875) 433–38, 481–94.

———. *Rechte Schriftauslegung.* No place: no publisher, no date.

———. *Rede bei den Oktober-Versammlungen zu Gernsbach 1878 über 1. Johannes 1,6 bis 2,6.* Lahr: Kaufmann, no date.

———. *Sagen, Sitten und Gebräuche der Munda Kolhs in Chota Nagpore.* Berlin: Buchhandlung der Goßnerschen Mission, 1871.

———. *Sieg und Leben in der Glaubenshingabe an den im Worte gegenwärtigen, völligen Erlöser.* Neumünster: Ihloff, 1899.

———. *Das völlige, gegenwärtige Heil durch Christum.* 5th ed. Berlin: Thormann & Goetsch, 1903.

———. *Die wahre Liebe und Menschenachtung eine sichere Bewahrung vor Unkeuschheitssünden.* Mühlheim: Evangelisches, 1887.

———. *Das Wesen der völligen Übergabe.* Lichtenthal: Kolportage Verein, 1900.

———. "Zur Geschichte der Heiligungsbewegung und ihrer Lehre." In *Das Reich Christi (RCJL)*, edited by Johannes Lepsius, 2/8:232–37. Berlin: Wiegand & Grieben, 1899.

Lepsius, Johannes. *Die Erste Eisenacher Konferenz. Pfingsten 1902 (26.–28. Mai). Bericht über die Verhandlungen.* Berlin: Deutsche Orient Mission, 1902.

———. *Verhandlungen der zweiten Eisenacher Konferenz.* Berlin: Deutsche Orient Mission, 1903.

Möller, Max. *R. Pearsall Smith: Ein Lebensbild.* Wandsbek: Bethel, 1910.

Monod, Théodore. *Looking unto Jesus.* No place: no publisher, no date.

———. *The Gift of God: A Series of Addresses.* London: Morgan and Scott, no date.

———. "Um was es sich handelt." In *Briefe über die Versammlungen zu Brighton: Versuch einer zusammenhängenden Darstellung und Beleuchtung der Smith'schen Bewegung*, by Gustav Warneck, 157–72. Hamburg: Walther, 1876.

Pfleiderer, Johann Gottlob. *Gnadauer Pfingstkonferenz 1888: Durch Begegnung zur Gnadauer Bewegung. Verhandlungen der Gnadauer Pfingstkonferenz (22.–24. Mai 1888).* New ed. by Johannes Dreßler. Berlin: Evangelische, 1987.

Rietschel, Ernst. *Lutherische Rechtfertigungslehre oder moderne Heiligungslehre? Ein Beitrag zum Verständnis der modernen Heiligungsbewegung mit besonderer Berücksichtigung des Buches von Th. Jellinghaus: Das völlige, gegenwärtige Heil durch Christum.* Leipzig: Dörffling & Franke, 1909.

Die Segenstage in Oxford. Reden gehalten bei den Versammlungen vom 29. Aug. bis 7. Sept. 1874. Basel: Spittler, 1875.

Smith, Robert Pearsall. *Die Heiligung durch den Glauben.* Basel: Spittler, 1874.

———. *Holiness through Faith: Light on the Way of Holiness.* New York: Anson D. F. Randolph, 1870.

———. *Das Geheimniß des Sieges.* Basel: Spittler, no date.

———. *Wandelst Du in der Heiligung?* 3rd ed. Basel: Spittler, no date.

———. "Der Weg der Heiligung." In *Jesus, der Befreier von Sünde: Erfahrungen aus dem inneren Leben*, by Robert Pearsall Smith and Hannah Whitall Smith. Basel: Spittler, n.d.

Wangemann, Hermann Theodor. *Pearsall Smith und die Versammlungen zu Brighton in ihrer Bedeutung für Deutschland.* Berlin: Herbig, 1876.

Warneck, Gustav. *Briefe über die Versammlungen zu Brighton: Versuch einer zusammenhängenden Darstellung und Beleuchtung der Smith'schen Bewegung.* Hamburg: Walther, 1876.

SECONDARY LITERATURE

Albrecht, Ruth. "Frauen." In *GdP*, 4:522–55. Göttingen: Vandenhoeck & Ruprecht, 2004.
Aldis, W. H. *The Message of Keswick and Its Meaning.* London: Marshall, Morgan & Scott, no date.
Arnold, Klaus. "Pietism." In *Global Wesleyan Dictionary of Theology*, edited by Al Truesdale, 408–10. Kansas City: Beacon Hill, 2013.
Barabas, Steven. *So Great Salvation: The History and Message of the Keswick Convention.* London: Marshall, Morgan & Scott, 1952.
Bärend, Hartmut. "Seminar/Bibelschule." In *ELThG*, 1:161. Wuppertal: Brockhaus, 1998.
Barth, Karl. *Geschichte der protestantischen Theologie des neunzehnten Jahrhunderts: Ihre Vorgeschichte und ihre Geschichte.* 6th ed. Zürich: TVZ, 1994.
Bassett, Paul M. "Holiness Movement." In *The Encyclopaedia of Christianity*, edited by Erwin Fahlbusch, 2:571. Grand Rapids: Eerdmans, 2001.
Bassett, Paul M., and William M. Greathouse. *Exploring Christian Holiness.* Vol. 2, *The Historical Development.* Kansas City: Beacon Hill, 1985.
Bauks, Friedrich Wilhelm. *Die evangelischen Pfarrer in Westfalen von der Reformationszeit bis 1945.* Bielefeld: Luther, 1980.
Baum, Markus. "Eberhard Arnold." In *BBKL*, 19:23–32, Nordhausen: Bautz, 2001.
Bautz, Friedrich Wilhelm. "Eberhard Arnold." In *BBKL*, 1:236–38. Hamm: Bautz, 1990.
———. "Friedrich Blecher." In *BBKL*, 1:620–21. Hamm: Bautz, 1990.
———. "Johannes Evangelista Gossner." In *BBKL*, 2:268–71. Hamm: Bautz, 1990.
———. "Seligman Baer." In *BBKL*, 1:341. Hamm: Bautz, 1990.
Bebbington, David W. *Evangelicalism in Modern Britain: A History from the 1730s to the 1980s.* London: Routledge, 1995.
Becker, Ingeborg. "Bibelschule." In *RGG*³, 1:1192–93. Tübingen: Mohr, 1956.
Beintker, Michael. "Baptism. IV. Dogmatics. 3. Protestantism. b. Reformed." In *Religion Past and Present*, 1:587. Leiden: Brill, 2006.
Beyreuther, Erich. "Eisenacher Bund." In *RGG*, 2:406. 3rd ed. Tübingen: Mohr, 1958.
Beyreuther, Erich. "Die Erweckungsbewegung." In *Die Kirche in ihrer Geschichte*, edited by Kurt Dietrich Schmidt and Ernst Wolf, 4:4–8. Göttingen: Vandenhoeck & Ruprecht, 1977.
Beyschlag, Karlmann. *Die Erlanger Theologie.* Erlangen: Martin-Luther, 1993.
Boardman, Mary F. *Life and Labours of the Rev. W.E. Boardman.* New York: Appleton, 1887.
Brecht, Martin. "Einleitung." In *GdP*, 1:1–10. Göttingen: Vandenhoeck & Ruprecht, 1993.
———. "Pfarrer und Theologen." In *GdP*, 4:211–26. Göttingen: Vandenhoeck & Ruprecht, 2004.
Brandenburg, Hans. "Theodor Jellinghaus." In *RGG*, 3:576. 3rd ed. Tübingen: Mohr, 1959.

Buttler, Günter. "Bibelschule." In *RGG*⁴, 1:1486–87. Tübingen: Mohr Siebeck, 2007.
Cochlovius, Joachim. "Theodor Jellinghaus." In *TRE*, 15:556. Berlin: de Gruyter, 1986.
Collins, Kenneth J. *The Scripture Way of Salvation: The Heart of John Wesley's Theology.* Nashville: Abingdon, 1997.
Cox, Leo. *John Wesley's Concept of Perfection.* Kansas City: Beacon Hill, 1964.
Dicker, Gordon Stanley. *The Concept of Simul Iustus et Paccator in Relationship to the Thought of Luther, Wesley and Bonhoeffer and Its Significance for a Doctrine of the Christian Life.* New York: Union Theological Seminary Press, 1971.
Dieter, Melvin E., ed. *The 19th-Century Holiness Movement.* Great Holiness Classics, 4. Kansas City: Beacon Hill, 1998.
———. *The Holiness Revival of the Nineteenth Century.* Metuchen, NJ: Scarecrow, 1980.
Dietz, Thorsten. "Der Einfluss der angloamerikanischen Heiligungstheologie auf Theodor Jellinghaus." In *Die neue Welt und der neue Pietismus. Angloamerikanische Einflüsse auf den deutschen Neupietismus,* edited by Frank Lüdke and Norbert Schmidt, 189–218. Berlin: LIT, 2012.
Drechsel, Joachim. *Das Gemeindeverständnis in der Deutschen Gemeinschaftsbewegung.* Gießen: Brunnen, 1984.
Ekholm, Dwight Allan. *Theological Roots of the Keswick Movement: William E. Boardman, Robert Pearsall Smith, and the Doctrine of the 'Higher Christian Life'.* Vienna: B.E.E., 1992.
Fischer, Otto, ed. *Evangelisches Pfarrerbuch für die Mark Brandenburg seit der Reformation.* 2 vols. Berlin: Mittler und Sohn, 1941.
Gäbler, Ulrich. "Geschichte, Gegenwart, Zukunft." In *GdP*, 4:19–48. Göttingen: Vandenhoeck & Ruprecht, 2004.
Graß, Hans. "Abendmahl. II. Dogmengeschichtlich." In *RGG*, 1:32. 3rd ed. Tübingen: Mohr, 1957.
Greschat, Martin, ed. *Gestalten der Kirchengeschichte.* 14 vols. Stuttgart: Kohlhammer, 1993.
Harford, Charles F., ed. *The Keswick Convention; its Message, its Method and its Men.* London: Marshall, 1907.
Hassel, Ulrich von. *Eberhard von Rothkirch und Panthen: Ein Lebensbild nach Briefen und Aufzeichnungen.* Berlin: Deutsche Ev. Buch- und Traktatgesellschaft, 1912.
Haußleitner, Johannes. *Grundlinien der Theologie Joh. Christ. K. v. Hofmanns in seiner eigenen Darstellung.* Leipzig: Deichert, 1910.
Hinrichs, Wolfgang. "Tillmann Siebel." In *BBKL*, 10:36–39. Hamm: Bautz, 1995.
Hofmann, Johann Christian Konrad von. *Der Schriftbeweis: Ein theologischer Versuch.* Vol. 1. 2nd ed.. Nördlingen: Beck, 1857.
———. *Schutzschriften für eine neue Weise alte Wahrheiten zu lehren.* 5 vols. Nördlingen: Beck, 1852–1856.
———. *Weissagung und Erfüllung im Alten und Neuen Testamente: Ein theologischer Versuch.* 2 vols. Nördlingen: Beck, 1841–1844.
Hollenweger, Walter. *Charismatisch-pfingstliches Christentum: Herkunft, Situation, Ökumenische Chancen.* Göttingen: Vandenhoeck & Ruprecht, 1997.
Holthaus, Stephan. "Baron Julius von Gemmingen d.J. (1838-1912): Publizist und Sozialreformer der Heiligungsbewegung." In *Mission und Diakonie, Kultur und Politik: Studien zum Vereins- und Gemeinschaftswesen in der Evangelischen Kirche im Baden im 19. Jahrhundert,* edited by Udo Wennemuth, 217–32. VVKGB 59. Karlsruhe: Ev. Presseverband, 2004.

———. *Fundamentalismus in Deutschland: Der Kampf um die Bibel im Protestantismus des 19. und 20. Jahrhunderts*. 2nd ed. Bonn: Kultur und Wissenschaft, 2003.

———. *Heil—Heilung—Heiligung: Die Geschichte der deutschen Heiligungs- und Evangelisationsbewegung (1874–1909)*. Gießen: Brunnen, 2005.

Jones, Charles E. *Perfectionist Persuasion: The Holiness Movement and American Methodism, 1867–1936*. Metuchen, NJ: Scarecrow, 1974.

Jung, August. *Vom Kampf der Väter: Schwärmerische Bewegungen im ausgehenden 19. Jahrhundert. Dokumente aus Freien evangelischen Gemeinden und kirchlichen wie freikirchlichen Gemeinschaften*. Witten: Bundes, 1995.

Kantzenbach, Friedrich Wilhelm. *Die Erlanger Theologie. Grundlinien ihrer Entwicklung im Rahmen der Geschichte der Theologischen Fakultät 1743–1877*. München: Evangelischer Presseverband für Bayern, 1960.

Kettler, Franz Heinrich. "Taufe. III. Dogmengeschichtlich." In *RGG*, 6:646. 3rd ed. Tübingen: Mohr, 1962.

Köberle, Adolf. *Rechtfertigung und Heiligung. Eine biblische, theologiegeschichtliche und systematische Untersuchung*. Leipzig: Dörffling & Franke, 1929.

Krause, Markus. "Robert Pearsall Smith—Impulsgeber für die deutsche Gemeinschaftsbewegung." In *Die neue Welt und der neue Pietismus: Angloamerikanische Einflüsse auf den deutschen Neupietismus*, edited by Frank Lüdke and Norbert Schmidt, 144–48. Berlin: LIT, 2012.

Kreck, Walter. "Abendmahl. III. Dogmatisch. 2. Ref. Lehre." In *RGG*, 1:37. 3rd ed. Tübingen: Mohr, 1957.

———. "Taufe. IV. Dogmatisch. 2. Ref. Lehre." In *RGG*, 6:647. 3rd ed. Tübingen: Mohr 1962.

Krug, Burkhard. "Carl Heinrich Rappard." In *BBKL*, 7:1361–62. Hamm: Bautz, 1994.

———. "Samuel D. Keller." In *BBKL*, 3:1321–22. Hamm: Bautz, 1992.

Kupisch, Karl. *Der deutsche CVJM*. Kassel: Pflugschar, 1958.

Lange, Dieter. *Eine Bewegung bricht sich Bahn: Die deutschen Gemeinschaften im ausgehenden 19. und beginnenden 20. Jahrhundert und ihre Stellung zu Kirche, Theologie und Pfingstbewegung*. Berlin: Evangelische, 1979.

Lindström, Harald. *Wesley and Sanctification*. London: Epworth, 1946.

Maddox, Randy L. *Responsible Grace: John Wesley's Practical Theology*. Nashville: Kingswood, 1994.

Melle, Otto. *50 Jahre Blankenburger Konferenz*. Bad Blankenburg: Harfe, 1936.

Mirbach, Wolfram. "Theodor Jellinghaus." In *BBKL*, 3:23. Hamm: Bautz, 1992.

Neander, August. *Geschichte der Pflanzung und Leitung der christlichen Kirche durch die Apostel, als selbstständiger Nachtrag zu der allgemeinen Geschichte der christlichen Religion und Kirche*. 3rd ed. Hamburg: Perthes, 1841.

Newmark, Peter. *A Textbook of Translation*. Hertfordshire: Prentice Hall, 1988.

Noble, Thomas A. *Holy Trinity: Holy People: The Historic Doctrine of Christian Perfecting*. Eugene, OR: Cascade, 2013.

Ohlemacher, Jörg. "Die Anfänge der Gemeinschaftsbewegung." In *PuN*, 15:59–83. Göttingen: Vandenhoeck & Ruprecht, 1989.

———. "Evangelikalismus und Heiligungsbewegung im 19. Jahrhundert." In *GdP*, 3:371–91. Göttingen: Vandenhoeck & Ruprecht, 2000.

———. *Die Gemeinschaftsbewegung in Deutschland: Quellen zu ihrer Geschichte 1887–1914*. Gütersloh: Mohn, 1977.

———. "Gemeinschaftschristentum in Deutschland im 19. und 20. Jahrhundert." In *GdP*, 3:393–464. Göttingen: Vandenhoeck & Ruprecht, 2000.

———. *Das Reich Gottes in Deutschland bauen: Ein Beitrag zur Vorgeschichte und Theologie der Deutschen Gemeinschaftsbewegung*. Göttingen: Vandenhoeck & Ruprecht, 1986.

———. "Theodor Jellinghaus." In *ELThG*, 2:985. Wuppertal: Brockhaus, 1993.

Packer, James I. *Keep in Step with the Spirit*. Leicester: Inter-Varsity, 1984.

Palmer, Phoebe. *The Way of Holiness*. New York: Palmer & Hughes, 1867.

Parker, Robert A. *The Transatlantic Smiths*. New York: Random House, 1959.

Pollock, John Charles. *The Keswick Story: The Authorised History of the Keswick Convention*. London: Hodder and Stoughton, 1964.

Pollock, John Charles and Ian Randall. *The Keswick Story: The Authorised History of the Keswick Convention—Updated*. Fort Washington: CLC, 2006.

Price, Charles, and Ian Randall. *Transforming Keswick*. Carlisle: OM, 2000.

Rappard, Dora. *C. H. Rappard, Inspektor. Ein Lebensbild von seiner Gattin*. Gießen: Brunnen, 1910.

Raser, Harold E. *Phoebe Palmer, Her Life and Thought*. Lewiston, NY: Mellen, 1997.

Rennstich, Karl Wilhelm. "Walter Jack." In *BBKL*, 2:1398–99. Hamm: Bautz, 1990.

Reuber, Kurt. *Mystik in der Heiligungsfrömmigkeit der Gemeinschaftsbewegung*. Gütersloh: Bertelsmann, 1938.

Ritter, Adolf Martin. "Church. 2.2. Historical Constructs and Theories. 2.2.7. The Reformation. 2.2.7.2. John Calvin." In *Encyclopedia of Christianity*, 1:486. Grand Rapids: Eerdmans, 1998.

Roeber, Klaus. "Gossner Mission." In *Quellenbestände der Indienmission 1700–1918 in deutschsprachigen Archiven*, edited by Erika Pabst and Thomas Müller-Bahlke, 45–54. Tübingen: Niemeyer, 2005.

Rothkirch, Fr. Eberhard von. "Eberhard von Rothkirch und Panthen." In *BBKL*, 8:824–25. Hamm: Bautz, 1994.

Ruhbach, Gerhard. "Abendmahl. b) theologiegeschichtlich." In *ELThG*, 1:6–7. Wuppertal: Brockhaus, 1992.

———. "Eisenacher Bund." In *ELThG*, 1:486. Wuppertal: Brockhaus, 1992.

Sauberzweig, Hans von. *Er der Meister—Wir die Brüder. Geschichte der Gnadauer Gemeinschaftsbewegung 1888–1958*. Offenbach: Gnadauer, 1959.

Schilling, Heinz. *Martin Luther. Rebell in einer Zeit des Umbruchs: Eine Biographie*. München: Beck, 2016.

Schleiermacher, Friedrich. *Der christliche Glaube*. Seventh edition. 2 vols. Berlin: de Gruyter, 1960.

Schmid, Urs. *Die Heiligungskonferenzen von Oxford (1874) und Brighton (1875) oder Die Amerikanischen Hintergründe der Konferenzen für 'Schriftgemäße Heiligung': In Oxford (1874) und Brighton (1875) und ihre Auswirkungen im deutschen Sprachraum*. ThD diss., Basel: Universität Basel, 1999.

Seidel, J. Jürgen. "Johannes Seitz." In *BBKL*, 14:1443–44. Hamm: Bautz, 1998.

Sloan, Walter B. *These Sixty Years. The Story of the Keswick Convention*. London: Pickering & Inglis, 1935.

Smith, Logan P. *Unforgotten Years*. Boston: Little, Brown, 1939.

Smith, Timothy L. *Revivalism and Social Reform in Mid-Nineteenth Century America*. New York: Harper & Row, 1957.

Sommerlath, Ernst. "Taufe. IV. Dogmatisch. 1. Luth. Lehre." In *RGG*, 6:647. 3rd ed. Tübingen: Mohr, 1962.
Spener, Philipp Jakob. *Pia Desideria—Umkehr in die Zukunft*. 5th ed. Giessen: Brunnen, 1995.
Stempel-de Fallois, Anne. *Das diakonische Wirken Wilhelm Löhes: Von den Anfängen bis zur Gründung des Diakonissenmutterhauses Neuendettelsau (1826-1854)*. Stuttgart: Kohlhammer, 2001.
Swarat, Uwe. "Johann Christian von Hofmann." In *ELThG*, 2:923-24. Wuppertal: Brockhaus, 1993.
Voigt, Karl Heinz. *Die Evangelische Allianz als ökumenische Bewegung*. Stuttgart: Christliches, 1990.
———. *Die Heiligungsbewegung zwischen Methodistischer Kirche und Landeskirchlicher Gemeinschaft: Die „Triumphreise" von Robert Pearsall Smith im Jahre 1875 und ihre Auswirkungen auf die zwischenkirchlichen Beziehungen*. Wuppertal: Brockhaus, 1996.
———. "Weling, Anna Thekla von." In *BBKL*, 23:710-15. Hamm: Bautz, 1998.
Wallmann, Johannes. *Der Pietismus*. Göttingen: Vandenhoeck und Ruprecht, 2005.
Warfield, Benjamin Breckinridge. *Studies in Perfectionism*. 2 vols. New York: Oxford University Press, 1931.
Wellenreuther, Hermann. "Pietismus und Mission." In *GdP*, 4:166–93. Göttingen: Vandenhoeck & Ruprecht, 2004.
Wenz, Gunther. *Geschichte der Versöhnungslehre in der evangelischen Theologie der Neuzeit*. 2 vols. München: Kaiser, 1984–1986.
Wesley, John. *The Works of John Wesley*. Bicentennial Edition. Oxford: Abingdon, 1975–.
———. *The Works of the Rev. John Wesley, A.M.*. An edition of the complete and unabridged *Works* reproduced by the photo offset process from the authorised edition published by the Wesleyan Conference Office in London in 1872 (originally edited by Thomas A Jackson). 14 vols. Repr., Kansas City: Beacon Hill, 1979.
Wesseling, Klaus-Gunther. "Christian Friedrich Spittler." In *BBKL*, 10:1031-35. Hamm: Bautz, 1995.
Weyer, Michel. *Heiligungsbewegung und Methodismus im deutschen Sprachraum: Einführung in ein Kapitel methodistischer Frömmigkeitsgeschichte und kleine Chronik einer Bewegung des 19. Jahrhunderts*. Stuttgart: Christliches, 1991.
White, Charles Edward. *The Beauty of Holiness: Phoebe Palmer as Theologian, Revivalist, Feminist, and Humanitarian*. Grand Rapids: Zondervan, 1986.
Wolfes, Matthias. "Paul Gennrich." In *BBKL*, 15:608-25. Hamm: Bautz, 1999.

www.ingramcontent.com/pod-product-compliance
Lightning Source LLC
Chambersburg PA
CBHW070327230426
43663CB00011B/2240